EMPOWERING STRUGGLING READERS

Solving Problems in the Teaching of Literacy

Cathy Collins Block, Series Editor

Recent Volumes

Empowering Struggling Readers

Practices for the Middle Grades

Leigh A. Hall
Leslie D. Burns
Elizabeth Carr Edwards

THE GUILFORD PRESS
New York   London

© 2011 The Guilford Press
A Division of Guilford Publications, Inc.
72 Spring Street, New York, NY 10012
www.guilford.com

Printed in the United States of America

This book is printed on acid-free paper.

Last digit is print number: 9   8   7   6   5   4   3   2   1

Library of Congress Cataloging-in-Publication Data

Hall, Leigh A.
  Empowering struggling readers : practices for the middle grades /
Leigh A. Hall, Leslie D. Burns, Elizabeth Carr Edwards.
      p. cm. — (Solving problems in the teaching of literacy)
  Includes bibliographical references and index.
  ISBN 978-1-60918-023-2 (pbk. : alk. paper)
  ISBN 978-1-60918-024-9 (hardcover : alk. paper)
  1. Content area reading—United States.   2. Language arts (Middle school)—
Correlation with content subjects—United States.   I. Burns, Leslie D.
II. Edwards, Elizabeth Carr.   III. Title.
  LB1050.455.H35 2011
  428.4071′2—dc22
                                                                          2010041737

About the Authors

Leigh A. Hall, PhD, is Assistant Professor of Literacy Studies at the University of North Carolina at Chapel Hill. She is a former middle school English and social studies teacher for the Alief Independent School District in Houston, Texas. Dr. Hall earned her doctorate in Curriculum, Teaching, and Educational Policy from Michigan State University in 2005, with specializations in literacy and teacher education. She is the recipient of the 2010 Early Career Achievement Award from the National Reading Conference/Literacy Research Association. Her research addresses issues relevant to adolescent literacy, struggling readers, middle school education, and teacher education. Her work considers whether and how students' identities as readers influence the decisions they make when reading and how teachers use information about students' identities to inform their practices and improve students' reading comprehension.

Leslie D. Burns, PhD, is Assistant Professor of Literacy at the University of Kentucky and a former English language arts teacher who worked in rural Kansas schools. He earned his doctorate in Curriculum, Teaching, and Educational Policy from Michigan State University in 2005, with specializations in English education and adolescent literacy. Dr. Burns focuses his studies on research-based standards for literacy and teacher education. He has published research on curriculum policy, identity development in education, and teacher education. He chaired the Conference on English Education's (CEE) Task Force for Political Action in

Education Reform, serves on the CEE's Standards Task Force, on behalf of the CEE Committee on Standards and Accreditation, and chairs the English Education Program at the University of Kentucky.

Elizabeth Carr Edwards, PhD, taught elementary school for 7 years before earning her doctorate in Reading Education from the University of Georgia in 2006. She is presently Assistant Professor of Literacy in the Department of Curriculum, Foundations, and Reading at Georgia Southern University, where she teaches undergraduate and graduate courses. Dr. Edwards has published research on elementary and middle grades vocabulary development in edited books and in journals such as *Reading Research Quarterly*, *The Reading Teacher*, and *American Educational Research Journal*. Her current research interests are vocabulary and sociocultural pedagogical theory.

Preface

Adolescent literacy has received a lot of attention lately. Much of this attention has been centered on "struggling readers," or students who fail to meet grade-level expectations in reading. Research and news reports suggest that many of our adolescents are struggling readers who will have difficulty in reading texts as adults.

While this is a critical problem that cannot be ignored, we also cannot help but see that students labeled as struggling readers tend to get a lot of bad press. We hear that they are lazy and unmotivated, and hate to read. We are told they don't like school and are uninterested in learning. Their low scores on reading tests and their report card grades seem to only reinforce this belief.

And yet, something doesn't add up. In our experiences as classroom teachers and researchers we cannot recall a single example of a kid who hated to read. Yes, nearly all kids can tell you something they dislike reading (like a textbook), but nearly all kids like to read something (like a magazine) or have a favorite topic they want to learn more about. They just don't necessarily like school reading or see how reading in school is relevant to their lives.

We began to think that too often we position the kids as being the problem. It's the kids who won't read. It's the kids who won't participate in discussions. It's the kids who won't write down their vocabulary definitions or answer the questions about the chapter. But what if the kids aren't the problem? What if the kids simply have a problem with the way school, and reading in school, is structured?

It is from these questions that this book was born. We considered what would happen if we took a close look at the discipline of English, considered how texts and reading instruction supported or marginalized struggling readers, and then thought about how to use texts to create instruction that would allow struggling readers a chance to find their place in school—a chance to fit in. No more pull-out programs. No more scripted curricula. No more giving some kids easier books to read. We wanted to offer a way for middle school English teachers to reach their struggling readers—and all their students—without feeling as if they were being pulled apart.

Each of the chapters in this book begins with a set of "focal points" to guide your reading and thinking about the topics discussed. Key ideas pulled from the text are highlighted in sidebars throughout the book. At the end of each chapter, you'll find questions for reflection (perfect for reading groups!) and a list of recommended print and online resources.

Chapter 1 begins by exploring what it means to be a struggling reader and how the label gets used in schools. We highlight how students labeled as struggling readers often know a great deal about reading and may possess skills that go unrecognized in schools. By considering how to draw on and connect their funds of knowledge to academic literacy practices, English teachers may find they can help struggling readers become more connected to classroom life.

Chapter 2 delves into the discipline of English. We take a look at the concepts the discipline privileges and how these concepts result in reading practices that may inadvertently reinforce the disadvantaged position of struggling readers. We consider how to use students' personal funds of knowledge and the concept of the "third space" to help students develop the various skills needed to read successfully in English.

Chapters 3 and 4 center on redesigning classrooms and instructional practices so that struggling readers' ideas are valued and respected. Chapter 3 focuses on creating classroom environments that support struggling readers in taking risks and thereby help them feel safe to read and discuss challenging texts. In Chapter 4, we examine how to further increase the engagement and motivation of struggling readers.

In Chapter 5, we consider the role that assessment can and should play in understanding both who our struggling readers are and how we might design instruction for them. We argue that, rather than drawing on traditional approaches to assessment, teachers should first assess students' various funds of knowledge and then use that information in selecting texts.

Chapters 6–11 focus on specific ways to provide instruction for struggling readers in English or language arts classrooms. While Chapter 6 focuses on comprehension strategy instruction, it takes up the problem of struggling readers deliberately avoiding the use of such strategies if they think that doing so will reveal their comprehension difficulties to others.

The chapter provides tools for helping teachers understand and navigate the crosscurrents between cognitive strategy instruction and the social status consequences that may ensue in English language arts classes.

In Chapter 7, Lisa Scherff from the University of Alabama looks at how English teachers can use young adult literature to improve reading comprehension while also teaching complex concepts such as race, feminist, or gender theory. Chapter 8 highlights how vocabulary instruction can go beyond teaching definitions of words by connecting students' own funds of knowledge to their vocabulary development.

Chapter 9 takes a look at how to structure discussions of texts in ways that make space for struggling readers while helping them read challenging texts. In Chapter 10, we present ways teachers can help struggling readers become better at reading online texts. In Chapter 11, Stergios G. Botzakis from the University of Tennessee further expands the discussions about reading and texts by considering the ways in which nonprint media can be used to support the reading skills development of struggling readers.

In Chapter 12, we take a step back from looking at instructional practices and consider how teachers can become active in their communities in ways that can shape policy and benefit the kids who need help the most. We present a variety of ideas to help teachers connect with one another locally and work toward goals that are relevant within their community.

Finally, in Chapter 13, David W. Moore from Arizona State University helps us think about how to put the ideas from this book into practice. He argues for the importance of considering a sociocultural approach to English education and carefully examining how our instructional practices position students as readers within our classrooms. Rather than lowering our standards for struggling readers, he suggests, we should figure out how to create more meaningful experiences for struggling readers so they can meet or exceed grade-level standards. None of this is easy or done overnight—or even within a single year—but through our collective effort it is something that we can accomplish.

Contents

EMPOWERING STRUGGLING READERS

1

Who Are Struggling Readers?

FOCAL POINTS

1. Struggling readers are constantly seeking ways to be successful in school.

2. The term *struggling readers* automatically marginalizes students who fall into that category.

3. Schools play a fundamental role in creating both good *and struggling* readers.

It may seem simple to describe "struggling readers." On the surface, they are the students who often have persistent difficulties in comprehending texts and learning academic subject matter. If you are a teacher, you may observe them sitting on the sidelines of your classroom, deliberately limiting their involvement with reading. They may even refuse to read or apply the reading skills and strategies you have provided extensive instruction on. In some cases, they might even disrupt class or remain completely silent. In general, such actions suggest that these students have largely withdrawn from classroom life. They don't seem to care about becoming better readers, and they don't seem interested in learning.

However, research investigating what it means to be a struggling middle school reader appears to indicate that many of these students are unhappy with their perceived status in classrooms and tired of sitting on the periphery. In fact, they often enjoy reading, want to learn, and wish to become better readers (Hall, 2007). Even when they appear disengaged or even resistant, they are likely listening and watching their teachers and classmates in an effort to learn (Hall, 2010).

When struggling readers limit their involvement with reading in school, it is often an understandable response to the repeated difficulties and frustrations they have encountered over the years (Lenters, 2006). Most recognize the difficulties they have with reading in school, but they don't know how to improve their situation. They would like to find a way to be full participants in classroom reading practices and contribute in meaningful ways, but they feel they have little to offer, and they may even feel ashamed of their perceived weaknesses (Hall, 2009).

UNDERSTANDING THE TERM *STRUGGLING READER*: A TYPICAL VIEW

Students who are considered to be struggling readers typically read one or more years below their current grade level but do not have an identified learning disability of any kind (Hall, 2005a; Spear-Swerling, 2004). They are often perceived as lacking the skills other students possess and use with little difficulty, such as analyzing information, defining vocabulary words, or applying reading comprehension strategies (O'Brien, Beach, & Scharber, 2007). The difficulties they have with reading are typically attributed to inadequate instruction or their own failure to fully engage with and learn from texts and classroom instruction. Based on these assumptions, common solutions for helping struggling readers include providing them with more intensive skills-based instruction, structuring lessons more effectively, and/or finding better ways to motivate them (Guthrie & Davis, 2003).

Struggling readers can have instructional needs that are much different from those of their peers who meet or exceed grade-level expectations in reading. For example, some struggling readers find it difficult to read words smoothly and easily and are still developing their fluency abilities. Others sound as though they are reading with great ease but don't always comprehend what they are saying (Rasinski & Padak, 2005). Some will recognize when they are failing to comprehend texts, but they don't know how to respond to the problem (Hall, 2005b). Others may focus on pronouncing words correctly without realizing that they should be creating meaning as they read (Pressley, 2004).

Because of their varying strengths and weaknesses, struggling readers are likely to need additional support to successfully comprehend texts and learn academic content (Allington, 2005). While there are many ideas for what this instruction might look like and how it might be implemented, the message often sent is that struggling readers need experiences that are markedly different from those of their nonstruggling peers—experiences that ultimately cost them opportunities to participate fully in normal classroom life. A typical response for addressing the needs of struggling readers is to provide them with additional reading classes that are separate and disconnected from their core subject areas (Allington, 2007). Despite the benefits these classes may offer, this approach fails to help students improve as readers within their own core academic classes.

When struggling readers do receive reading instruction in their subject-matter classes it is often limited and infrequent. The types of texts available for struggling readers to read in school may also be limited in terms of genre, topic, and degree of difficulty. Reading texts in school may be restricted to reading and answering prescribed questions that require students to identify low-level facts or to focus on finding a single correct interpretation (Mraz, Rickleman, & Vacca, 2009). Such experiences do not provide struggling readers opportunities to think about and reflect on what they are reading or consider other interpretations.

Overall, struggling readers are often portrayed as students with problems who experience failure with reading in school and who have little to offer. It is often assumed that the problem resides within *them* and that curriculum and instruction can simply be adjusted in ways that can "fix" them, should they choose to fully engage with it. But how accurate are our understandings about struggling readers? Are they really students with reading difficulties who have, for whatever reason, failed to become proficient readers in school, or have we lost perspective on an issue that is not as straightforward as it may appear?

THE STRUGGLING READER CRISIS: MYTH, REALITY, OR SOMEWHERE IN BETWEEN?

For over 34 years, the National Assessment of Educational Progress (NAEP, 2005, 2007, 2008) has consistently recorded that the majority of middle school students have persistent difficulties in comprehending print-based texts. NAEP results have uniformly shown that most students both enter and leave middle school with the capability of being able to do little more than extract basic facts from classroom texts. Many will experience difficulties in critically evaluating information, making inferences, and applying what they read in school to their lives. These findings are of great concern. By the time students finish the eighth grade, after all, their reading abilities are one of the strongest predictors of their success—or, rather, lack of it during and beyond high school (ACT, 2008).

The reading difficulties middle school students experience do not suddenly begin at the outset of the sixth grade, nor are they specific to any one type of student. NAEP (2007) data have shown that fourth graders have similar types of reading problems as eighth graders. Most students who have reading difficulties early on in school just continue to struggle until they graduate. It is estimated that over 8 million students—nearly

40%—in grades 4–12 fail to achieve grade-level standards in reading, a factor that contributes to many students' decision to drop out of school (National Institute for Literacy, 2007). Students with reading difficulties come from all racial, ethnic, and economic backgrounds. However, the majority of these students are black or Hispanic and eligible for school lunch programs (NAEP, 2007).

The reading difficulties middle school students experience do not suddenly begin at the outset of the sixth grade, nor are they specific to any one type of student.

Despite the negative portrait these statistics paint, struggling readers actually possess a great deal of knowledge about reading that is not always recognized, valued, or fully utilized in schools. Researchers have shown that struggling readers engage in complex and rich literacy practices in their homes and communities (Alvermann, Hinchman, Moore, Phelps, & Waff, 2006). They may read traditional print texts and the Internet for pleasure or to gain specific information that addresses questions important to them (Moje, Overby, Tysvaer, & Morris, 2008). Some students who struggle with reading in school form out-of-school book clubs with their peers or engage in reading with their parents. Others use reading as a way to network with peers who share a common interest such as video gaming, sports, or auto repair.

Struggling readers actually possess a great deal of knowledge about reading that is not always recognized, valued, or fully utilized in schools.

The skills and concepts struggling readers learn while using these texts help them define their world and raise important questions for them about their place in it (Heron-Hruby, Hagood, & Alvermann, 2008). Those skills also support their development as literate individuals and help them redefine what it means to be a reader. It may seem surprising, but just because a student struggles to read in school does not mean he or she doesn't read at all.

In fact, struggling readers' out-of-school literacy practices challenge our understanding of what it means to have reading difficulties in school and how struggling readers are afforded space to grow as readers—or not. For these students, their regular and often diverse reading habits outside of school suggest they see reading as having a regular place and purpose in their lives. From their point of view, reading may not always be about succeeding in school, making a good grade, or completing an assignment. Instead, it may be a way to connect with peers, explore their own world, and learn things they find relevant to their own life.

However, being identified as a good reader in school often means engaging with classroom reading practices in the ways deemed valuable by teachers, school administrators, and educational policymakers (Alvermann, 2001a; Moje et al., 2008), ways

> **Struggling readers' out-of-school literacy practices challenge our understanding of what it means to have reading difficulties in school and how struggling readers are afforded space to grow as readers—or not.**

that do not always connect to the lives of struggling readers. Students who reject or cannot engage in the reading practices often emphasized in schools risk being labeled as "struggling" no matter how enthusiastically they may engage in reading on their own time. Because of their difficulties in reconciling personal and educational reading practices, they find themselves marginalized in their own classrooms.

HOW STRUGGLING READERS DEFINE THEMSELVES

Understanding who struggling readers are means considering their perspectives on reading both in and outside of school. Struggling readers are usually aware of their comprehension problems. By the time they reach middle school, they have had the chance to determine what counts as being a good or poor reader in school and numerous opportunities to see how their reading abilities compare to those of their peers (McCarthey, 2001). Many have had multiple experiences in school that suggest they are not good readers, may never become good readers, and that they have little to offer.

Leigh spoke with three middle school students, Sarah, Nicole, and Jason, about their experiences with reading. Each of them read below grade level and, according to their teachers, consistently had problems in comprehending and learning from the texts used in school. The students recognized their comprehension difficulties too and saw themselves as being poor readers.

Sarah was a sixth-grade student who read on a fourth-grade level when the year began. Her teachers labeled her as struggling, and she told Leigh that she was "probably the worst reader in the entire sixth grade." Still, there were aspects about reading that she enjoyed.

"I like to read big books," said Sarah. "At home there's this one book I'm reading called *Beautiful Bible Stories*, and then I'm reading *Chicken Soup for the Teenage Soul*—and that's all the books I'm basically reading right now. I was reading *The Secret Garden*, but it was boring. I liked the movie, though."

When Leigh noticed that Sarah focused only on what she read at home, she asked Sarah to discuss what she was reading in school. Sarah replied, "Well, in English I was supposed to read *Island of the Blue Dolphins*, but I didn't."

"Why not?"

"I don't know," Sarah shrugged. "Too hard. I couldn't read it."

"Are you reading something now in your English class that you like?" Leigh asked.

"Nope. It's all too hard, so I don't do it. It's not like at home, where I can just go get another book to read if I don't like the first one. I'm supposed to read whatever the teacher gives me, but I can't."

This excerpt reveals a complex side to Sarah's reading practices. Her actions indicate that at home she approached texts in ways that are characteristic of good readers. She read for pleasure on a regular basis, and when she did not like a book she eventually stopped reading it. She did not find reading boring but noted that on her own time she was free to stop reading books that did not capture her interest or were too difficult. She was also free to find books that better suited her taste or goals, a practice that mirrors how most people approach reading and using texts in everyday life.

Leigh's discussions with Nicole and Jason revealed they also read at home for pleasure but were frustrated by the reading they were expected to do in school. When Leigh first met Nicole, a seventh grader, she was told by one of her teachers that Nicole "doesn't read really well and needs a lot of help." At the time, Nicole was reading on a fifth-grade level and described herself as "not the best reader." When Leigh asked her to talk about her experiences with reading, she responded by sharing how much she enjoyed reading series books at home:

> "I like to read series [books]. Like right now I'm reading the *Left Behind* series for kids. It's about, like, what happens when Jesus comes down to earth. I'm on number 25, and there's like 31. What's cool is sometimes there's the same characters, but it doesn't all happen the same way. I usually read it at home. I have to finish my homework first! I'm also reading *Holes*. I saw the movie too."

Although Nicole was an avid reader at home, she made it clear that she did not enjoy reading at school. Like Sarah, she found the books her teachers selected to be "superhard" and "impossible to understand." Nicole explained that, in order to get by in school, "you read just enough to make it look like you know the book. There's no point to this stuff. It's just too hard. When I go home, I get to read all the good stuff I like."

Jason was an eighth grader who read on a fifth-grade level. When Leigh asked him to describe himself as a reader, he explained: "I'm not the best—that's for sure! Most people read faster and better than me." He further stressed the points made by Sarah and Nicole:

> "I really like to read, but not in school. They're always telling you what to read in school, and I don't always like it because it's so hard. I read lots of magazines at home, but I want to read more books. I like scary books. My cousin has a bunch that I borrowed."

Leigh's discussions with Sarah, Nicole, and Jason suggest that, although they were interested in reading, they were unable to enjoy reading in school. Like all readers, middle school students like to self-select books to read for pleasure and information (Kottke, 2008; Weih, 2008). However, they are expected to spend their school days reading texts that present significant challenges and seem irrelevant to their lives (Allington, 2007).

It is not surprising, then, that Sarah, Nicole, and Jason found reading in school to be a difficult, boring, and frustrating task. It was only on their own time and with texts they self-selected that they were able to connect reading to their lives and read texts they could fully engage with. At home, they engaged in literacy practices they could learn from, be successful in, and enjoy—all expectations they could not fulfill when reading at school.

REDEFINING THE TERM *STRUGGLING READER*

Helping struggling readers fully participate in classroom reading practices means redefining our concept of "struggling readers." We recognize that categorizing students as readers is a part of school culture, and we cannot pretend that labels do not exist. They do, and they have real consequences for how we treat students, how we design instruction for them, and how they get positioned to engage in classroom reading practices. What we *can* do is provide a broader definition for understanding and working with students who fail to meet the criteria set forth in schools for being categorized as a good reader.

McDermotte and Varenne (1995) and Alvermann (2001a) have argued that institutions like school create the category of "struggling reader" and then make that status a reality for some students. Schools too often view reading—and readers—through a deprivation lens. Students either have the skills and cognitive abilities that enable them to be identified as good readers, or they don't. Often such classifications are made based on our perceptions about what students should be able to do at a particular age or grade level.

Viewing struggling readers through a deprivation lens can lead to literacy instruction that is framed by an autonomous model of literacy (Street, 1985). In an autonomous model of literacy, reading is based solely on the ability to acquire and apply a specific set of skills such as decoding, identifying basic facts, or reading at an appropriate rate. Reading is seen as a simple process where decoding words on a page leads to comprehension. From an autonomous view, teaching reading is about identifying what skills students lack and creating instruction to help them improve and catch up.

In an autonomous model of reading, the skills one needs to be a good reader are considered to be universal, that is, the same across all contexts. The social, cultural, and historical contexts that frame students' home and school lives are seen as irrelevant to their reading abilities. When students struggle, it is assumed that they are either not trying hard enough or need additional skills-based instruction. Because school officials generally think in terms of the autonomous model for reading, the curriculum tends to ignore students' social and cultural funds of knowledge (Moll & Gonzales, 2001; Moje et al., 2004) that might otherwise be used to support their success as readers. As a result, the autonomous model of literacy not only generates the traditional culture of reading in school but also sets the stage for many students to fail through no fault of their own.

Our definition of struggling readers and framework for how to work with them are situated in Street's (1995) ideological model. In comparison to the autonomous model, an ideological model of reading views reading as a complex social practice that means more than just saying words correctly or answering comprehension questions at the end of a text. While learning skills like decoding is necessary and important, students' development as readers also depends on providing them with explicit information about how reading works in school, allowing them a choice and voice in classroom activities, and helping them find relevance by connecting reading practices with the knowledge and experiences they bring to school.

"Good readers" and "struggling readers" exist, then, because schools create a culture that supports the categorization of some youth as successful and others as failing. However, as Alvermann (2001a) notes, "Adolescents who struggle with reading are part of the same cloth from which good readers come. Neither group stands alone in opposition to the other, both are bound up in the cultural contexts they inhabit" (p. 683). We interpret Alvermann's statement to mean that schools create a culture from which particular types of readers are born. Despite the different labels that might exist, both

> **"Good readers" and "struggling readers" exist because schools create a culture that supports the categorization of some youth as successful and others as failing.**

struggling and good readers are products of the same culture and ways of thinking that ultimately create who they become.

Our research and experience with middle school readers show us that labeling students as "struggling" is a dangerous practice with serious long-term consequences. If so many of these same students can read outside of school, then why do they so often appear unable to read in our classrooms? If they can in fact read, then we must consider that it isn't our students who need fixing—it's *us*. If we truly believe all of our students are capable of learning to read in school and if we know they are not learning enough to be successful in our classrooms, then our first task is to think hard about our assumptions and methods as English teachers.

Rather than subscribe to an either–or view of reading ability, we choose to see *all* students (and all adults) as *developing* readers. The term *developing reader* does not suggest that we are all still developing our phonemic awareness or our ability to decode texts. Rather, it means that the skills, strategies, and knowledge we use to approach and interact with texts in a variety of contexts are constantly growing and changing as a result of the social, cultural, and academic experiences we have during our lives.

Throughout this book we occasionally use the term *struggling reader* because we recognize that it is a common one, an established one, familiar to most people and regularly used in schools. It is also an important term to use because it reflects the culture of schooling that middle school students have been brought up in. Understanding how to respond to the reading needs of middle school students means being responsive to the effects this term has had on how we teach and the options students have had for participating.

However, we also use the term *marginalized reader* to describe and discuss students who often fail to meet the reading demands of school. According to Moje, Young, Readence, and Moore (2000):

> Marginalized readers are those who are not connected to literacy in classrooms and schools. Specifically, we identify as marginalized adolescents those who are not engaged in the reading and writing done in school, who have language or cultural practices different from those valued in school; or who are outsiders to the dominant group because of their race, class, gender, or sexual orientation.

We maintain that students are only struggling readers because we have positioned them to struggle by teaching them how to read in certain ways instead of others. In this book we seek to understand the limitations of this label and provide ways for helping students overcome it. We believe that, by explicitly teaching students how to read in an academic setting and helping them use their personal funds of knowledge, we can reposition so-called struggling readers to participate in their own development and to find both success and satisfaction in school learning. By aligning our practices with students' needs and making academic reading more relevant to their daily lives, we can move away from seeing students as either more or less competent. We can see them instead as capable individuals who use school to amplify their opportunities to define the powerfully literate adults they are to become.

SUMMARY

Responding to the needs of struggling readers is a complex issue that involves understanding them from multiple perspectives, including cognitive, motivational, social, and cultural perspectives. While struggling readers are likely to make up a high percentage of students in classrooms, they are certainly not the only students whose reading needs must be attended to. Struggling readers sit alongside students who meet or exceed grade-level standards in reading. Therefore, instruction must attend to a diverse range of readers (Dennis, 2008).

While struggling readers may have unique needs, the goal in working more closely with them is not to provide them with instruction and reading assignments that further alienate them from classroom life but rather to engage them in ways that make them an integral part of classroom reading practices. There is no single answer, no simple set of rules, no one size fits all approach that will enable you to best respond to the needs of struggling readers. To be successful, you will need to view both them and your interactions with them from multiple angles.

Addressing the literacy crisis faced by many of our nation's middle school students is not about working *on* them. Rather, it is about working *with* them in new ways that enable them to progress in their development as readers. It is about helping them understand what you are trying to help them achieve, and it is about listening to and respecting who they are and want to be. The resistance that is said to characterize adolescents who are positioned as struggling readers is often misperceived as unwillingness to learn. It is anything but that! Struggling readers earnestly want to change their social status in classrooms and be involved with the curriculum. They want to work alongside their peers as full and capable participants who have something meaningful to say. Responding to the literacy

The resistance that is said to characterize adolescents who are positioned as struggling readers is often misperceived as unwillingness to learn. It is anything but that!

crisis is about helping them gain access to the reading practices that can help them find their voices in school.

Questions for Reflection

1. How do *you* help struggling readers fully engage with the curriculum and classroom reading practices?

2. What kinds of texts do your struggling readers typically read in school? What do they read at home?

3. How do you respond to students who believe they are incapable of reading and who refuse to participate?

RECOMMENDED RESOURCES

Gallagher, K. (2009). *Readicide: How schools are killing reading and what you can do about it.* Portland, ME: Stenhouse.

Larson, J. (2007). *Literacy as snake oil: Beyond the quick fix* (rev. ed.). New York: Peter Lang.

Miller, D. (2009). *The book whisperer: Awakening the inner reader in every child.* San Francisco: Jossey-Bass.

2

Promoting Disciplinary Reading Practices in English Language Arts

FOCAL POINTS

1. English is an academic discipline that has many useful applications in relation to everyday life, a complex history and traditions, and specialized terms, concepts, and ways of demonstrating knowledge.

2. When marginalized students are specifically taught to understand how the discipline "works," they are better able to complete academic reading tasks.

3. By drawing on students' funds of knowledge from outside of school—whether from the home, the community, or the Internet—teachers can make academic content more understandable.

Anyone who has taught English in middle school has at some point heard a student mutter (or cry out), "This is so *boring!* Why do we have to do *this* stuff?" The object of that student's scorn may have been your favorite novel, the poem you thought everyone would enjoy, or the vocabulary game you created to help study for this week's quiz. "Boring" is the battle cry of many marginalized readers. Is that all there is to it? Is English class just soul-killing for some young people?

Although our students might not always share our enthusiasm in school, most English teachers are passionate readers, and we have a thousand reasons why students should love the subject the way we do. Les, for example, wouldn't teach English today if he hadn't fallen in love with books from his youth like *Superfudge, The Hobbit, The Catcher in the Rye,* and many others. We can all point to books that fired our imagination, entertained us, and changed how we thought about the world. We chose to teach English in part because positive encounters with texts inside and outside of school made it seem fun. But not everyone likes English, and today's students don't always come to school with the same kinds of reading experiences we enjoyed when growing up.

Engaging in the traditional practices of English isn't always comfortable or familiar to 21st-century students. Although they have been asked to read in school for years by the time they reach the middle grades, they often do not understand there are differences between reading for pleasure and reading for academic purposes. They may not feel comfortable writing and talking about what they read in formal ways. Many marginalized readers, in particular, struggle because they do not understand that English class requires certain ways of knowing and doing that aren't necessarily the same as those used for reading and communicating in other situations they know.

When they enter middle school, students experience the in-depth study of such subjects as English for the first time, and they are confronted with specialized terms related to language and text, more complex modes of reading and writing, and special ways of demonstrating understanding. They are expected to analyze texts not only for literal comprehension but also to understand how they work. In nonschool situations they just enjoy good stories, magazine articles, or websites without noticing how they work. They are *assigned* in school to write about the content and structure of language from their reading in specified ways, but it is unusual for teachers to spend much time helping students understand *why* they read and respond in those ways. Too often, students are not provided instruction in *how* to fully participate in English, such as when teachers ask students to discuss their reading without helping them explicitly to think about how large-group discussions work. Marginalized readers can find themselves stuck on the periphery of classroom life because they lack *disciplinary literacy*—knowledge of how and why subject area content is supposed to be used in school (Greenleaf, Schoenbach, Cziko, & Mueller, 2001; Moje, 2008). When students exclaim that they are bored with reading in English, what they often mean is they don't have the information they need to participate confidently and enjoy it (Jago, 2003). Unless we help marginalized readers learn how our discipline works, they will continue to sit uncomfortably on the periphery rather than participate. They will continue to struggle.

In this chapter we discuss the nature of English and the need to teach students disciplinary literacy by helping them connect what we do in classrooms with their diverse *funds of knowledge*—formal and informal knowledge they bring with them into our classrooms from their everyday lives beyond school (Moll & Gonzales, 2001). We'll examine the purposes and history of our field to understand why English has traditionally focused on some topics rather than others, and we'll explore the typical content taught in middle schools today as it relates to the teaching of reading. We'll explore how to help marginalized readers become full participants in our classrooms by explicitly teaching the vocabulary, concepts, and ways of reading, writing, talking, and thinking that they need to know. We'll conclude by describing how to bridge students' out-of-school knowledge with the reading demands of English.

DISCIPLINARY LITERACY AND ENGLISH

Although teaching students disciplinary literacy may seem like common sense, most contemporary school professionals do not approach reading instruction in this way, even in English. Instead, they tend to implement a style of content area reading instruction in which students are taught literacy strategies such as predicting, using context clues, and using graphic organizers *in addition to* transmitting the content of the basic curriculum. This common approach generally assumes the autonomous model of literacy we mentioned in Chapter 1, where reading is simply decoding and comprehending text in general. But, although this model seems straightforward, it has complicated teachers' work by treating reading instruction and content knowledge as separate projects. In fact, even English teachers complain that reading instruction takes time away from their main job of "covering" the subject (Moje, 2008).

According to Moje (2008), although we often treat reading as a basic skill in every school subject, teachers are mistaken when they assume that reading in English class, for example, is the same as reading in science class or even in social studies, where students might read texts similar to some they encounter in English. The ways in which readers pay attention to and create meaning in different disciplines vary. In science, for example, readers may focus particularly on reading analytically to understand the steps in chemical processes or the components of ecological networks and relationships. In history classes, readers are often focused on cause–effect relationships and chronological sequences related to significant events. In English, readers may also read to understand processes, cause–effect, and chronology, but they do so for reasons peculiar to English class, particularly in relation to literary reading.

In literary analysis, students focus on reading to understand grand themes about human nature, society, and life in general, as well as focusing on the ways in which figurative as well as descriptive language is used poetically and symbolically to create meaning for both moral statements and aesthetic pleasure. This is not to say that a history or science text necessarily lacks any pleasurable qualities—many, in fact, possess such qualities. However, in science and social studies classes students are not usually expected to read aesthetically or to learn about, analyze, and apply composition techniques in relation to their own lives, other literary texts, and the world around them. Reading in the discipline of English is unique to those particular applications. Accepting that fact, one important job that middle school teachers have is teaching students reading skills and concepts in ways that enable them to understand the particular ways of communicating in English classes. Making the discipline's reading processes explicit is key to all students' success.

When discussing the disciplinary nature of reading for English, even the name given to our subject is controversial. Middle grade curricula often refer to the subject as "language arts" or "English language arts" (ELA), and the title has been a point of contention among educators. *Language arts* is generally considered a set of related topics rather than a formal discipline and is the label often assigned to elementary-level teaching. *English* is the traditional label in higher grades because secondary education tends to be organized in relation to academic work in colleges and universities, where the discipline originated. In higher education, *English* primarily addresses the formal study of literature and cultural theory along with secondary focus on composition, rhetoric, and linguistics. In K–12 *language arts*, the curriculum addresses a much broader array of topics, including not only literature, composition, and grammar but also speaking, listening, communications media, and reading. Theoretical study is generally absent in secondary classrooms, and the focus in middle grades is on practical literacy and communication skills rather than abstract analysis. Because of its unique position as a bridge between elementary school and high school, the middle school curriculum might label the subject one way or the other. For our purposes in this book, we use the term *English language arts* thereby highlighting *both* the disciplinary roots of the subject *and* what we see as the underlying *literacy* aspects of our classroom work in middle school—namely, teaching students how reading, writing, and other modes of communication work within the discipline of English.

> One important job that middle school teachers have is teaching students reading skills and concepts in ways that enable them to understand the particular ways of communicating in English classes. Making the discipline's reading processes explicit is key to all students' success.

No matter what label we choose, it is useful for all teachers to know something of English's history and origins as an academic discipline. A *discipline* can be defined as a particular area of academic study that has a unique purpose in relation to everyday life, a shared history that affects activities, and special concepts and skills for participating in a learning community (King & Brownell, 1966). That history is rarely discussed during teacher education, but knowing it reveals important information about what we teach today and why.

PURPOSES, GOALS, AND ACTIVITIES FOR TEACHING ENGLISH

Most English language arts teachers would agree that our subject doesn't just help students appreciate language and literature but also makes them better people. At its heart, the purpose of ELA is to study language, signs, and texts to interpret, explain, and evaluate human nature and experience. As people engage with the discipline, they use reading, writing, speaking, listening, and visual representations to communicate. They concentrate on analyzing print and nonprint texts for themes and patterns to understand language and society. When communicating about texts, they cite evidence of how structures and content relate to their prior knowledge and personal experiences to increase understanding about the world around them. According to the National Council of Teachers of English (NCTE; 1996a, 2006), studying English makes collective experiences more meaningful, demonstrates both commonalities and differences in language and culture over time, promotes respect for diversity, and enhances aesthetic appreciation, critical thinking, and personal growth.

Academically speaking, an additional disciplinary goal of ELA is to help participants think systematically and creatively from multiple perspectives. To do this, our subject draws on knowledge from such fields as literature, literary theory, reading, composition, rhetoric, speech, history, philosophy, linguistics, psychology, and the like (Luke, 2004). For example, when teachers guide students to read Christopher Paul Curtis's *The Watsons Go to Birmingham—1963* (2000), we do not simply hand out copies of the book and concentrate solely on the content. Rather, most ELA teachers organize a unit of instruction that includes teaching background information about racial inequalities at the time of the novel's setting, key aspects of the civil rights movement at that time, the nature of society in the American South during the early 1960s, and more. We supplement the novel with history, cultural analysis, psychological and philosophical information about race and prejudice, information about current events that have been influenced by the history, and usually some discussions of our students' experiences related to prejudice, stereotypes, and diversity today. Doing so enhances the experience and pleasures of reading Curtis's novel, but more importantly it provides students with the cognitive supports and information they need to fully comprehend the text and use it to create meaning for themselves.

We use multiple theories and practices from these fields—literary theory, philosophy, history, and psychology—to derive conclusions and communicate interpretations of the novel, and normally there is no single correct answer to the questions we raise. Such literary theories as feminism, colonial theory, new historicism, and reader response, for example, provide diverse perspectives for thinking about a book and what it can teach us. Historical interpretations help us put the story in context and evaluate its credibility and purposes. Using these disciplinary tools, we read not only to understand but also to *do* things with texts and solve problems in the real world (New London Group. 2000). These ways of reading in English are not always clear to students, and so we must make them explicit during classroom activities so that students understand the purposes of each perspective, activity, and experience. It is not that reading a novel like *The Watsons Go to Birmingham—1963* is intended to indoctrinate our students into certain viewpoints about race and class in our society; rather, the purpose is to help them learn how to read it from multiple perspectives and evaluate it to make interpretations in ways that lead to improved analytical skills. Explicit instruction creates a foundation for disciplinary literacy that helps students learn how to talk and think in ways that promote their own participation and success.

If we think about English in terms of its goals and resulting activities—such as learning to read and think from multiple perspectives—it becomes clear that being literate in our subject means more than just being able to read for literal comprehension, or to offer simple plot summaries focused on predetermined "correct" responses. Being literate in the discipline of English means being able to understand language and use texts for multiple purposes and audiences in a wide variety of situations. It means learning how to participate in such activities as interpreting texts and articulating personal connections with them through the use of reader response techniques, learning to question and evaluate the assumptions and perspectives of authors, and using evidence and knowledge to justify particular interpretations.

The goals, purposes, and activities described above are the products of a complicated history and tradition in ELA. It is helpful to trace its historical development in the United States from the late eighteenth century to the present because key moments in our history can help teachers and students alike understand why English works the way it does now. That understanding can enable them to work together in school more productively.

THE HISTORY OF THE ENGLISH CLASS— AND ITS CONSEQUENCES

Surprisingly, the origin of what we now call "English class" in the United States is not rooted in public education but rather in the Christian church (Brass, 2009; Lacquer, 1976). To some extent, this derivation explains our discipline's focus on personal growth and its desire to explain the world, explore human nature and society, and ultimately understand the meaning of life. As far back as colonial times, churches used both religious *and* secular stories to educate children about morality and social values, and stories were used as parables for teaching the "right" ways to think and act. During the Industrial Revolution of the early and mid-1800s, however, the influence of religion in American daily life declined, and many feared that the movement of the population from tightly knit rural communities to unstable and chaotic cities was causing moral decay. Educators began promoting secular literary study as a way of preserving morality in the postindustrial age (Protherrough & Atkinson, 1991).

During the same period, universities began instituting mandatory reading lists for all students seeking to enter higher education. Their rationale was that a college education required students to be familiar with a certain body of cultural knowledge (Western civilization and history), an idea that survives to this day (Hirsch, 1988, 2006). Prior to the end of the 19th century, secondary and higher education was mostly restricted to the upper classes, and literary study was an activity for the social elite intended to reproduce "correct" speech and conserve traditional Anglo culture and values. With the turn of the 20th century, however, the United States experienced mass immigration by mostly poor and non-English-speaking people from all over the world. Educators began advocating public schooling for *all* children irrespective of ethnicity or social class. The call was issued in part so that new citizens would be trained to speak and behave in ways deemed crucial to maintaining civility in the larger community's life.

Without excusing the racist, classist, and elitist practices that resulted from their beliefs and actions, educators at that time sought to create a unified "American" culture through public schooling, and schooling was a key ingredient in the recipe for what's traditionally been called America's "melting pot." Because canonical literature was thought to embody "high" culture and "correct" language use at that time, literary study was viewed as a useful topic for *all* children to study. By 1900 "English" was well established as a required academic subject (Applebee, 1974; Hook, 1979; Shumway & Dionne, 2002; Sperling & DiPardo, 2008).

Although other subjects like reading and composition were included in the English curriculum from the start, literature has always been central because of its perceived role as a repository for correct language and values. In fact, by the 1930s, educators and members of the public alike began to regard English teachers as the *guardians* of language and the "preachers of culture" (Mathieson, 1975). The aura of spiritual refinement that was tied to literature early on in our country's development continued throughout its history and still echoes today. For example, when the National Council of Teachers of English (1996a) asserts that literature must be seen as "the core, the humane center" of the curriculum for students, "adding delight and wonder to their daily lives" (p. 18), we can see how enlightenment is still a major focus of classroom work. Literature is thought to generate humanitarian impulses in students, make their lives more pleasurable, and open their minds to new ideas and points of view. Literary analysis of canonical texts is still by far the most valued activity in university English departments because of these purposes, and some scholars view factual reading, writing, linguistics, film, and other media as beneath their dignity because of classic literary study's perceived power for spiritual enlightenment (Miller, 1991; Scholes, 1985; Shumway & Dionne, 2002).

Whether the subject's overweening emphasis on literary study has been reasonable or not, it has certainly been detrimental to the explicit teaching of reading in secondary schools. Because of it, ELA in the upper grades nowadays focuses less on *teaching* reading as on *requiring* students to read in order to interpret texts in certain ways. The ability to read fluently for literal comprehension is often just assumed. In fact, of all the topics in ELA, reading is perhaps the most disregarded because at the highest levels of the discipline it is treated as a *prerequisite*.

> **Because of its emphasis on classic literary study, ELA in the upper grades nowadays focuses less on *teaching* reading as on *requiring* students to read in order to interpret texts in certain ways.**

Because of its dominant role in the subject's history, literary study constitutes nearly the entire university-level curriculum for any individual studying English and preparing to become a teacher. In fact, by today's definitions, a highly qualified English teacher must have either a bachelor's degree in English or at least a concentration in English coursework. That focus seems reasonable in the context of the discipline's history, but it has been unfortunate in terms of preparing teachers to work with middle school students, especially marginalized readers. Because university study mostly consists of activities that assume that aspiring teachers are already fluent readers themselves, little attention is paid to helping them understand how reading works. Prospective ELA teachers usually take coursework in grammar, composition, rhetoric, and linguistics, but they are rarely given sufficient training to teach children how to read in ways relevant to disciplinary English (Marshall, Smith, & Schaafsma, 1997). Instead, new teachers tend to assume that basic reading skills are taught at some earlier point during children's schooling. They sometimes take their own students' reading abilities for granted, and research shows that graduates who become ELA teachers do not think they need to help students learn how to read—any more than social studies, science, or math teachers do (Lillis, 2003). Rather, they see themselves as *literature* teachers, and that focus is reflected in national standards and state curricula. As a result, most teachers do not teach the explicit tools for disciplinary literacy that their students need in order to participate successfully in reading activities.

The historical and traditional emphasis of literature in ELA curriculum has had consequences for both what we teach in middle grades and why. Most teachers continue to view reading as something learned during elementary school, and once it is learned they believe it is unnecessary to revisit it later. Middle school students who have reading difficulties often get left behind. They have few opportunities to learn, practice, and improve. Unsure of how to participate, they position themselves on the margins, frustrated and possibly unwilling to try.

We are not arguing that literature and the knowledge of language and culture that results from its study should be eliminated from middle school ELA—it should not. We are simply describing how ELA became a school subject and examining the role of reading instruction in our field. Despite general lack of teacher training, the need to teach reading is embedded in nearly every aspect of curriculum standards for ELA teaching. Knowing that, we must acknowledge that *the literary focus of the discipline has in many ways prevented us from teaching students as well as we can.* Knowing many students arrive unprepared to participate, ELA teachers must go beyond today's norms and explicitly teach disciplinary literacy to help *all* students better comprehend the special characteristics of school reading.

Having reviewed some of the history of our discipline, we are better positioned to understand the motives and purposes that underlie our subject, and we can now decide *how* best to teach our students to read. One challenge that becomes clear is the need to help *all* students find relevance in classroom reading irrespective of their prior experiences or background. Another challenge is to make reading instruction a normal part of classroom work rather than something extra we have to teach in order for marginalized students to catch up. Before we can explore these problems, though, we need to examine the content or scope of study that has developed from the discipline as part of its history. The content of the teaching and classroom activity is set forth in a planned set of learning experiences we commonly refer to as the ELA curriculum.

> One challenge that English teachers confront is the need to help *all* students find relevance in classroom reading irrespective of their prior experiences or background. Another challenge is to make reading instruction a normal part of classroom work rather than something extra we have to teach in order for marginalized students to catch up.

THE ENGLISH CURRICULUM

The ELA curriculum specifies the concepts and skills individuals must learn in order to participate in our discipline. Two documents published by the NCTE—*Standards for the English Language Arts* (1996b) and *Guidelines for the Preparation of Teachers of English Language Arts* (2006)—specify the curriculum at the secondary level and are useful in thinking about teaching middle school reading. The *Standards* state what all students should know and be able to do as a result of studying English, and the *Guidelines* state what teachers must know, do, and believe in order to be successful. While it would be impossible to describe all of the content required for coverage in a few pages or even a full chapter, it's useful to consider an overview of the ELA curriculum from the perspective of reading instruction.

The K–12 *Standards* assume students will practice reading on a daily basis, even though reading is not always the focus of instruction. Reading is thoroughly integrated in nearly every standard, and the NCTE's *Guidelines* for teachers reinforce that integration. According to NCTE policies, reading instruction should never be treated as separate from the study of language, composition, literature, media, speech, or inquiry. Rather, *these topics should be taught, studied, and practiced through activities with real purposes in ways that are relevant to the daily lives and personal experiences of students*. In other words, the professional standards that teachers are expected to uphold actually set the stage very well for teaching disciplinary literacy by using students' individual funds of knowledge.

The ability to read serves as the foundation for most other activities in our discipline. Students' abilities to think and communicate through writing and other media all result from knowledge they gain by decoding, comprehending, and evaluating a variety of print and nonprint texts they can then use as models for communication. The literacy skills they gain enable them to participate in broader communities, appreciate and respect diverse peoples and languages, and become more capable (NCTE, 2006). English teachers are expected to treat comprehension as "the heart of the reading act," and they are expected to teach not only literary interpretation but also the skills that constitute the elements of reading, including "phonemic, morphemic, semantic, syntactic, and pragmatic systems of language and their relationship to the reading process" (p. 32). As we discuss later, these seemingly elementary-level reading practices are still important in the middle grades and beyond; they are simply addressed in more sophisticated ways as students learn and grow (Bruner, 1960/1977).

FOUNDATIONS OF READING IN THE ENGLISH CURRICULUM

Forming a foundation for reading in the middle grades entails teaching students to learn and apply basic skills and strategies through the study of multiple genres and textual modes. It means studying language for reading at the *word, sentence, and connected text levels* (for an in-depth discussion of vocabulary instruction, see Chapter 8). In turn, that means teaching students explicitly about *using context clues* to increase comprehension and studying *vocabulary* and *orthographic patterns* (the predictable ways words and sentences are constructed). By studying orthographic patterns, readers can generate rules and principles for determining the meaning of unfamiliar words. Practicing these skills over time increases *automaticity*—the ability to comprehend words and sentences automatically—and reduces the reader's cognitive load so that he or she can concentrate on analysis and interpretation. Automaticity is the key to *fluent reading*, and fluency is largely developed through regularly, repeated opportunities to read and recognize patterns in the ways words and sentences work (Krashen, 1993).

Building fluency is most often accomplished by providing regular opportunities to read developmentally appropriate texts orally and silently to improve not only speed but also accuracy, phrasing, and expression based on clues from *text features* like punctuation, paragraphing, and syntax. At the word level, students need to study *the terminology of word parts*, such as synonyms, antonyms, homonyms, and homophones. They should also practice identifying patterns and terms for the *syllabication* of words, including prefixes, suffixes, and common roots. Understanding these basic features of language helps students comprehend differences between *literal and nonliteral meanings* of words, opening the way to more sophisticated explorations of concepts like denotation and connotation. By regularly practicing and reinforcing these seemingly elementary structures with increasing interest and appreciation, formerly marginalized readers can become increasingly fluent and even learn to find specific information in a text by *scanning* or *skimming*.

Many middle grade teachers may view reading fluency as a skill predominantly addressed by elementary school teachers. However, even by the end of the eighth grade many students are not yet fluent enough to move beyond decoding and word-by-word comprehension (Rasinski & Padak, 2005). Providing marginalized readers with opportunities to understand how language works and to develop automaticity while talking about meaningful ideas is essential for enlisting their full participation in middle school classrooms.

GENRES, COMPREHENSION, AND INTERPRETATION

In addition to studying language at the word and syntax levels, students should also study how whole texts convey meaning. They must learn how different *modes of fiction and nonfiction* work, including narrative, expository, analytical, and descriptive writing. In addition to teaching students how common types of text are structured, teachers should name and model *reading comprehension strategies* that students can apply in various situations (for detailed discussions of reading comprehension instruction, see Chapters 6 and 7).

Comprehension strategies include *activating and drawing on prior knowledge, making predictions* based on evidence and prior experiences with similar narratives and genres, and *generating clarifying questions, literal questions, and inferences* about what a text is trying to convey. Students should explore how texts use such conventional structures as *chronology, cause and effect, comparison and contrast, description, classification, and logical sequencing.* Using their understanding of these terms and conventions, students should learn to *paraphrase and summarize* readings and document their comprehension (for detailed discussions about the relations among reading, writing, and discussion, see Chapters 9 and 10).

Explicit instruction about the foregoing topics should inform daily extended reading practice. Using texts about topics that are relevant and useful for students' daily lives, teachers should not only identify the structures of those texts but also help students use that knowledge of terms and concepts for strategic reading—explaining how different reading strategies work, how texts are studied and talked about in classrooms, and *why* they are studied in the first place. For example, it is not enough to simply help students memorize the elements of a given plot for Friday's quiz or test; rather, in addition teachers should coach students to use those same literary elements as useful tools for strategic reading (Jago, 2003). If students understand that the first part of a narrative normally introduces the setting, important characters, and the central conflict, they will be more prepared to recognize important information and use it to create meaning, formulate predictions, ask questions about the text, and connect to other texts, their lives, and the world in general.

By recognizing that the plot structure of a story generally involves typical conventions, students can read a story more intentionally and better map information to increase their comprehension and analytical skills. When they learn such concepts and their functions in reading (instead of, for example, merely memorizing plot elements or characterization techniques as lists for recall on a test), they gradually come to feel more comfortable with academic texts for the remainder of their school careers, whether one is talking about poems, plays, folktales, legends, mythology, historical fiction, realistic fiction, mysteries, science fiction, or fantasy. These genres share various elements in common as well as unique ways of structuring narratives, arguments, and information. In order to fully participate in the ELA curriculum, marginalized readers must learn to use generic knowledge to make sense of academic questions asked in school. As they learn how genres work, they gain disciplinary literacy and move beyond simple comprehension. They become ready to practice *interpretation*.

Interpretation may be considered the highest level of ELA activity. The ability to interpret texts enables students to fulfill the primary goal of the discipline, namely, making meaning of human nature and understanding how society works. Interpretation involves learning to both infer and be able to explain an author's purposes, messages, and themes based on evidence, knowledge, and experiences. It is most often accomplished in schools by charting textual evidence and data, mapping it, organizing it graphically, outlining it, and noting it so that the resultant information can be composed in coherent statements about meaning and significance.

These academic operations are by no means commonly practiced by readers outside of school. They must be recognized as academic tasks, and they should be frankly treated as means for thinking systematically and creatively in academic work as students learn to use them. As students gain familiarity with interpretive processes like these, they can begin using such devices as *propaganda, bias, rhetorical appeals, figurative language, rhyme, alliteration, description, and dialogue.* These devices become tools and cues for creating meaning when reading rather than terms to be memorized and regurgitated on objective tests. They enable students to manipulate language in both reading *and* writing—that is, using ELA in their everyday lives to communicate and achieve goals. This is the essential goal of disciplinary literacy in ELA.

SUPPORTING MARGINALIZED READERS IN MIDDLE SCHOOL ENGLISH

While most ELA teachers acknowledge that skills like strategic reading and concepts like the elements of literature are appropriate to middle grade instruction, many view instruction about more basic reading skills as the exclusive task of their elementary school colleagues. Consequently, issues like fluency and grammar study are treated mostly as matters of review rather than opportunities for enrichment. However, middle grade research shows that these topics are central to a full-fledged curriculum, especially for marginalized readers, since these foundations are better taught as practical reading techniques rather than as topics for remediation in mainstream classrooms.

Lain (2003) encourages middle grade teachers to consider six traits of the reading process as they teach disciplinary literacy: decoding (semantics, syntax, graphophonic cues, syllabication), building context (activating prior knowledge), comprehending (literal), interpreting (inference, thematic), synthesizing (applications—text–text, text–self, and text–world connections), and evaluation (drawing conclusions, reflecting). These six aspects of reading occur simultaneously rather than one by one in a rigid process, and treating some as elementary and others as more advanced can prevent marginalized readers from learning to use the fullest array of reading tools possible. When we limit reading instruction to a few advanced aspects of the process rather than the complete act, marginalized readers have no chance to meet grade-level expectations. Instead, we've assumed our students are already fluent and strategic readers, and that is neither a safe nor healthy assumption if we seek to support their success.

For example, although teachers might wish to concentrate on interpretation and evaluation of texts during middle school, Fang (2008) points out that a strong grasp of syntax is significantly related to improved reading comprehension. She recommends providing regular opportunities for all students—especially marginalized readers—to practice "syntactic anatomy" to improve fluency and automatically recognize the relationships between different clauses in a sentence. Rather than handing students a laundry list of grammar terms and worksheet exercises to teach these seemingly remedial skills in isolation from daily reading, teachers can help students study how sentences from texts they are reading are put together—how their "anatomy" works. In doing so, students work with peers in small groups to solve genuine problems in their reading by applying grammar as a comprehension tool rather than as a subtopic all to itself. Working together, students across all ability levels benefit from the conscious use of academic practices to learn and participate in the discipline.

Treating grammar as integral in the ways described above moves middle school ELA beyond elementary practices. Teachers can show students how identifying subjects and predicates in a sentence will help them understand any text better, and students can begin treating grammar study as a way to solve problems rather than as an abstract exercise that has no use outside the classroom. When marginalized readers have difficulty in understanding a sentence, teachers can coach them to use their knowledge of syntactic anatomy to decode the things they read.

Similarly, middle grade teachers do not have to interrupt content instruction to help struggling readers become fluent. Repeated reading, for example, is a technique often used in elementary classrooms to build fluency by having students read the same text over and over until they are familiar with the words and structures. As they practice, students gain vocabulary through repetition and slowly improve automaticity. However, most middle school students may quickly grow tired of so much repetition, and that style of repeated reading may be inappropriate. Teachers should focus on more substantive content in the upper grades.

Still, there are more sophisticated ways middle grade teachers can design activities where repeated reading becomes a kind of invisible practice that fosters fluency. For example, in the process of studying plot structure, teachers can assign students to read a text for surface comprehension and then reread sections of that text to analyze its narrative components (exposition, rising action, climax, falling action, resolution). Applying yet another literary element like conflict, the teacher can instruct students to reread portions of the text a third time to map how conflicts develop, merge, and resolve. In this way rereading happens as a matter of course while students focus on content and thereby become more fluent during the process. Reading becomes more integrated without taking time from important mandated content.

Middle grade reading instruction *should* focus on higher-level comprehension, vocabulary enrichment, interpretation, and analysis of text features (Fisher & Frey, 2008). But that focus doesn't negate either the need or the opportunity to engage in fluency and word study at the same time, especially in classrooms where marginalized readers need practice (Slavin, Cheung, Groff, & Lake, 2008). The key is to build such practice into regular activities so that marginalized readers gain experience and engage with grade-level curriculum at the same time.

When deciding whether to teach certain reading skills in the middle grades or not, consider this: if students in your classroom cannot read the texts you are teaching, their ability to learn content is significantly limited. In the long run, teaching students how to read by using disciplinary concepts supports *greater* content coverage because they are more able to participate and use new content to communicate. Integrating reading instruction with content instruction *enhances* learning.

BEYOND TRADITION TO DISCIPLINARY LITERACY AND "THIRD-SPACE" TEACHING

As we discussed in Chapter 1, the currently dominant label of *struggling readers* positions a large cross-section of our students as less capable, slower, and otherwise deficient. When we consider that teachers rarely give students explicit instruction about how ELA works along with guidance about how to participate in school, we are forced to consider that it is not the students' fault, or their parents', or their culture's, and so on. We are forced to consider the notion that our curriculum is poorly designed. We are forced to consider whether our expectations are reasonable. Is it fair to expect adolescents to catch up when they've never been explicitly taught how our unique academic discipline works? Is it ethical to position them as less able when they've never been provided *systematic* opportunities to understand how schoolwork relates to everyday life?

If we assume that all our students should already know how to read for school when they enter the middle grades, then we will not spend much time teaching them specifically how to read in our discipline when they reach us. In very real but institutionalized and indirect ways, we blame marginalized readers for not learning what we have neglected to teach them. This is not to say that students aren't occasionally resistant, or lazy, or less able than their peers. Sometimes they are; but in general adolescents are functionally literate readers outside of school. Knowing that, ELA teachers can begin to address this problem by *first* examining their own assumptions about teaching, learning, reading, their students, and the subject of the English language arts. In this manner, we can consider how disciplinary literacy works and design instruction so that students can access that knowledge more readily and relate it to life beyond school.

In order to successfully teach disciplinary literacy in ELA, we recommend that middle grade teachers link classroom study to students' *funds of knowledge* in everyday life (Moll & Gonzales, 2001). According to Moje et al. (2004), funds of knowledge are sources of experience, information, and understanding that people bring to any given learning process. Funds of knowledge can be considered as perspectives or frames of reference. For example, middle school students bring knowledge with them to school that has its roots in their family and community lives, such as the work their parents do at home and in their jobs, or their religious and cultural practices in their local communities. People also understand the world based on knowledge gained from popular culture such as television, film, music, art, and the other forms of mass media they consume. If we consider students' everyday lives outside of school to be a kind of "first space" for learning and thinking, and school to be a "second space," we can consider blending the two to create a "third-space" alternative where teachers help students draw these separate funds of knowledge together (Guitiérrez, 2008). Teaching ELA in this "third" space connects school learning more seamlessly with information and ideas students already know and understand. Therefore, third-space instruction fosters disciplinary literacy.

Third-space teaching may sound overly abstract at first, but its underlying principle is simple and straightforward. By using students' home and community knowledge as a legitimate part of academic study, teachers reduce the amount of new knowledge students need to absorb in order to participate meaningfully in class discussions. It means selecting texts that focus on culturally and socially relevant topics that students can relate to with greater ease. By using familiar and relevant topics and literacy practices to teach ELA, we empower students to make far greater contributions to classroom learning experiences. And by reducing the amount of new information students require to participate, we also reduce their cognitive load so they can concentrate on practicing advanced reading comprehension strategies and the kinds of interpretation required by middle grade curricula.

> **By using familiar and relevant topics and literacy practices to teach ELA, we empower students to make greater contributions to classroom learning experiences, and we reduce their cognitive load so they can concentrate on practicing advanced reading comprehension strategies.**

SUMMARY

Creating opportunities for learning disiciplinary literacy in third-space classrooms is not simple. Traditional ELA curricula strongly emphasize learning basic facts and routine processes in isolation rather than learning how disciplinary structures work and applying them in authentic ways. However, we believe third-space teaching and disciplinary literacy are the keys to helping marginalized readers—and indeed all students— gain full access to a truly valuable education and thereby move in from the periphery of our classrooms. In the next chapter, we focus on ways teachers can create learning environments that support this new form of teaching and learning.

Questions for Reflection

1. Knowing that the full scope of the ELA curriculum goes beyond comprehending traditional literature, what are five essential things your students need to know about how English works in school?

2. What knowledge and experience do your students bring to your classroom from outside of school? How can you connect what they know and do to the curriculum you are required to use?

3. How might a focus on *reading* instruction rather than *literary study* change the way your school approaches ELA teaching, especially for marginalized readers who have been labeled as "struggling"?

RECOMMENDED RESOURCES

Luke, A. (2004). The trouble with English. *Research in the Teaching of English*, *39*(1), 85–95.

McCormick, K. (1994). *The culture of reading and the teaching of English*. Manchester, UK: Manchester University Press.

National Council of Teachers of English. (2004). On reading, learning to read, and effective reading instruction: An overview of what we know and how we know it. Retrieved March 11, 2010, from *www.ncte.org/positions/statements/onreading*.

National Council of Teachers of English. (2006). *Guidelines for the preparation of teachers of English language arts* (rev. ed.). Urbana, IL: Author.

Wilhelm, J. (1997). *You gotta be the book*. Urbana, IL: National Council of Teachers of English.

3

Designing Classroom Environments That Support Literacy Development

FOCAL POINTS

1. Classroom environments can either reinforce or *change* students' positions as struggling readers.

2. Properly designed classroom environments can enable struggling readers to take on a leadership role with their peers.

The classroom environment plays a crucial role in students' development as readers (Bass, Dasinger, Elish-Piper, Matthews, & Risko, 2008; Triplett, 2007). Environments can be created that encourage the reading development of *all* students, or they can create contexts where some students are inadvertently privileged and others silenced. Classroom environments help set the tone for whether and how students can participate.

Marginalized readers' relative involvement with reading practices is often closely linked to their perception of how they are positioned within the class.

The classroom environment is particularly important in working with marginalized readers and helping them gain full access to classroom reading practices. Marginalized readers' relative involvement with reading practices is often closely linked to their perception of how they are positioned within the classroom (McCarthey, 1998). As noted in Chapter 1, when students are positioned as struggling readers, they are often treated as if they have little or nothing to offer in school. They are likely to believe their participation will not be valued and therefore may understandably minimize their involvement with reading.

However, when marginalized readers believe their ideas about texts are heard and respected, they are more likely to participate. Triplett (2007) has argued that classroom environments can be designed in such a way as to minimize, if not totally eliminate, the possibility of being treated as a marginalized reader. Creating such environments requires examining the current "climate" of our classrooms and our assumptions about both "struggling" readers and "good" ones. The language we use with our students, the books we select, and how we invite participation all send messages about who should participate, how often, and what the result should look like. Therefore, classroom environments have the potential either to help marginalized readers gain greater access to classroom reading practices or, alternatively, to continue to reinforce their current low status.

Compton-Lilly (2008) argues that there are two critical requirements for creating environments where marginalized readers can succeed and fully participate. First, it is important to recognize, understand, and respond to students' cognitive abilities as readers. This requirement means knowing how and why students do or do not use their personal skills and strategies when reading and, additionally, identifying areas in which they need further instruction. However, understanding students' cognitive abilities as readers does not mean focusing on what students cannot do well. Rather, it means identifying students' *strengths* and creating opportunities for students to utilize those strengths while addressing areas that need more attention.

Second, creating positive classroom environments for marginalized readers means appreciating their diverse social and cultural backgrounds and how these might usefully contribute to their self-identification as readers. By the time students reach middle school, they have had many experiences at home and school that have shaped their overall conception about what it means to be a reader and what does and does not count as reading (Alvermann, 2001b). For example, students who are continually told that there are clear right and wrong answers to their interpretations of text may quickly learn that reading is about identifying specific facts or simply regurgitating the text back to their teachers. Alternatively, students who experience reading as an act of examining and questioning ideas and exploring varying

> Creating positive classroom environments for marginalized readers means appreciating their diverse social and cultural backgrounds and how these might usefully contribute to their self-identification as readers.

interpretations may view reading as a complex act that is often used to deepen their understanding of ideas (Aukerman, 2007).

For students positioned as struggling readers, their understanding about who they are and what they are capable of doing with texts is grounded in the experiences they have had with reading. As a result, their decisions about how they should engage in classroom reading practices are filtered through the lens of their experiences. For example, Derek, an eighth grader, explained in a questionnaire given at the start of the school year that he was "a bad reader" who "can't read at all." He explained that trying to engage in classroom reading practices was pointless because he was never successful and everyone knew it. Therefore, creating an environment where struggling readers can be successful means understanding that their past experiences with reading shape their current ones.

STRUGGLING READERS' THOUGHTS ON CREATING POSITIVE CLASSROOM ENVIRONMENTS

Struggling readers' understanding about what does and does not contribute to a positive classroom environment can harken back even to the first grade. It is often during these first few years of school that students first get positioned as struggling readers and therefore begin to regard themselves in that light. Their repeated experiences of being labeled as struggling readers for many years should spur teachers to come up with ideas for better structuring classroom instruction to help them become more active participants.

Helping struggling readers become fully engaged with classroom reading practices means findings ways for them to feel secure enough to openly and freely participate. Leigh Hall's (2009) examination of Sarah, a sixth-grade struggling reader, showed a student who enjoyed reading, often read at home in her spare time, and was interested in becoming a better reader so she could learn more in school. However, Sarah felt afraid to participate in classroom reading practices because she worried that doing so would expose her to teachers and classmates as a poor reader—something she dreaded because of the socially negative label.

Sarah's fear of being publicly identified as a poor reader guided most of her decisions about how to engage in classroom reading practices. Over the course of the year-long study, Leigh learned that Sarah would never ask for help when she did not understand what she read. She would limit her participation in discussions to saying only what she knew to be "100% right," and she even restricted how she applied the reading instruction her teacher gave.

Teachers can help struggling readers feel more secure in participat-

Teachers can help struggling readers feel more secure in participating by first understanding what might limit their involvement in classroom reading practices.

ing by first understanding what might limit their involvement in classroom reading practices. This information can be acquired in a number of ways, including having informal conversations with students or asking them to write about how they would describe themselves as readers and why. Throughout the year, teachers can ask struggling readers to privately share with them what is contributing to any lack of participation or what is helping them feel more confident. Through such continual discussions teachers can better gauge what is and is not working within the environment and be immediately responsive.

Struggling readers can also benefit by seeing that they are not the only ones who encounter difficulties when they read. In their interactions with texts, struggling readers may believe they are the only ones who have difficulty in deriving meaning from what they read. However, when struggling readers come to realize that it is normal to encounter difficulty in interpreting text, they may begin to open up and feel they can participate more actively (Hall & Nellenbach, 2009).

For example, David, a sixth grader, explained to Leigh how he believed that most students in his class "understand what we read in here" and "get it right away." David thought that most of his peers did not experience the difficulties that he did. However, his teacher insisted that class members regularly discuss readings in small groups, and portions of these discussions specifically focused on identifying and discussing areas of confusion.

While David admitted he was initially "scared to participate" for fear of "looking dumb," over time he began to see that all the students in his group—even those he supposed were "really smart and really good readers"—had some difficulty in understanding the texts they read. He explained:

> "I thought that maybe there would be one other person in here who didn't read well. But I learned that's not true. *Everyone* has problems understanding these things. Sometimes I know it good, but someone else—like Kim, who's a really good reader—doesn't. And so I can explain it to Kim and that helps her, and sometimes she explains things to me. And it doesn't matter because we're all reading and helping each other."

When students believe their actions and thoughts about text are important and helpful for both themselves and their peers, they begin to recognize they have strengths and that there is more to them as readers than what they cannot do. Their confidence can start to grow, which in turn can change how they participate with texts both individually and as a member of their class. When students' experiences with reading become more positive, they can start seeing the act of reading as something that is useful in their lives (Dunston, 2007).

Therefore, creating an environment that helps struggling readers feel they can fully participate in classroom reading practices without having negative repercussions requires understanding what guides their decisions about participating. Although struggling readers may often be viewed as unmotivated, discussions with them have revealed that they are likely to be highly motivated to read and learn but afraid to step into the larger social context that a class presents (Hall, 2007, 2009). Getting them to become fully engaged with classroom reading practices, then, means creating an environment where they feel safe to take risks and explore texts without worrying that their actions will result in negative experiences.

SELECTING TEXTS: THE READABILITY APPROACH

The selection of texts is a critical part of the classroom environment. Most middle school students are expected to read texts that are too difficult for them and often have little choice in their selection (Allington, 2007). Schools and districts often mandate that all students read the same texts at a similar pace. When struggling readers are expected to engage with difficult texts on a regular basis, their experiences may serve as a reminder that they cannot read as well as their peers (O'Brien, 2006). As a result, they may severely limit their involvement in classroom reading practices.

One way teachers can approach selecting texts is to consider a text's readability in relation to the reading level of the student. Many people have argued that helping struggling readers gain access to texts in school is mostly about successfully matching them with texts that are written on their own reading level (Allington, 2007; Brown, Morris, & Fields, 2005). Throughout their school career, struggling readers have likely been assigned texts that were not successfully leveled for them (Mesmer, 2006). The term "leveled texts" is meant to "represent a progression from more simple to more complex and challenging texts," (Brabham & Villaume, 2002, p. 438). Thus, a text rated as Level 1 would be considered easier than a text rated as Level 5.

The intention behind using leveled texts is to enable students to improve their ability as readers while also learning useful content. Teachers assess students or review their assessment scores and then match them with texts that are considered to be an appropriate level of difficulty. This matching process is supposed to result in students reading texts that are neither too difficult nor too easy but appropriately challenging based on their cognitive capabilities.

However, other researchers have challenged this approach. O'Brien, Stewart, and Beach (2009) have argued that the difficulties students may have with texts are not simply contained within the text itself or based on skills students do or do not possess. They note that, while students' abilities to access a text are based on how well the text is written, the readability of a text is just one factor in a much larger picture. They point out that the accessibility of a text is also influenced by the reader. Prior knowledge, interest in the topic, and purpose for reading all affect the extent to which students view a text as being accessible (O'Brien et al., 2007). Matching students to texts based solely on levels assumes that the "diversity of students' social, cultural, and experiential backgrounds can be whitewashed when matching readers to books" (Dzaldoz & Peterson, 2005, p. 222).

While there is likely a benefit to having students read texts written at a given range of readability levels, it is also important to consider how students regard these texts. Middle school struggling readers are likely used to reading texts written on their instructional level, particularly during their elementary school years, when guided reading groups are often the predominant practice. Given that struggling readers are defined as students who read below grade level, they normally read texts considered to be "easier" than those assigned to students who read at or above grade level. When students continually observe that they have to read easier texts than their peers, it reinforces the idea that they are less capable and have less to offer. Additionally, struggling readers have expressed that they would like to read more difficult and challenging texts and would welcome help in learning how to do so (Hall, 2007). Consider the comment that Karla, an eighth grader, made to Leigh:

> "I like to read hard books and argue about stuff, 'cause not everyone agrees with you and then you have to explain it to them. And that helps you understand it better. The more you explain something, the better you understand it. Reading hard books alone is hard 'cause if you don't talk about it then it don't always make much sense."

Karla's comment suggests that teachers might want to consider being more open to having students engage with texts they might normally consider too difficult. Halladay (2008) suggests that students profess to enjoy texts considered too difficult for them and that some are able to comprehend more than teachers might expect. While difficult texts can be challenging, they do not need to be avoided altogether.

A CULTURALLY RELEVANT APPROACH
TO SELECTING TEXTS

Rather than making students' reading levels the primary factor in select-ing texts, texts can be chosen that take students' social and cultural backgrounds into account. A culturally relevant approach to text selec-tion requires understanding students' lives both in and out of school and selecting texts that will help students better understand themselves as well as the world around them (Ladson-Billings, 1992). As students develop new understandings, teachers can help them use what they learn to challenge and change their world. Ultimately, a culturally relevant approach to text selection helps empower students rather than, in effect, accepting passive reinforcement of the status quo (Larrotta & Gainer, 2008).

A culturally relevant approach to selecting texts is often discussed in terms of helping students from diverse backgrounds gain greater access to texts. However, it can be particularly useful for helping marginalized readers gain greater entrance to classroom norms by providing space for them to offer ideas and raise questions central to their lives and the lives of their peers (Dzaldoz & Peterson, 2005). As marginalized readers become more connected with the texts and participate more in readings and discussions, they thereby have the opportunity to practice the read-ing skills they need to develop. Such experiences enable them to find a meaningful way into texts that connects not only with the curriculum but also more meaningfully with their lives.

Teachers can engage in a culturally relevant approach to text selec-tion by drawing on their students' personal funds of knowledge. They can select texts that are connected to and utilize the diverse experiences and knowledge that students bring with them to class. However, select-ing texts via a culturally relevant approach does not mean that texts are chosen *solely* based on students' interests or that they necessarily feature characters or individuals sharing the same social, economic, or cultural background. While this outcome may sometimes result, it is by no means wholly realistic or foreordained. Teachers also have to actively consider the disciplinary knowledge that must be imparted to *all* students and the literacy skills required in successfully receiving it.

For example, Tatum (2006) documented how a seventh- and an eighth-grade teacher used young adult literature to help students under-stand issues relevant to them while also helping them develop knowledge and skills central to the ELA discipline. One teacher, for example, used the text *Slam* (Myers, 1995) to help his students consider how to engage in school in ways that would be productive for them while also help-ing them realize their dreams. By allowing students' social and cultural backgrounds to frame their text selection and instruction decisions, the teachers found that students were able to connect texts to their lives both in and outside of school. Additionally, the teachers reported that students improved as readers, with many demonstrating significant increases on the standardized reading test. Students previously classified as struggling readers who had shown little interest in reading were suddenly begging to take novels home, asking to read more, and had increased their participation in classroom reading practices.

THE ROLE OF LANGUAGE IN CREATING CLASSROOM ENVIRONMENTS

In addition to considering how texts are selected and used, we can also focus on language's important role in shaping classroom environments and in helping students gain access to texts (Johnston, 2004; Vygotsky, 1978). Through language, students learn what behaviors and social interactions are seen as more and less valuable by their teachers and peers. Language suggests to students which characteristics they should acquire and which they should discard.

For marginalized readers, their understanding of how to respond to instruction, texts, their teachers, and one another are shaped and reshaped through the messages they hear in classrooms (Egan-Robertson, 1998; Sarup. 1996). Students who engage or attempt to engage with texts in the ways valued in a classroom often receive more privileges while those who do not risk being marginalized (Hall, 2010). Therefore, the language used in classrooms not only communicates to students what you believe they need to do in order to succeed but also what they need to do in order to achieve a higher social status in class.

Before we look at how language shapes students' interactions with texts, let's consider an example you might find in your own life. Imagine for a moment that you are attending a professional development seminar on how to create reading instruction that addresses the needs of marginalized readers. At the beginning of the seminar the instructor distributes a packet of readings to you and says the following:

> "I've given you a lot of readings that will help you think about how to teach marginalized readers and some new ideas that can help how you instruct them. I want to caution you, though, that these readings are very difficult, and most people can't understand the main ideas in them or even begin to think about how to implement what is presented. If you don't understand something, you can ask me for help. However, I'm bound to be pretty busy since there are so many

of you. You can just ask one another for help or ignore the hard parts."

What would your reaction be upon hearing such an introduction? What kind of mood and tone would it set for the seminar, and what might it suggest that the instructor thought about you as a reader and learner? One possible message that might logically be taken from this introduction is that, while the readings might be challenging, the real problem is that most people in the room do not have the ability to comprehend them. If so, why bother assigning these readings at all, particularly if the instructor cannot provide sufficient support for everyone to comprehend them? Why would you want to try to complete these readings, much less participate in the seminar? Through language alone, the tone would already be set that you are unlikely to succeed.

Now consider an example in a middle school classroom setting. Ms. Rosenberg has distributed a text and explains to her class what she wants them to do as they read on their own:

> "I really want you all to work on sharing ideas with one another. It's okay if you read something in here and don't know exactly what it means. Just consider what you think it might mean. Sharing ideas, talking, asking questions—these are things that are going to help all of us learn."

Ms. Rosenberg's language indicates that she values her students discussing ideas and exploring different meanings in the text. An implicit message found in her statement is that she does not want students to be passive or silent or keep their ideas to themselves. She believes that failing to share ideas about texts will likely limit learning both on an individual level and class level.

There are several ways you can evaluate how you talk to students—and particularly marginalized readers—about how they should engage with texts. One approach would be to audiotape or videotape a short segment of class or have a colleague come in and observe. In reviewing the segment, you or your colleague can consider how students are told to (1) engage with the text, (2) address comprehension difficulties, and (3) interact with you and their peers. Some characteristics you might look for in your language include:

> Are students told to read silently, or can they talk about the text and ask questions with both you and their peers?
> Can students read with a partner? If so, are conditions attached to this?

Are students asked to share the "right" answers about a text, or are more open-ended responses encouraged?

Are students provided with reminders for how to address comprehension difficulties, or are they expected to already know what to do?

A second approach would be to ask your students to explain their understanding of what is valued in your classroom. This approach can help you see how students are making sense of and internalizing what you say and if you are being heard the way you wish to be. Providing time for students to give a written response will allow marginalized readers the opportunity to share their ideas without concern. The following questions are examples of what you might ask students:

"When I assign something to read, what do I expect you to do?"

"When you don't understand something that you read, how do I expect you to handle the problem?"

"How do I expect you to participate in discussions about the readings?"

"How do I feel about you talking with your classmates about the readings?"

In setting up these questions, it is important to make clear to students that you want them to tell you how they understand what it is you want them to do. You are not asking them to explain what they actually do. For example, a student might understand that when you assign something to read, you expect him or her to read the text in its entirety unaided. However, he or she may choose to read only a portion of the text for numerous reasons. While these reasons are important, for this particular response you want students to explain how they understand what you are telling them to do.

THE LANGUAGE OF READING AND OF BEING A READER

In addition to communicating expectations for how students engage with texts, language can also communicate what it means to be or become a particular type of reader. Teachers can use language to explain how they see their students as readers. Likewise, students use language to tell their peers what they think of their reading abilities and to communicate what they think of their own abilities.

Marginalized or poor readers are likely to be presented as students who experience problems with texts, while good readers are likely to be presented as having a variety of skills that contribute to their learning as well as the learning of others.

When discussing what it means to be a reader, students are often presented with two key options, namely, being a good reader or being a poor one (Hall, Johnson, Juzwik, Wortham, & Mosley, 2010). Teachers often explain to students what it means to be a good or poor reader in terms of skills—what they can or cannot do. Marginalized or poor readers are likely to be presented as students who experience problems with texts, while good readers are likely to be presented as having a variety of skills that contribute to their learning as well as the learning of others. For example, consider the following explanation about what it means to be a poor reader:

> "Poor readers have a hard time understanding what they read. When something doesn't make sense to them, they don't know what to do about it. They often skip over things they don't understand without trying to use a strategy or even ask for help."

This example suggests that poor readers understand very little of what they read and either cannot solve their difficulties or choose not to. The example does *not* suggest that poor readers have useful skills or abilities they could use during reading to improve their comprehension. As such, the example suggests that poor readers can do very little when reading and therefore have little to offer their classmates.

Contrast the example of poor readers against a statement that might be made about good readers:

> "Good readers understand most of what they read, but sometimes they have questions. When they do, they use strategies like rereading or asking themselves questions to help. They also participate frequently in class and share what they have learned from reading. Good readers share their ideas and questions with the class, and this helps us all learn more."

In this example, good readers are defined in terms of what they *can* do. They are positioned as having few, if any, comprehension difficulties, and instead are presented as asking insightful questions about texts. They are also shown as having skills and abilities they can use to gain information that they then share with their peers. Here, good readers are seen as students who have important insights that their classmates would benefit from hearing.

Students use the information they are given to form their understanding about what it means to be a particular type of reader and where they fit in relation to these definitions. While their prior experiences inform how they see themselves as readers, their understanding of those experiences can be either reinforced or changed within classrooms. Explanations about what it means to be a particular kind of reader have the potential to help struggling readers gain greater access to classroom reading practices or alternatively, to continue to shut them out by positioning them as being able to do very little and not having much to offer.

When students hear that poor readers have comprehension problems and do not know how to address them, they can respond in several ways. First, students who identify themselves as poor readers may limit their interactions with texts. These students may believe they are incapable of engaging with texts and may respond by withdrawing. Students who identify themselves as good readers may believe that poor readers have little to contribute. They may therefore limit their interactions with these students and cause these students to feel even further alienated from classroom life.

With these considerations in mind, it becomes all-important to understand how students identify themselves as readers, the rationale for their self-identifications, and how *you* describe the different types of positions students can take up as readers in your classroom. As discussed earlier, an effective way to do this is to document how you talk to your students about what it means to be a reader within your classroom. In reviewing what you say, consider the following:

Do you describe specific reading identities, such as the "good" reader or the "poor" one?

Do certain students or certain types of students get positioned as being better readers than others?

Students can provide you with written feedback where they explain (1) how they would describe themselves as readers and (2) why they think this description is accurate. This type of feedback not only helps you get a sense of *how students see themselves* but also helps you understand how students conceptualize what it means to be a particular type of reader. For example, if students believe being a good reader is all about saying words quickly or correctly, you may discover that they are less concerned with or aware of the importance of creating meaning from the words.

HOW STUDENTS GET POSITIONED IN CLASS:
THE ROLE OF PRIMARY AND SECONDARY KNOWERS

Definitions of good and poor readers position students in many ways, particularly in terms of what they can contribute. These definitions can result in some students being positioned as primary knowers and others as secondary knowers. Primary knowers are the individuals within a classroom who hold a great deal of power and are perceived as smart. They often determine what counts as right or wrong and set a standard for the actions that are acceptable in the classroom.

Secondary knowers are seen as being less knowledgeable and therefore having less to contribute than primary knowers. Students who are identified as struggling readers are often considered secondary knowers and have little authority in classrooms. The ideas and questions offered up by secondary knowers are rarely seen as valid and helpful unless a primary knower takes interest in them.

In most classrooms, the teacher is considered to be the key primary knower (Berry, 1981). It is usually the teacher who decides what knowledge is valued and, in the case of reading, which interpretations of texts are the right ones. However, students can also be positioned as primary knowers. Within classrooms, typically there are students perceived by their teachers and peers as having a wealth of information to offer. Normally the best-advantaged positions are filled by students who are regarded as good readers and whose interpretations of texts are generally in agreement with those of their teacher.

Consider the following exchange between Rosa, who was viewed as one of the best readers in her class, and Martin, who was positioned as a struggling reader. In the example, Martin and Rosa have been reading Scott O'Dell's (1960) *Island of the Blue Dolphins*. Martin shares his interpretation of the text with Rosa, who disagrees:

> MARTIN: I thought it was good that Karana jumped off the boat to be with her brother.
>
> ROSA: No. She could have killed herself, and now they are all alone on an island.
>
> MARTIN: But another ship will come for them, and that was her brother. She had to help him.
>
> ROSA: I don't think that's right at all. She should have done what the captain said.

MARTIN: Yeah, you're right. The captain is in charge. She shoulda listened to him.

While Martin and Rosa initially had different views on what Karana should have done, it was Martin who changed his stance to conform to Rosa's. Students like Martin who get positioned as secondary knowers, and who do not have their ideas validated by primary knowers often relinquish their ideas and align with the person who serves as the primary knower. As a consequence, ideas like the one presented by Martin are effectively silenced and students are sent the unfortunate (and inaccurate) message that ultimately there is a single correct interpretation of a text.

Students who are get positioned as struggling readers often recognize that they are assigned a lower status in the classroom and respond by decreasing their involvement and participation as a direct consequence. Devon, a sixth grader, explained to Leigh that he had been well aware of his position since the first grade:

> "I don't think I'm a very good reader. I've always thought that since first grade. I never got anything right—like when the teacher calls on you and stuff. I can't answer the questions, or she'll ask me what I think and I'll say it but then she'll say 'No' or ask me another question. And everyone knows I'm not right. And that happens all the time. So, now I'm just pretty quiet, I guess. I got tired of hearing I was wrong all the time, and I am."

Contrast Devon's statement with that from one of his classmates, Robin, who was considered to be a good reader:

> "Reading is easy. I always know the answer. Teachers always call on me when they ask hard questions or if nobody raises their hand. And a lot of times I get to help out other kids who don't read good. Like, if they don't know what something means, I tell them. And I like that because I think it helps them learn."

Devon's and Robin's experiences highlight what it means to be positioned as a primary versus a secondary knower in school. While the teacher may continue to be seen as the ultimate authority, Robin's position as a good reader gave her the power to authorize her classmates' interpretations of texts. Devon, however, seemed unable to interpret texts in ways that his teachers found relevant. As such, he was positioned as a secondary knower, or someone who had much to learn but little to offer.

REPOSITIONING STRUGGLING READERS

Creating environments where struggling readers can succeed means helping them be seen as primary knowers—or at least what Aukerman (2007) calls *possible knowers*. Students become possible knowers when they are given the space to express their interpretations of text without having to conform to someone else's interpretation. Aukerman (2007, p. 90) argues that in order for students—and, in particular, struggling readers— to succeed they "*must* be in the position of one who knows, seeks to know, and discovers—and who has the authority to make claims about what a text says and means and what s/he thinks of that." Classroom reading practices, then, must be restructured to position *all* students as people who have something to offer and that create new spaces where diverse students recognize themselves as knowledgeable others who have something worthwhile to contribute to the class's cumulative knowledge.

> **Students become possible knowers when they are given the space to express their interpretations of text without having to conform to someone else's interpretation.**

However, creating such structures is not simple. First, classes are normally structured so that teachers are (most naturally) in an authoritative position. While teachers' definably authoritative role may be necessary to some degree, Aukerman (2007) points out that this role often extends to their serving as the final arbiter for what counts as reading. For example, while reading a given text, the teacher may ask students to explain what the passage means. Normally, it is the teacher who determines which interpretations the students provide are correct. When students routinely see that teachers have the ultimate power to determine what is valued or seen as correct, the ways they engage with reading—if they decide to engage at all—are likely to be structured toward what the teacher demands and values. As a result, reading instruction and the discussion of texts may well develop with relatively little input from students' original ideas and questions.

Repositioning struggling readers as primary or (especially) possible knowers requires examining the traditional authoritative role teachers take within their classrooms. Instead of structuring ELA classes so that students must identify the answers the teacher finds most acceptable, additional space should be created to allow struggling readers to share their ideas and to have those ideas fully explored, questioned, and (if need be) challenged in a serious manner.

Such instruction means placing real value on what struggling readers think—even if their ideas initially sound off base. Within a class, all students need to question and consider their own ideas as well as the ideas of their peers—*but without feeling they must move toward a single correct and shared understanding.* Disagreements (even those that are never resolved) are acceptable, and discussions that end with questions remaining can and probably should become the norm.

When struggling readers are allowed to explore in greater detail their own perspectives, and experience having their ideas explored by others, the experience can expand their understanding about who they are as readers and what they are capable of doing. Having something worthwhile to contribute to the class can leave struggling readers feeling empowered and likely to participate more in the future. For example, one student explained:

> "I always thought I was a bad reader. All my life. You know, I can't read as well as my friends or my sisters or anyone really. But then I started to notice that sometimes other people find it hard to read too—even people I thought could read pretty good! It's like, hey, I'm not the only one who thinks this is hard. And sometimes my ideas seem to help other people get it or think of new things. And that's really cool because I didn't know I could do that."

SUMMARY

This chapter has highlighted some critical factors in creating environments that can help struggling readers gain greater access to texts. At the heart of these recommendations is how students are positioned in classrooms. Many struggling readers have had multiple negative experiences with reading in school, leading them to believe they have little to offer. Helping struggling readers believe they can engage with texts is largely about helping them see that they have a legitimate place in their ELA classes as contributors.

One way to help struggling readers feel increasingly comfortable in contributing is through the language that we teachers use and promote among our students. Language tells students what it means to be a reader, what counts as reading, and who is considered to be a "good" or a "poor" reader within a classroom (Hall et al., 2010). So long as we willingly let polarized definitions of good and bad readers influence our classroom interactions, students will continue to take up and enact those enviable and unenviable roles.

Merely providing struggling readers additional space where their perspectives and ideas can be seriously considered allows them to become valuable contributors in their classrooms—something they very much want to experience. As struggling readers are encouraged to transform themselves into possible and even primary knowers, seeing firsthand how their ideas help others learn and grow, they invariably increase their interactions with texts. And, as their interactions increase, they gain greater confidence in their reading abilities and are more likely to develop their reading skills.

Questions for Reflection

1. What messages (direct or indirect) do you communicate to your students about reading?

2. How does your classroom environment serve either to empower students or to reinforce existing positions and stereotypes?

3. How are texts selected and presented to students?

4. How are students who are labeled as either good or struggling readers positioned in your classroom or within your school?

RECOMMENDED RESOURCES

Compton-Lilly, C. (2007). *Re-reading families: The literate lives of urban children, four years later.* New York: Teachers College Press.

Compton-Lilly, C. (2008). *Breaking the silence: Recognizing the social and cultural resources students bring to the classroom.* Newark, DE: International Reading Association.

Delpit, L., & Dowdy, J. K. (Eds.). (2008). *The skin that we speak: Thoughts on language and culture in the classroom.* New York: New Press.

4

Engaging and Motivating Marginalized Readers

FOCAL POINTS

1. Marginalized, or struggling, readers tend to be disengaged readers at school. However, they have good reasons for their lack of motivation to engage with traditional academic subject matter.

2. High reading motivation and engagement attributes are strongly related to higher levels of learning and achievement.

3. Teachers should seek to activate both *intrinsic and extrinsic* means of motivating marginalized readers to better encourage them to engage in reading activities.

4. Teachers can best motivate and engage marginalized readers by drawing on their personal knowledge and extracurricular activities, making these naturally more relevant to academic work.

Research shows that students can improve their scores on standardized tests by reading more and receiving explicit strategy instruction (Guthrie, 2002). Beyond this obvious type of preparation, however, most teachers seek to help their students—especially those who are struggling readers—develop *internal* motivation to read for the rest of their lives. To achieve that goal, teachers must consciously create environments that are specifically designed to support reading motivation and engagement. In this chapter we discuss reading motivation, reading engagement, and the *engagement perspective* (Guthrie & Wigfield, 2001) that teachers can use to draw on students' collective funds of knowledge in the discipline of English.

Defined most basically, motivation is a reason or collection of reasons for acting in a particular way. An individual's motives may lead to engagement in an activity or to avoiding engagement. That is, motivations may be either positive or negative. *Reading* motivations, then, are reasons for students to participate (or not) in activities that involve reading.

An individual might read because she (or he) is motivated to acquire information or merely for pleasure. She might use the Internet to read movie reviews and decide whether a new film is worth seeing, or she might read vampire novels like *Twilight* (Meyer, 2006)—both for pleasure and to relate to her friends who read the same books. On the other hand, she might *avoid* reading because certain peers regard it as "uncool." Alternatively, or in addition, she might believe reading is something she isn't good at doing in school. If she's struggled with academic reading in the past, she might naturally feel reluctant to participate, as doing so would risk her feeling embarrassed and less intelligent. Depending on a student's motives in a classroom, she may or may not be willing to *engage*—that is, participate actively and purposefully. Her reading engagement depends heavily on both her reading motivations and her reading *self-efficacy*, that is, her beliefs about whether or not she can read successfully in particular situations (Deci & Ryan, 2000).

Engaged reading is strongly associated with increased reading achievement (Guthrie & Wigfield, 2001). Reading successfully on a regular basis contributes to a self-sustaining pattern of motivation for lifelong learning and a persistent sense of efficacy. The more students read, the better they become at reading. The better they are at reading, the more they comprehend new texts and persist when they encounter challenging reading situations such as the ones they experience more and more in middle school. The more they comprehend school texts, the more successful and engaged they will be when reading in English class. So it goes. When middle school teachers provide students with regular opportunities to practice reading in a fully supportive and engaging environment, those students will become more skillful, independent, and willing readers. The effects of purposeful, motivated reading engagement are so profound that engaged 13-year-old readers generally comprehend more than non-engaged 17-year-olds, compensating for over 4 years of actual schooling (Guthrie & Wigfield, 2001).

It is no surprise that marginalized readers who have become motivated to avoid reading and believe they will be unsuccessful also tend to be disengaged readers during school. They read without interest or purpose, resist reading, refuse to participate in reading-related activities, and even try to disrupt class to avoid reading. After years of low grades and negative messages about their abilities, most struggling readers have concluded they can't succeed and have moved to the periphery of the classroom. They don't necessarily like it, but they see no solution except to voluntarily withdraw to the sidelines and strive to preserve their self-image as best they can. By deliberately disengaging, they seek to protect themselves from abject failure by just not trying.

Part of the reason some students struggle with reading assignments during middle school is that school reading doesn't reflect their out-of-school reading practices, and they don't know how to participate in the ways that are most valued in English class. The middle school curriculum generally removes or decreases students' opportunities to *choose* what they read, which frustrates their ability to summon up and maintain positive motivations. They find fewer opportunities to talk about texts in ways they understand and value, and they are tested for skills that they don't regard as really relevant to their lives (Oldfather & McLaughlin, 1993). As we noted in Chapter 2, students are rarely given explanations or instructions to help them understand how reading in English class works as compared to the reading they do outside of school or in other subjects. And because they are punished for their seeming lack of ability or willingness to participate (through low grades, and the like), they become motivated to avoid reading altogether (Guthrie, Coddington, & Wigfield, 2009). The conditions that could lead to positive reading motivations, increased reading efficacy, and focused reading engagement for marginalized readers are often missing from school.

The conditions that could lead to positive reading motivations, increased reading efficacy, and focused reading engagement for marginalized readers are often missing from school.

Although middle school English classroom environments are not always designed in ways that support higher reading motivation and engagement, there are several conditions and practices teachers can work toward that are found to increase both student participation and success. In this chapter, we examine the conditions teachers need to establish for marginalized students to engage when reading and to participate with positive motivations. We will explain why engendering positive motives for engaged classroom reading is the heart of reading instruction. First, we explain the terms *reading self-efficacy, reading motivation,* and *reading engagement* in greater detail. Then we explore Guthrie and Wigfield's (2001) *engagement perspective* for secondary reading instruction. Finally, we conclude by suggesting how middle school teachers can motivate, support, and maintain students' engagement by connecting the engagement perspective to students' unique funds of knowledge.

READING SELF-EFFICACY, MOTIVATION, AND ENGAGEMENT

Fundamentally, a student's motivation is closely related to his sense of self-efficacy (Wigfield, 1997). A student's *self-efficacy in reading*—confidence in his or her ability to understand texts and achieve reading-related goals—goes a long way toward determining that student's likelihood of academic success (Guthrie & Davis, 2003). When readers feel more confident about their ability to understand and participate, they become more willing to persist even when challenged by new texts or problems. When middle grade students experience early and ongoing success, they develop a *continuing impulse to learn* and subsequently engage in reading more purposefully (Oldfather & Dahl, 1994; Thomas & Oldfather, 1997). They become more motivated because of the positive feelings that success generates in their minds.

Many studies, however, find that reading motivation declines for students as they move from elementary to middle school. The reasons are complex, but one factor is that teachers pay less attention to the conditions required to maximize students' reading efficacy (Alvermann, 2002). To continue building their confidence and comfort with school reading, teachers must continually support students' autonomy. According to Reeve and Jang (2006), when teachers consistently design activities that support students' success by preserving and recognizing their competence, interests, preferences, values, and control, students' efficacy increases, and they develop intrinsic motivations to participate and learn. These findings suggest that teachers must create environments in which they position previously marginalized readers as possible and even primary knowers (as discussed in Chapter 3).

Beyond the basic definitions we have offered so far, "reading motivation" can be defined as a blend of internal and external reasons for reading during school. Motivation may be intrinsic (where participation is attributable purely to personal enjoyment and/or interest) or extrinsic (where such external inducements as rewards, praise, or higher grades are key) (Otis, Grouzet, & Pelletier, 2005). Generally, intrinsic motivators lead to greater long-term success than extrinsic motivators, although extrinsic motivators are not inherently negative. Used exclusively, external rewards may only temporarily enhance students' willingness to read. The overuse of extra credit, prizes, or special privileges can actually lower students' engagement in future reading situations where such inducements are not granted. Still, when teachers use external motivators judiciously along with supportive classroom practices that encourage intrinsic interest and pleasure, students' motivations to read will increase, and students will engage more over time. As Otis et al. (2005) report, when students decide reading will benefit them in any consistent way over time, they often begin to regulate their own behavior in ways that generate intrinsic motivation.

The motivation to read comes from many sources. Interest and attitude play a significant role (Guthrie & Alao, 1997; Schiefele, 1996; Schraw, 1997), and so does freedom to choose both texts and purposes for reading (Schraw, Flowerday, & Reisetter, 1998). Support from caring teachers may play a central role, and so does positive social interaction (Wentzel, 1997). Intrinsic reading motivation often requires providing students with opportunities to choose what they read for enjoyment, to provide knowledge they view as useful in achieving social goals, and satisfy their curiosity about topics they find relevant to their lives. These intrinsic motivators have been linked to higher achievement on standardized reading tests, but they also support reading for its own sake (Guthrie et al., 2009).

As important as it is for teachers to think about how to increase positive intrinsic motivations, it's also necessary to keep in mind that marginalized readers who struggle in school often come to class with negative motivations that lead them to avoid participation. They devalue reading in their lives and even resist using strategies and classroom instruction that would otherwise help them succeed (Guthrie et al., 2009). Often, as a direct result of their negative experiences, marginalized readers will fake reading, refuse to do homework that requires reading, or even misbehave to get out of situations that require reading.

However, when marginalized readers have sufficient motivations to read in a supportive and intentional classroom environment, they become more likely to engage. Reading engagement can be defined as willing, focused, active participation in reading. Engaged reading is characterized by purposeful use of strategies to achieve goals (Guthrie, Alao, & Rinehart, 1997; Guthrie & Wigfield, 2001). Engaged readers comprehend better and have stronger reading outcomes than disengaged readers (Guthrie et al., 2006). The question, then, is this: How can middle school teachers generate positive motivations in English class that lead to reading engagement?

Guthrie and Wigfield (2001) outline an *engagement perspective* teachers can use to guide their work toward these ends. In the following sections we detail the engagement perspective and explain how teachers can use research to create situations in which marginalized learners find and use motivations that increase their confidence, help them engage positively and purposefully, and participate fully in English class.

THE ENGAGEMENT PERSPECTIVE

Generating reading motivation and engagement requires that teachers establish six key conditions in their classes, conditions that are neither typical nor simple to generate. In this era of highly routinized standardized testing and instruction, teachers must work consciously to achieve them. We will discuss five conditions for reading engagement, including establishing knowledge goals, delivering explicit strategy instruction, providing choices and an abundance of interesting texts, designing real-world interactions and supporting collaboration (Guthrie et al., 2006).

Establishing Knowledge Goals

Establishing knowledge goals for reading provides students with clear purposes for reading in English class. Such a pedagogical move seems like common sense, but often teachers simply assign students to "Read Chapters 1–3" for a class without explicitly explaining what they want them to learn or practice. Providing knowledge goals such as "Read Chapters 1–3 to identify the setting and point of view used in the story" gives readers a focus for their work. When teachers specify a discipline-related goal, they thereby guide students in analyzing the text more manageably rather than implying that they should comprehend everything about the text on the first reading. In addition to lightening students' cognitive loads while focusing their attention on learning specific reading skills, articulating discrete knowledge goals enables students to better concentrate on learning specific terms and concepts, a key to disciplinary literacy.

Designing Explicit Strategy Instructions

To complement knowledge goals, teachers should explicitly introduce, model, and assign students reading comprehension strategies they can readily put into practice, such as predicting, summarizing, and questioning the content of a text. These first two conditions alone can have a significant positive impact on students' reading comprehension over time. Grolnick and Ryan (1987) found that when students received knowledge goals for reading, their comprehension increased more than with students who were simply told to read and "try hard" on a test. Similarly, Schunk and Rice (1993) demonstrated that "providing clear goals for reading tasks ... increased self-efficacy and strategies for text comprehension" (p. 408), while Spires and Donley (1998) found that strategy instruction resulted in higher comprehension and positive attitudes among students. Focusing students on attainable goals and showing them how to use strategies explicitly (rather than merely telling them to use strategies) helps them experience reading success early and often, thereby improving their self-efficacy and increasing motivation to read more often.

Providing Choices and an Abundance of Interesting Texts

Providing a variety of interesting texts and allowing struggling readers greater latitude in choosing what they read also increases motivation and engaged reading in school (Ivey & Broaddus, 2001; Kottke, 2008). Adolescents often struggle with school reading not because they can't read but because school texts don't interest them (Allington, 2007; Lenters, 2006). When students can choose the texts they read, the tasks they complete using those texts, and/or the peers they interact with while reading, their motivation increases and they become more purposefully engaged (Guthrie et al., 2006). Similarly, when students are allowed to read about topics they find interesting or when those texts are presented in interesting formats via digital media or reader's theater, they become more likely to engage for intrinsic reasons.

Even in contexts where the availability of obviously relevant texts is limited, teachers can frame reading tasks by picking themes that are meaningful to students' personal lives and values. The teacher can then support students in choosing from a range of optional tasks that demonstrate their learning. For example, while reading Lois Lowry's *The Giver* (1993), students might be given the option to (1) compare and contrast two characters from the novel, (2) write a script and make a video interpreting those characters' behavior or the text's tone in a pivotal scene or chapter, or (3) design and explain a soundtrack of popular music they would use to enhance and communicate the meaning, themes, tone, and mood of the story. These alternatives provide structure *and* choice so that teachers can maintain order even as students show their learning in a variety of ways and demonstrate disciplinary knowledge. When students have choices, their intrinsic motivation increases, and when they don't they become more likely to disengage and/or develop negative motivations related to reading in school (Lenters, 2006).

Designing Real-World Interactions

Another way for teachers to increase students' motivations for engaged reading is to deliberately include real-world interactions whenever possible. A real-world experience with a text in English class might consist of, for example, listening to and interviewing a Holocaust survivor while reading Jane Yolen's (2004) *The Devil's Arithmetic* or Anne Frank's (1953) *The Diary of a Young Girl*. It might involve participating in a mock trial of Alexander T. Wolf, the narrator of Jon Scieszka's and Lane Smith's (1996) *The True Story of the Three Little Pigs*. Or it might consist of simulating the pure darkness and chill of the dungeon in Edgar Allan Poe's (2000) short story "The Pit and the Pendulum" by considering such concepts as mood, tone, and symbolism. It is not that students need literally to experience the situations they read about, but that they receive multiple opportunities to become involved with the texts they read instead of sitting silently while their teacher tells them what those texts mean. Dialogue journals, guest speakers and field trips, creative drama activities, and mock debates all constitute real-world concrete interactions that stimulate students' thinking in ways that increase positive reading motivation. They all support comprehension and provide knowledge goals and interest for engaged reading irrespective of the individual student's ability level.

> **Students need to be able to choose among varied opportunities to become involved with the texts they read instead of sitting silently while their teacher tells them what those texts mean.**

Supporting Collaboration

One of the reasons why real-world interactions related to school texts increase reading motivation and engagement is that they require students to interact with others. According to Guthrie and Davis (2003), collaboration creates interdependence among students as they work toward shared goals. Collaborative activities can also be designed so that students are given explicit opportunities to participate in the norms of English as a discipline. For example, during reading activities teachers can coach students to practice using terms and applying concepts—again, not simply interacting with one another for the sake of fun but, rather, consciously working toward knowledge goals. By providing repeated opportunities to hear and apply disciplinary terms and concepts, teachers help students to retain knowledge that enables them to understand and succeed better academically (Marzano, Pickering, & Pollock, 2001). Such experiences increase students' self-awareness, build up their confidence and self-efficacy, and thereby result in more motivated and engaged reading.

By the same token, students' reading motivation increases when they believe their teacher cares for and understands them as individuals. Positive interactions between teachers and students can be pivotal. According to Klem and Connell (2004), middle school students are three times as likely to report being engaged when they feel their teachers are supportive. When teachers overtly demonstrate warmth and encouragement, students feel more comfortable, welcomed, capable, and motivated to exert effort (Skinner & Belmont, 1993). Displaying warmth does not mean that a teacher shouldn't challenge students or push them to work hard. It means the teacher must consciously show all students he or she believes they can succeed. Naturally enough, when readers try harder, teachers give them more praise and enthusiastic support (Klem & Connell, 2004). When they seem to resist, teachers may actually withdraw support or punish them. Based on such findings, if teachers want *struggling* readers to improve, they must demonstrate even more overt caring and support for them than their better-performing cohorts (which, in any teaching situation, seems particularly apt).

The five conditions described above create an engagement perspective that teachers can consciously use to design instruction and increase students' self-efficacy related to reading. The engagement perspective opens the way to generating positive reading motivations that in turn lead to more successful reading. As a result of increased and engaged reading, students tend to understand more and continue reading more over time. In the next section, we discuss how assessing students' individual funds of knowledge can help teachers create situations that improve reading motivation and engagement, with a focus on using students' *textual lineages* (Tatum, 2008a) to generate the kinds of third-space contexts for reading instruction that we discussed in Chapter 2.

ASSESSING FUNDS OF KNOWLEDGE
FOR ENGAGEMENT

Although we discuss assessment in much greater detail in Chapter 5, it is still important to ask here how teachers can assess students' personal funds of knowledge and prioritize content to increase reading motivation and engagement. One way is to help students map their "textual lineages" (Tatum, 2008a) and use their histories as readers to determine their reading and literary repertoires—the prior knowledge, experiences, and understanding of text genres and elements they can use to understand the texts they read in middle school English classes (McCormick, 1994).

As was noted in Chapter 2, all students bring unique knowledge and experience to school with them; they are not blank slates or empty vessels for teachers to fill. They are active consumers of books, magazines, films, television programs, websites, popular music, and more. Although some of these media do not focus on reading alphabetic print, they all share genres and patterns related to disciplinary knowledge in English. Many of these texts are especially memorable and meaningful to students—more so than many of the printed texts they are assigned in school. Along with books, they make up an adolescent reader's textual lineage (Tatum,

2008a). Actively recruiting these alternative texts to help teach reading can increase students' positive motivations.

According to Tatum, teachers can motivate and engage students in reading by helping them identify texts they believe they will always remember and then asking them to explain why those texts were meaningful (Tatum, 2008b). Texts from this lineage make a student feel differently about himself or herself, affect his views about himself, and move him to act for particular reasons in his life. As Tatum found, such texts have "enabling qualities" that motivate students to seek more knowledge they can use to identify themselves in ways they see as important (2008b, p. 10). Such texts, then, can be suggestive of other related texts a teacher might use to teach reading comprehension strategies and disciplinary concepts in English that have real-world connections, that interest students, and that respond better to their needs for choices in school assignments.

Often students see ethnic and gender connections with the texts they read as the qualities that make a text relevant, memorable, or motivating. However, drawing on textual lineages is mostly a matter of supporting students' personal identification with texts they read *in school*—but striving for authenticity in reflecting their emotions, responses, behaviors, living conditions, and actual experiences in life as well as their multiple identities as members of a given race, friends, family members, young adults, males and females, athletes, computer users, dancers, skateboarders, and so forth (Tatum, 2008b). These personal connections are one reason why young adult literature is often helpful in enabling marginalized readers to engage with texts they read in English class. In young adult (YA) literature they are more likely to encounter characters, topics, and themes they are familiar with and interested in from their own lives.

Drawing on students' textual lineages as funds of knowledge requires moving away from traditional text selection in ELA curricula. If you want to motivate and engage adolescent readers, bring their lineages to the fore in academic study. Their increased engagement will lead to improved scholastic achievement, which is the overall goal in school. Using their lineages to determine what texts to use for instruction will raise questions that connect to their actual needs for motivation and engagement.

Understandably, some teachers might initially object to using nonprint texts from students' lineages to teach reading. Many adults worry that popular culture texts are of low quality and are inappropriate for study in school. That can be true; but that is true for print texts, too. There are countless books readers might find interesting but that would be inappropriate for academic study. However, there are also countless popular print and nonprint texts students identify in their textual lineages that have much to offer in academic study.

When students consume popular culture texts—print or nonprint—they do not just consume particular storylines and ideas; they also absorb structures that they then recognize and that help them participate in future textual interactions. They develop what McCormick (1994) calls a literary repertoire. They encounter metaphors, similes, and other figurative language through their reading of song lyrics. They recognize symbols in advertising. They learn irony through experiences with comics and graphic novels. Through their "readings" of television sitcoms and other genres they learn story grammars—predictable arrangements of elements that are used to construct both print and nonprint texts. If the student is familiar with sitcom structure, he or she can easily understand and predict the storyline of just about any similar text. Films across all genres use traditional literary plot structures, and adolescents' already fluent understanding of how narrative, informational, and poetic structures work in popular media provides teachers with rich sources of prior knowledge. By realizing that students are already familiar with disciplinary concepts from the popular culture texts they consume outside of school, teachers can help them similarly understand and engage with academic texts.

When teachers help students think systematically about the textual lineages they bring to school, they can help them articulate knowledge of these disciplinary concepts as they read new texts. As students access English in relation to their everyday lives, they also learn how school texts work,

> **By realizing that students are already familiar with disciplinary concepts from the popular culture texts they consume outside of school, teachers can help them similarly understand and engage with academic texts.**

and they can make sense of school practices because their teachers have connected their prior experiences to academic knowledge goals.

More than simply activating prior knowledge, teachers' use of students' textual lineages as funds of knowledge also gives marginalized readers a voice in classroom discussions. While a teacher focused on unfamiliar academic texts usually shuts most struggling readers out, a teacher who invites students to talk about their own pop culture experiences with reading enables them to speak with authority. As we know from research, when students feel more successful, their efficacy, motivation, and engagement increase dramatically.

Conversely, when teachers refuse to acknowledge any value in students' popular culture, they imply that the texts and knowledge students bring from outside of school are inferior and undesirable. Because of disciplinary history and traditions, many English teachers are predisposed to label television, pop music, and film as "trash" that "rots the brain." This inclination is unfortunate, as scholars have demonstrated that pop culture consumption can actually improve a person's thinking skills (Johnson, 2005). It may be difficult for teachers who value books so much to equate a movie with a novel in terms of quality, but doing so helps adolescents appreciate real-world applications of English and therefore achieve at higher levels. When teachers help students identify and use their textual lineages, they generate knowledge and experiences that can anchor academic study and the successful construction of new knowledge for reading in school.

SUPPORTING READER AUTONOMY

The engagement perspective described above, paired with attention to students' textual lineages and their unique fund of knowledge, leads teachers to think systematically about the conditions that marginalized readers need to enhance their motivations to engage in school reading. At the heart of this way of thinking is the concept of supporting learners' autonomy—their ability to act on their own and participate in their own education (Reeve & Jang, 2006). In addition to establishing the six conditions of the engagement perspective, there are other ways teachers can support purposeful engagement in middle grade English.

As we noted earlier, teachers can increase reading motivation and engagement simply by demonstrating special concern for marginalized readers. This particular initiative consists in making it clear to such readers that you believe they can read and succeed. It means communicating genuinely high and supportive expectations. But what does such behavior look like?

Demonstrating support means listening to and affirming students' knowledge and perceptions. We've already emphasized that teachers should affirm the value of texts and knowledge students bring from their out-of-school reading experiences. In addition, teachers can support students' autonomy by acknowledging their prior experiences in school as legitimate and relevant to current classroom activities. When students say they are bored, we should listen. When they complain that activities are difficult, we should acknowledge their discomfort. When they wonder why they are being asked to read a particular text or complete a certain activity, we should take their questions seriously and offer them responses beyond such statements as "Because it will be on the test" or, worse, "Because I said so!"

Teachers who clearly respond to students help them feel like partners in their own learning. Such listening is related to other forms of autonomy support. By listening and adjusting activities and content to students' perceived needs, teachers can give students the active role they crave and increase their positive motivations to read. When a student demonstrates keen interest in computer gaming and design, for example, we can respond by generating options within a reading-related

Demonstrating support means listening to and affirming students' knowledge and perceptions. When they say they are bored, we should listen. When they complain that activities are difficult, we should acknowledge their discomfort. When they wonder why they are being asked to read a particular text or complete a certain activity, we should take their questions seriously.

assignment for that student to design a videogame related to academic text. When a student asks if she or he can draw a picture instead of writing an essay, we can work with that student to design a project that enables her to use her desire and still support her use of textual evidence to demonstrate her comprehension. When students find a teacher-suggested topic uninteresting, we can ask them what they would like to talk about in relation to a text and use their suggestions instead, thereby further involving them while still connecting to the disciplinary content.

The more teachers listen and respond, and the more they support extended talk about texts in ways students choose, the more likely students are to act as primary knowers. Doing so contributes to putting into practice the conditions of the engagement perspective, and with it increased student motivation, engagement, and comprehension over time. None of this is to argue that teachers should allow students total freedom to read anything they want or do anything they please. Middle school students have to learn disciplinary concepts and skills, and that requires teachers to create assignments students would not always choose or identify on their own.

Because students cannot know everything they need for reading success in school, part of our job as teachers is to provide rationales for classroom activities. Les Burns often uses analogies (Marzano et al., 2001) to help students understand why he requires them to practice reading comprehension strategies in his classes. For example, many youth are active in sports or music. In basketball, they enthusiastically practice fundamentals that help them play better. Coaches teach them the step-by-step mechanics of shooting free throws or layups in basketball, and they practice these motions over and over. Les asks the students why they do this in sports, and they never fail to reply that they do it because it helps them play more naturally. Practice makes them better so that they enjoy the game more. Similarly, students who sing or play musical instruments explain that they practice scales and other exercises for the same reasons.

When they review these analogies, Les helps them apply the same rationales to their reading in English class. When he asks students to identify elements of characterization and then use evidence from a text to illustrate what characters look like, he explains that practicing during class will help them understand characterization with less effort when they read on their own so they can comprehend more readily and enjoy reading more. They might still find practice tedious sometimes, but they understand the purposes of classroom activity, and they almost always recognize that the work pays off in both improved grades and greater satisfaction.

When rationales for classroom work are clear and responsive to students, the teacher can further enhance students' autonomy and positive motivations by giving them both praise and positive informational feedback. As Reeve and Jang (2006) suggest, teachers can coach marginalized readers by saying "Good job!" and "That's great!" while also asking how they made certain connections or used textual evidence to make predictions (p. 211). When students struggle, as they often will, teachers can encourage them by going beyond saying "Almost!" or "You can do it" by further elaborating, for example, with "You're on the right track, and you can do it. What other words do you know that have that same prefix? What do they mean?" These kinds of hints and affirmations lead students to feel more valued in English class, and they move closer to acting as primary knowers. And by acknowledging that reading in school can be hard work even as we praise them, teachers can consistently help marginalized readers see that they are making progress and experiencing real success.

Beyond these coaching behaviors, teachers must give marginalized readers more time and opportunities to read (Ivey & Fisher, 2005). While it seems obvious to say this, it is remarkable that when students struggle with reading they are often given remediation that reduces their opportunities to read whole texts, let alone choose topics they find interesting. Teachers may even prevent students from gaining self-efficacy and positive motivations by focusing on drills, more frequent testing than normal, and activities that require them to work alone. Such conditions make reading and learning academic content even harder for students who already struggled by removing the conditions of the engagement perspective they actually need in order to succeed.

Again, none of this is to say teachers should not offer direct instruction. While students sometimes need to "just" read, marginalized readers also need direct instruction to learn. Research-based instructional strategies like collaborative learning groups, activating prior knowledge, and teaching background knowledge for reading comprehension make significant positive differences in students' learning (Marzano et al., 2001). According to Marzano and colleagues (2001), explicit teaching and use of collaborative learning for reading such as jigsaw groups, think–pair–share activities, and literature circles can increase achievement by as much as 28%. Using advanced organizers that preview topics students will read about can improve learning by as much as 17%. And teaching students to demonstrate their comprehension by using nonlinguistic representations such as graphic organizers, illustrations, videos, and other media can improve learning by as much as 40%. These instructional strategies help foster the engagement perspective, support the use of students' personal funds of knowledge about texts from outside of school, provide clear rationales for classroom activities, and contribute to increased efficacy, motivation, and engagement.

Perhaps most importantly, the engagement perspective underscores the utility of going beyond prepackaged reading programs schools often purchase in attempting to remediate struggling readers. Many programs provide standardized instruction and extrinsic motivation for reading engagement. They are often advertised as "teacher-proof" systems that require students to read grade-level texts (which may or may not be suitable) and answer low-level comprehension questions unconnected to students' lives (Ivey & Fisher, 2005). Such programs often obstruct middle school readers' development of intrinsic motivations (Biggers, 2001) by making them feel that they are forced to read books they don't care about solely to pass tests. In short, such programs are not successful in improving reading instruction (Thompson, Madhuri, & Taylor, 2008). As Biggers (2001) reports, "Students who *are* motivated by competitions also show a high degree of reading avoidance, particularly for more difficult reading tasks or reading outside of school requirements" (p. 73, emphasis added). Prepackaged reading programs actually *de*motivate and *dis*engage students from reading. Marginalized readers are far better served when teachers approach reading instruction by using the engagement perspective to draw on learners' personal fund of knowledge and textual lineages.

CHALLENGES AND POSSIBILITIES
FOR ENGAGED READING

It would be a mistake to pretend that using the engagement perspective will always result in little utopias where marginalized and previously unmotivated and/or disengaged readers suddenly crave Dostoevsky's or Hemingway's writings at age 13. Although most of the recommendations discussed in this chapter seem like common sense, they are not necessarily easy to implement in today's schools.

To be as realistic as possible, we must acknowledge that sometimes we can't truly reach a student. Some will resist our best efforts, no matter what. Some have serious problems with learning or have so little experience with reading that we can't meet their needs without extreme measures that might include pulling them out of the classroom for individualized instruction in the pure decoding of text. Some students resist reading not because they lack the ability to do it but simply because they never will be interested in school. Some students disengage due to personal issues, social pressures, cultural values, or other issues far beyond any teacher's control. Further, middle school is traditionally the time when adolescents begin specializing in some subjects rather than others as they consider various career paths. While we English teachers certainly argue that our subject is important for everyone, the expanded curriculum encourages young people to choose, and English class may just not seem relevant, no matter how much choice we offer or how much caring we show.

In addition, we have to admit that today's schools require us to deal with standardized tests and accountability for student learning defined by outside agencies. That often means our curriculum is designed in ways that prevent us from implementing aspects of the engagement perspective we know would be better for our students (and ourselves).

The structure of schooling alone can make it difficult. How can we afford even 15 minutes for silent reading when the class lasts only 50 minutes and we have to cover grammar, literature, writing, vocabulary, and more? How can we provide students with texts that reflect their identities and experiences when we don't even have enough textbooks for each student, let alone a variety of texts that would interest kids more? Many of us work in schools and communities where there isn't access to technology that would enable marginalized readers to demonstrate understanding by using alternative media. And even where we do, our students may lack access to the resources they need when they leave our classrooms at the end of the day.

The key is to consider that the individual conditions described here are parts of a *perspective*—a way of looking at and thinking about reading instruction that significantly improves reading motivation and engagement. Knowing that students require a variety of interesting texts, we can work with librarians and administrators to build both central and classroom libraries toward that end. Knowing that students gain motivation from reading about topics *they* consider relevant, we can choose the texts we use more strategically. Knowing that they engage better when they are taught to interact and given time to read during class, we can plan more efficiently and use time more wisely. Knowing that our own overt behavior makes a real difference, we can conscientiously act in ways that research tells us make our students develop intrinsic motives. We may not be able to do it all, but we can always use the engagement perspective to support students more systematically than we might otherwise.

> **Knowing that students gain motivation from reading about relevant topics, we can choose the texts we use more strategically. Knowing that students engage better when they are taught to interact and are given sufficient time to read during class, we can plan more efficiently and use time more wisely.**

SUMMARY

Providing students with a classroom environment that supports engaged reading does not have to take time, energy, or focus away from learning ELA content. The engagement perspective increases *all* students' opportunities. In Chapter 2, we discussed the characteristics of English, noting that our discipline encourages its own peculiar ways of talking, thinking about the world, and demonstrating knowledge. Classroom sessions designed while keeping the engagement perspective uppermost in mind support students' abilities to participate by having them read a wide variety of texts, making connections between text, self, and the world outside of school, and incorporating each student's own unique funds of knowledge and textual lineages so that reading becomes more enjoyable and easier to comprehend. The engagement perspective not only motivates students to read but also ultimately helps teachers cover *more* of the ELA curriculum better than they can by using traditional methods, textbooks, and activities.

Although building an engaging environment for reading in English class is essential, some students may refuse to engage or otherwise fail and continue to struggle. As Cambourne (1995) points out, our efforts may result in little or no engagement in reading unless our students agree to "have a go" at participating (p. 185). We cannot "fix" struggling readers, but we *can* provide the structures, content, opportunities, and encouragement for them to join us and improve. The more often teachers engineer classroom reading experiences that give students choice, variety, goals, strategies, collaboration, and real-world connections, the more likely students are to value reading both in and out of school.

Questions for Reflection

1. How does research on the engagement perspective change the ways you think about students who resist reading?

2. What kinds of media do your students say they enjoy and consume most outside of school? How could you use those texts to help students discover what they already know about reading in your classroom?

3. How would you sequence reading lessons so that students experience success early and often, and thereby develop stronger efficacy and motivation?

4. Based on your school's and community's resources, what options do you have for providing students with more variety and choice in their classroom reading?

5. Think of a text you are required to teach in your school. List three to five ways your students could choose to demonstrate their comprehension of that text. How could you use these options to generate engaging tasks that still helped students learn important skills and content knowledge?

RECOMMENDED RESOURCES

English Journal, Vol. 93, No. 3. Issue theme: Popular Culture.

Lowe, J. (2005). Creating an A+++ classroom library. Retrieved March 18, 2010, from *www2.scholastic.com/browse/article.jsp?id=4136*.

Morrell, E. (2004). *Linking literacy and popular culture: Finding connections for lifelong learning*. Norwood, MA: Christopher-Gordon.

5

Assessing Reading Performance and Students' Funds of Knowledge

FOCAL POINTS

1. Traditional ELA reading assessments are important—but insufficient for helping marginalized readers succeed.

2. Teachers need to assess both what students already know and what they do outside of school in order to make classroom work most relevant.

3. Teachers can cover academic content and meet standards better by connecting instruction to students' own funds of knowledge.

4. Assessing students' funds of knowledge enhances but does not replace academic instruction and testing.

So far in our discussion of teaching marginalized readers in middle school English language arts, we have noted that students come to school with considerable prior knowledge about how texts work and that many students labeled as "struggling" are actually active readers outside of school. By understanding students' general knowledge and their reading of texts outside of school, middle school English teachers can create a kind of "third space" (Guitiérrez, 2008; Moje et al., 2004) in classrooms where students use their funds of knowledge to learn disciplinary content and practices (Moje, 2008). When teachers systematically link curriculum with texts and knowledge from students' lives beyond school, they can reposition formerly marginalized students to become possible or primary knowers (Aukerman, 2007) who become central to their own learning and participate more fully than they were when labeled as "struggling." When they are supported in such environments by implementing the engagement perspective described in Chapter 4 (Guthrie & Wigfield, 2001), marginalized readers become more likely to develop positive motivations, improve their reading skills, and engage in ways positively correlated with increased reading achievement. This whole process begins with the fundamental act of assessment.

In this chapter we discuss how assessing each individual student's funds of knowledge is the first step in positioning middle grade readers for success in English. We begin with a discussion of traditional assessments used in middle grade classrooms and review reading assessment standards. Next we describe an approach to reading assessment in which teachers use data about students' funds of knowledge to choose texts and methods that address the ELA curriculum while also meeting the needs of marginalized readers. We conclude with a discussion of how this alternative approach to assessment repositions formerly struggling readers in more positive ways and actually supports teachers in meeting state and national test standards.

TRADITIONAL READING ASSESSMENT
IN MIDDLE SCHOOL

Countless textbooks offer reading teachers the formulas and techniques associated with traditional reading assessments. Like most professional educators, we believe the assessment of students' prior knowledge of academic concepts, ongoing learning, and periodic evaluation should influence curriculum development and inform instructional practices. Assessment is the systematic collection and analysis of data before, during, and after a learning episode, in which information is used by teachers to evaluate instruction, provide feedback for learners about their progress, and analyze the overall nature of teaching and learning during a given time period in a particular place.

Assessment data are referred to as *formative* when they are used to document and revise the teaching and learning process. Data become *summative* when they are used to evaluate or otherwise rank the quality of teaching and/or learning during a specific time span. Whether formative or summative, assessment data are primarily intended to generate a context for teaching and learning that guides future activity. As such, we consider all assessment to be formative and meant primarily to support student and teacher success rather than primarily to test them, especially as applied to educating marginalized readers.

A review of literacy research and scholarship reveals very little specific information about particular assessments or systems for secondary-level reading education. Many studies and discussions refer to standardized reading tests and their positive and/or negative effects on teaching and learning (Guthrie, 2002; Johnston & Costello, 2005; Lee, 1998). Others discuss the validity or reliability of such tests for understanding patterns in student learning or policy reform (Linn, Baker, & Dunbar, 1991; Sarroub & Pearson, 1998; Thomas & Oldfather, 1997). But most resources discuss traditional approaches that are likely already familiar to middle school English teachers.

Examples of traditional reading assessments, for example, include but are not limited to criterion-referenced tests (standardized tests that assess individual students' recall and application of specific content knowledge and skills) and norm-referenced tests (standardized tests that compare students' relative abilities in a particular skill or subject, based on statistical averages for their age group, grade level, gender, race, etc.). Criterion- and norm-referenced tests are typically administered only at the state and national level. But the majority of reading assessments in US middle schools are teacher-made (Ornstein, Lasley, & Mindes, 2005). For example, teachers create multiple-choice and short-answer quizzes to assess students' literal comprehension of texts they read, as well as matching and true-or-false tests. They create essay prompts that require students to analyze, synthesize, and evaluate their reading in ways that are believed to reflect higher-level thinking skills, or they use similar assessments offered in standardized textbooks.

While such quizzes and tests are frequently used as summative assessments of students' understanding, teachers also employ assessments to guide their use of instructional materials during the process of teaching and learning. For example, teachers may employ various formulas to make sure the texts they use are appropriate for a certain grade level, or they may use cloze tests to assess students' general ability to read or their readiness to engage with more complex material.

Less formally, teachers assess middle school readers during instructional units by observing patterns of behavior across classes and grade levels. According to Roe and Smith (2005), such observations include monitoring student discussions about reading, analyzing anecdotal notes from teacher–student conferences to document whether and how students use reading strategies, documenting students' abilities to retell and summarize information from readings, and using checklists and rating scales to document growth in fluency and vocabulary. In some states and schools, teachers also analyze portfolios in which students collect and describe documentation of their individual progress as readers over time. All together, these assessments can be used to establish measurable goals for reading instruction and to generate data about whether or not students attain those goals.

All of the assessments noted above are widely described in most textbooks about reading instruction. In today's climate of testing and accountability in education, they are frequently required and implemented as a matter of routine in middle schools across the United States. Because of their prominence, we choose only to mention them in passing here, the assumption being that practically all middle school English teachers already use them. There is an additional type of assessment that is too often missing from middle school reading instruction that would make traditional assessments more productive, namely a basic assessment of students' individual fund of knowledge from outside of school.

Our approach reflects the Standards for the Assessment of Reading and Writing set forth by the International Reading Association (IRA; 2009). IRA's standards stipulate that students' interests should come first in any assessment (standard 1). Starting with assessment of one's own funds of knowledge reflects the fact that teachers are the most important actors in assessment (standard 2) and that students, their families, and their local community conditions all play significant roles in both designing and applying assessments (standards 1, 5, 8, 9, 10, and 11). While IRA notes (and we agree) that traditional assessments are important for accountability, the standards also stress that the primary purpose of assessment is to *improve* teaching and learning, *not* merely to document or evaluate them (standard 3). That primary purpose of continuous improvement requires us as teachers to think critically about how assessment drives curriculum and instruction (standard 4). It requires us to make sure assessments are fair and equitable for our students (standard 6), and it requires us to change them when they are not (standard 7). Assessing individual students' funds of knowledge enables teachers to meet IRA's rigorous standards in ways that support *all* students, especially marginalized readers, as they learn to read and succeed in school.

WHY ASSESS STUDENTS' FUNDS OF KNOWLEDGE?

Because summative testing and evaluation are by far the most common types of assessment used in schools today, many teachers might reasonably ask why they should spend time documenting students' funds of knowledge gained *outside* of school when both the students and teachers will be held accountable most for the knowledge gained *inside* the school. Actually, in truth, starting the reading assessment process with data collection about students' knowledge, interests, experiences, and the use of texts beyond school is really a way to make traditional assessments *more* effective.

Learning to assess and use each student's funds of knowledge is not intended to replace traditional reading assessment. It *enhances* assessment in ways that scientists have established are basic to valid and reliable testing. As Johnston and Costello (2005) note, "Assessment is a social practice that involves noticing, representing, and responding to children's literate behaviors, rendering them meaningful for particular purposes and audiences" (p. 258). In support of this perspective, Johnston and Costello point out that all assessment "should be grounded in current understandings of literacy and society" (p. 256). The most profound implication of grounding assessment in the *current* understandings of literacy and society is that traditional academic texts used for teaching youth to read are in many ways out of date when used on their own. They can only be made useful if teachers have the data needed to link those traditional texts with students' current knowledge and daily experiences.

> Learning to assess and use each student's unique funds of knowledge is not intended to replace traditional reading assessment. It *enhances* assessment in ways that scientists have established are basic to valid and reliable testing.

Saying that traditional texts and assessments are insufficient is not to say that they totally lack value; on the contrary, traditional texts and assessments *can and should* be used in schools. They can be useful in helping students learn important concepts, skills, and cultural capital they need for participation in 21st-century society. But traditional assessments and the curricula they reflect are unlikely to be *sufficient* for 21st-century students—especially marginalized readers. As Moje et al. (2004) point out, traditional academic texts can get in the way of students learning how to participate, understand, and communicate in the ways we value most for classroom work. Thomas and Oldfather (1997) point out that the ways we assess students send important messages about how we see them as people. When we offer 21st-century students texts and tests that ignore, discount, or subordinate their own interests, practices, and experiences in favor of testing them for their familiarity with academic texts selected without their input or consideration, we literally position those readers for failure in spite of our intention to help them.

By starting the reading assessment process with documentation of each student's funds of knowledge, teachers can send all students the essential message that their everyday *local* knowledge and uses of reading are considered important, valuable, and useful in ultimately succeeding in the discipline of English. This acknowledgment can bolster their efficacy as readers, encouraging their academic *resilience*—"a disposition to focus on learning when the going gets tough, to quickly recover from setbacks, and to adapt" (Johnston & Costello, 2005, p. 257). As Johnston and Costello describe it, generating resilience through assessment counteracts the creation of "brittleness" in some students that comes from testing them for mastery in high-stakes environments where the risk of failure leads to avoidance and ego-defensive behavior, both of which negatively correlate with reading achievement (Guthrie et al., 2009).

When marginalized readers are supported in both learning and practicing English language arts via tasks and texts they find meaningful and authentic, they perform differently and usually more successfully. Traditional assessments typically presume that performance of a skill or application of a concept in one context can reliably represent that individual's knowledge and ability in all contexts, but that is not necessarily true (Johnston & Costello, 2005). Young people often treat knowledge from other parts of their lives as distinctly different from school knowledge. As a result, they don't always see their existing skills and knowledge as highly relevant to academic learning (Moje et al., 2004).

By documenting their knowledge and skills and then using that data to help students see how their own experiences connect with disciplinary knowledge, teachers can take the first step in positioning formerly marginalized readers as primary knowers. These marginalized readers' understandings of and experience with texts, structures, genres, and concepts from film, television, magazines, multimedia, and other texts they read every day are both highly relevant and useful in ELA classes. Their newly acknowledged literacies can become central to their ultimate understanding academic practices and disciplinary knowledge (Monnin, 2009).

ASSESSING STUDENTS' FUNDS OF KNOWLEDGE: A PROTOCOL

In their research about the nature of students' knowledge outside of school, Moll, Amanti, Neff, and Gonzalez (1992) and Moje et al. (2004) have attempted to devise comprehensive categories for the various types of knowledge ("funds") that children bring with them to school. The goal of their research is to systematically consider how educators can use such knowledge to design curriculum and instruction that responds to students' needs in local communities while also helping them succeed in the current U.S. system of educational accountability.

Students' various funds of knowledge come from many sources, and knowledge may cross categories or overlap contexts. In this section we offer a protocol—a systematic process—for asking questions and documenting the kinds of knowledge, skills, interests, activities, and texts that middle school readers engage with in their everyday lives. Our categories and questions are derived from research on these funds of knowledge, reading motivation, and scholarship about authentic assessment (Friese, Alvermann, Parkes, & Rezak, 2008; Ivey & Broaddus, 2001; Moje et al., 2004; Moll et al., 1992; Risko & Walker-Dalhouse, 2007). It is important to emphasize that our protocol is intended as a model rather than a recipe for assessing students. It is not intended to provide a laundry list of questions to ask all students everywhere in exactly the same way. Teachers working with diverse children across different classrooms and communities can and should modify categories and questions, depending on their particular contexts. Questions should also be rephrased as appropriate in ways that young adults can understand and respond to easily.

One of the great challenges noted in research about students' various funds of knowledge is the practical impossibility of teachers visiting the homes of all their students, gaining full access to their communities, and talking with all of the individuals or documenting all of the activities that inform those students' understanding and experience. Such in-depth assessment is all but impossible. However, individual teachers (and certainly groups of teachers at the departmental or school level) can collect data by simply interviewing students in their classroom and asking them to respond directly to questions about their activities and reading practices outside of school. These questions need not be overly intrusive. They can be asked and discussed in class through conversation as teachers demonstrate genuine interest in their students' lives. In fact, teachers can explain that they are interested in learning these things about students' lives specifically because doing so will help them make sure students get what they need to succeed, and that the information will be used to make school more relevant and accessible to everyone.

The following set of figures offers five categories and sets of questions any classroom teacher can use or adapt to assess students' funds of knowledge and thereby make more responsive decisions about curriculum and instruction. Figure 5.1 includes questions in the category of Family and Home Life Funds, Figure 5.2 includes questions in the category of Community Funds, and Figure 5.3 the category of Personal Activity Funds. Figure 5.4 includes questions in the category of Popular Culture Funds, and Figure 5.5 the category of General Knowledge/Current Events Funds.

By asking students about their family structures, relationships, working lives, domestic activities, and household routines or traditions, teachers gain data about students' funds of knowledge as areas of skill and interest, vocabularies, and norms for social interaction that may vary by culture and social class. Similarly, by asking them about their neighborhoods and communities, teachers gain data about students' languages,

1. Describe your family.
2. Where did your family come from? What do these origins mean to you and your family?
3. Do you have any brothers or sisters? How old are they? How would you describe your relationships with them?
4. Describe your parents.
5. Do you have other relatives you are close to? Where are they? How are they important to you?
6. What do you talk about with your family when you are together?
7. What kinds of things do you do with your family when you are together?
8. What are your roles in your family?
9. What traditions does your family have? What do these traditions mean to you?
10. What things do you believe your family values most? What do these values mean to you?
11. What kinds of chores do you and your family members do at home?
12. What kinds of work do you see your mother doing? How do you help her?
13. What kinds of work do you see your father doing? How do you help him?
14. Do you work outside of your home and school? What kinds of work do you know how to do?
15. Do your brothers and sisters work outside of home or school? If so, what do you know about the work they do?
16. What kinds of reading and writing do your family members and you do? Do members of your family read or write for pleasure and work? Do you?
17. How do you think your family has affected who you are as a person?
18. Does your family have any special goals or expectations for what you do, how you behave, or who you will become? If so, how do you feel about these goals and expectations? Why?
19. What goals do you have for yourself in life?

FIGURE 5.1. Family and home life funds of knowledge.

expectations and understanding of social interaction, patterns of activity, consumer knowledge and values, communication styles, and even schedules (Moll et al., 1992). Asking students what they read and why they read it (or not) most obviously helps teachers understand how and why a group of students is likely to respond to a text used in the classroom (Ivey & Broaddus, 2001). Teachers can then use the data to select texts more strategically, adapt instructional techniques, and teach disciplinary content and processes using scenarios students are more likely to understand and more readily relate to. Similarly, learning more about what a group of students typically knows or believes about interacting with authority figures outside of school can help a teacher make important decisions about what tone to take during class, how to choose language

1. Where do you live? What's it like there? What's the geography like? What kinds of homes do people live in? What do you see every day?
2. How would you describe your neighborhood to someone from a different part of the world?
3. Who lives in your neighborhood? What do you know about them? How do you feel about them?
4. What do you know about the kinds of work people from your neighborhood do?
5. Name the most important or popular places in your community. What meaning do these places have for you?
6. What activities do you participate most in your neighborhood? Why?
7. What do you think are the most important values of people, overall, in your neighborhood? Why?
8. What kinds of organized activities take place in your community? Are there festivals, or sports, or special events that are important? What do these mean to you?
9. In your opinion, what are the most important things you've learned from living in your community? Why are these things meaningful to you?

FIGURE 5.2. Community funds of knowledge.

the students will respond to during instruction, and how to manage and motivate various individuals and groups.

We recognize that middle school students are highly diverse, even within a single supposedly homogeneous classroom. Any single class's answers to these questions are likely to vary a great deal. Perhaps more importantly, some students may feel uncomfortable answering questions about their family and home lives in school. Some students might be

1. When you have free time, how do you spend it? Why?
2. What do you like to do for fun? Why?
3. What kinds of things do you do when you are with friends? Why?
4. What kinds of things do you enjoy doing on your own? Why?
5. What do you look for in a friend?
6. What makes you a good friend?
7. Do you have any hobbies? How did you learn about them? What do they mean to you?
8. Are you involved in any organized activities like sports, theater, dance, music, or arts and crafts? Why?
9. Do you participate in any other organized activities like youth groups, volunteer organizations, church activities, or the like? What do you get out of being a part of these groups?

FIGURE 5.3. Personal activity funds of knowledge.

1. What books have you read recently? Why?
2. What books have you read in your life that were meaningful to you? Why?
3. What's your favorite kind of thing to read? Why?
4. What's a good book or story you read in school recently? What made it stand out for you?
5. What magazines do you read? Why?
6. What are your favorite television shows of all time? Why?
7. What television shows are you watching right now? Why do you like them?
8. What are your favorite movies? Why?
9. What are the best movies you've seen lately? Why did you like them better than others?
10. If you use the Internet, which sites do you visit? Why?
11. What do you use the Internet for most?
12. If you have a computer, what do you use it for most?
13. Do you use email? How often? What do you use email for most? Who do you email? Why?
14. Do you have a cellphone? How do you use it? Do you use text messaging? How often? Why do you text, and who do you text with most?
15. What are your favorite kinds of music? What artists or groups do you like to listen to most? Why? What music are you listening to right now? Why do you like that music more than other kinds? Are there any kinds of music or performers that you do *not* like? Why?
16. If you listen to the radio, what do you listen to? Why?
17. What video games do you play? What do you like about those games? Are there games you don't like? Why?
18. What makes you want to read, watch, play, or listen to something? How do you decide? What makes you dislike reading, watching, playing, or listening?
19. Which celebrities do you like? What makes them special for you? Which celebrities do you dislike? What do you dislike about them?
20. How do feel when teachers use music, TV shows, movies, and other things you enjoy outside of school to teach English?

FIGURE 5.4. Popular culture funds of knowledge.

anxious about sharing personal information. Others may be intensely private based on cultural values, and some may simply feel embarrassed to disclose certain information. On the other hand, we realize too that some students may be overly eager to share and may go far beyond the intent of assessing their funds of knowledge. We encourage teachers to be explicit with students about the purposes of assessment, namely, to learn more about them as individuals and understand where they come from, what they know, what they like, how they learn, and what they do related to reading and learning in school. Assessing their funds of knowledge is

1. Have you ever traveled to other places? Where? Why?

2. What did you learn by traveling to other places?

3. What are your favorite places to visit? Why?

4. Where would you travel if you could go anywhere you wanted? Why? What would you do there?

5. What are the most important things happening in the world today? Why are these most important for you?

6. Who are the most important or influential people in the world today? Why do you think they are important?

7. What makes you want to pay attention to current events?

8. What makes you decide to ignore a news story? What makes you want to learn more?

9. What makes you want to learn something new? When you want to learn something, how do you usually do it?

10. Who do you learn the most from? What makes them good teachers?

FIGURE 5.5. General knowledge/current events.

not intended to make students reveal private matters or confess personal problems to authority figures. The point is to learn *with* them and see how their everyday lives can be linked with the things they will learn and do during English class and to make the curriculum more acceptable to them as readers.

> The point of assessing students' funds of knowledge is to learn *with* them and see how their everyday lives can be linked with the things they will learn and do during English class and to make the curriculum more acceptable to them as readers.

We also realize that our protocol is almost certainly incomplete. The questions and categories are in some ways arbitrary. As noted, teachers should adapt the questions and adjust the categories in any way that generates the most (and most useful) data for *their* context.

Even more importantly, teachers must remember that data collected by assessing students' funds of knowledge doesn't replace the need to teach ELA content, but rather *supplements and complements* that disciplinary knowledge. A teacher, for example, who uses students' knowledge of video games is not "teaching video games" in English class and should never allow students, colleagues, administrators, or parents to misconstrue this limited use. Rather, that teacher is using systematically collected assessment data to identify and use topics, models, and text features of video games to help students understand, talk about, and practice disciplinary knowledge and skills in reading for English language arts (for more detailed information and examples, see Chapter 11). When teachers explain to interested parties how their use of students' funds of knowledge benefits their academic success, the teachers invariably experience support and encouragement from these parties.

Using video game knowledge (or any other atypical kind) doesn't lead to a disregard for disciplinary knowledge and academic work. Rather, it *augments* that knowledge and work by providing topics that frame disciplinary practice in ways marginalized readers find especially compelling, thereby increasing their motivation. Their ready familiarity with such funds of knowledge makes them feel more able to understand academic reading content and practices—increasing their self-efficacy. Their knowledge about texts and topics from these funds positions them as primary knowers who have clear and valuable contributions to make during classroom discussions and activities related to school reading.

Consequently, assessing and using students' funds of knowledge to contextualize reading instruction in English leads to the kinds of engagement that we know correlate positively with increased learning, improved motivation, and lifelong reading. This outcome includes improved performance related to standards and standardized assessments (Guthrie, 2002). Having offered a protocol for assessing students' funds of knowledge, in the next section we describe how those data can be used to guide reading instruction.

USING FUNDS OF KNOWLEDGE IN TODAY'S SCHOOL SYSTEM

Friese et al. (2008) assert that selecting texts solely on the basis of students' interests and knowledge outside of school is not acceptable. We agree with that proposition. Just because the majority of students in a particular classroom enjoy a particular television program, book, film, or musical genre does not mean that the text they enjoy so much is appropriate or useful for academic instruction. We definitely do not subscribe to the clichéd notion that TV "rots the brain," but we absolutely acknowledge that some texts are inappropriate for use in teaching students to read. After all, the texts may involve content that is excessively profane or otherwise adult, or the texts simply may lack quality in terms of their structure, content, and production. All media formats—including the novels and poetry typically valued in English language arts—include texts that most would deem to be low-quality in terms of content, production, or both. However, just as there are obviously high-quality literary texts teachers can use to help students learn to read, there are also high-quality nontraditional texts from outside of school that are useful too.

All quality texts, whether print or nonprint, involve the use of structures, genres, techniques, topics, and patterns that reflect diverse content in the ELA curriculum. The teacher's role in applying assessments about students' specialized funds of knowledge is to make clear connections between their funds of knowledge and the disciplinary content and practices involved in reading. There is content unique to ELA that students need to learn for success in school and real knowledge that needs to be taught in anticipation of state-level assessments. However, just as teachers should avoid choosing texts and topics based on students' interests alone, they should also not select texts and topics solely on the basis of mandated and/or state-level assessments that fail to respond to students' personal knowledge and literacy needs.

> All quality texts involve the use of structures, genres, techniques, topics, and patterns that reflect diverse content in the ELA curriculum. The teacher's role in applying assessments about students' specialized funds of knowledge is to make clear connections between their personal knowledge and the disciplinary content and practices involved in reading.

The key is to blend traditional assessment data with data from the assessment of students' funds of knowledge to generate a more balanced and responsive curriculum and supportive instructional practices. Greenleaf et al. (2001) correctly note that, "helping students master academic literacy practices ... does not mean a return to isolated skills-based instruction" (para. 25). However, it is equally true that teaching comprehension strategies, text structures, and vocabulary through the use of systematically assessed and *relevant* topics, content, and activities helps marginalized readers make sense of academic texts and increases their reading achievement in school.

As we discuss in greater detail in Chapter 11, we recognize that many teachers may feel strongly that using pop culture texts such as movies, music, and television programs involves "dumbing down" the curriculum as compared to using traditionally defined "classic" books and poems in school. However, exclusively using texts that *fail to interest* students— as many classic novels and poems apparently do—results in decreased motivation, frustration for readers who struggle to comprehend those texts, and lower-quality engagement. Moje et al. (2004) found that popular culture was not only an important fund of knowledge unto itself but perhaps *the most important fund of knowledge available* for teaching students reading in schools. They found that using popular culture texts—especially music—helped students feel more able to engage with their peers in ways that supported their identities, increased their sense of efficacy as readers, and therefore supported higher levels of engagement and reading achievement.

The use of students' funds of knowledge related to pop culture texts like music is perhaps obvious for most English teachers. Popular music lyrics are easily used to provide students with familiar texts that use poetic structures commonly taught in the discipline. Lyrics involve rhythm, rhyme, alliteration, and many other types of figurative language. They also use traditional poetic structures such as stanzas, refrains, and choruses. Just like traditional poetry, they involve topics such as love, family, identity, friendship, war, death, change, loss, and countless others that can be used to generate themes for reading, writing, speaking, listening, visually representing, and blending the language arts in ways that are essential for success in school and life. It may be less obvious how assessment of students' home lives, family structures, and work experiences are useful in teaching reading.

Assessing students' funds of knowledge is not just useful in terms of selecting texts and topics students find interesting. Doing so also provides information about what they value most, how they interact with different kinds of people in their daily lives, how they are used to using language, how they understand their own roles and responsibilities in life, and more. So, for example, a teacher might learn that the majority of students in the classroom have parents who work in factories—or in managerial jobs, or in service industries—thereby suggesting particular familiar topics and themes that could be useful in selecting texts and designing activities. In addition, the teacher might find that the majority of students are used to communicating with adults and peers outside of school in ways that are highly interactive and in which people are not only expected to seek attention but to *compete* for it based on cultural or community values. In such a case, the teacher can use that assessment data to understand why certain students might appear to speak out of turn during classroom interactions and recognize when and how to teach such children the modes of participation required in English as an academic discipline. At the same time, the teacher can use assessments of students' family and community funds of knowledge to more fully compreheend their need for collaborative learning techniques, explicit instruction, and relevant content to systematically support and affirm their identities while still teaching them the content and practices required by the formal curriculum.

By the same token, a teacher might find that a particular group of students comes from a family or community background in which children are expected to be highly deferential to adults and authority figures and therefore inclined to wait for instructions and information as a matter of respect. In such cases, the teacher could use that information not only to select texts that help students understand their own lives but also to design instruction that systematically provides opportunities to work in ways they find comfortable while progressively acquiring skills they need for social contexts where expectations differ—as well they might in school and working life.

Students' family and community funds of knowledge may reveal a great deal about how students view and use different kinds of texts and communications. Teachers are often shocked when they discover that students do not already know certain vocabulary, elements of fiction, writing and reading conventions, or ways of communicating that are expected and valued in middle school. By beginning the assessment process for reading instruction with students' funds of knowledge, teachers can learn more about what, how, why, and whether students read and write for various purposes. Based on that information, they can then collect additional data and further analyze the information to anticipate students' needs for ELA reading.

For example, if students come from family, community, and work backgrounds where reading and writing are not commonly used, teachers can better anticipate the specific concepts, skills, and practices students will need in order to participate in class. If they come from backgrounds in which computer and Internet access is rare, marginalized readers may require more direct instruction and opportunities to learn and practice keyboarding, using search engines, and evaluating the utility of various Internet websites (Moje et al., 2004). If students are actively participating in peer cultures where text messaging is commonplace or routine, then teachers can decide both when and how they might use that activity to engage students in communication during reading activities. And, of course, the data collected about students' extracurricular lives should always be used to help choose texts, adapt them in selective ways, and assign them at opportune times to help students learn in ways that are maximally helpful to them.

By collecting such detailed specific data about middle schoolers—especially marginalized readers—teachers can gradually integrate their heightened understanding of the students' worldview into traditional instructional practice. As Risko and Walker-Dalhouse (2007) recommend, teachers can integrate students' specialized funds of knowledge into formal instruction by separately identifying the content to be taught (topics), the problems embedded in that content (opportunities for higher-order thinking), the disciplinary element that students should learn as a result of the instruction (skills and concepts), and finally students' prior knowledge, "including patterns of language used in their community, at home, and with peers" (p. 99). Teachers can use this approach to design instructional activities and assessments that are responsive to the knowledge of readers who may have been marginalized in past classroom experiences.

English teachers can and should continue to teach students the skills and content they need to do well on such traditional assessment tools as essays, quizzes, and standardized tests. They can also help students learn to participate in their own reading instruction by creating assessments in which students use their funds of knowledge to "perform, create, produce, or do something" that involves higher-order thinking, represents "meaningful instructional activities," involves "real-world applications," and enables them to move step by step toward a classroom environment that helps marginalized readers eventually become primary knowers (Corcoran, Dershimer, & Tichenor, 2004, pp. 213–216).

There can be little doubt that teachers can better support marginalized readers when they assess funds of knowledge beyond school. However, such data can be used wisely or poorly. Moll et al. (1992) warn that educators must avoid stereotyping students based on findings about funds of knowledge. For example, assessment data showing that a particular group of students enjoys hiphop or country music does not mean that all those students are equally fans of that music genre or that implementing references to just any hiphop or country music will necessarily be useful in enhancing reading instruction. Similarly, finding that even a majority of students in a class feels comfortable communicating in competitive ways does not necessarily mean that every reading activity should therefore emphasize competition.

Before applying such assessments wholesale, teachers must ask their students what certain texts mean to them, how they use them, why they communicate in certain ways in certain situations, and so forth. Based on how they refine the funds of knowledge data, teachers can best determine what students need for success in school and how to structure classroom interactions to the greatest advantage. Without that considering the data's implications carefully, teachers risk alienating students even more, or stereotyping them, or failing to connect their specialized knowledge to disciplinary content in ways that prove productive for all.

Teachers must take steps to assure that they keep up with students' ever changing and expanding knowledge and experiences in order to keep reading instruction relevant and responsive to their needs—especially when working with marginalized readers.

Importantly, the funds of knowledge data useful for teaching reading in one classroom are not always the same data that will be useful for teaching in another classroom—or even necessarily anywhere else in the same school (Moje et al., 2004). What students know, do, and value in one neighborhood or household or geographic location may vary greatly when compared with students in another group. Teachers must take steps to assure that they keep up with students' ever changing and expanding knowledge and experiences in order to keep reading instruction relevant and responsive to their needs—especially when working with marginalized readers. As is true with any form of assessment, teachers must periodically collect, review, and analyze new data to make adjustments and consistently improve their methods. Such ongoing purposeful assessment is the ultimate goal enshrined by the International Reading Association's standards (IRA, 2009).

SUMMARY

Even as we strongly encourage middle grade English teachers to work with so-called struggling readers to systematically assess their specialized funds of knowledge, we realize that current demands for accountability and testing make it difficult to implement that approach as fully as we might like. However, as Marsh (2006) concludes, "If we do not ensure ... teachers are aware of the realities of children's out-of-school literacy lives, shaped as these are by popular culture, media, and new technologies, then we are likely to continue to have literacy curricula ... that are anachronistic and inadequate" (p. 173). If teachers allow themselves to simply implement the curriculum and tests required by schools and states without regard for students' existing knowledge, values, and practices, then they will inevitably perpetuate the current situation in which many students "struggle" because they aren't given the time, resources, reasons, or opportunities they need to be successful (Ivey & Broaddus, 2001; Scherff & Piazza, 2008).

Still, it is impossible to ignore the workplace conditions and political realities of public schools and high stakes reading assessments that get in the way of responding to marginalized readers' needs (Lee, 1998). Current standards and state/federal accountability systems constrain curriculum to an extreme degree that makes it difficult and even risky for teachers to integrate students' funds of knowledge. Lee notes that students (as well as parents, administrators, and teachers) may resist assessments that don't look like traditional schooling because they may violate their assumptions about what they think should happen in school (teachers lecturing to students who sit quietly in rows, completing worksheets, taking multiple-choice tests, reading particular "classics," etc.). Most teachers probably need to take two-steps-forward, one-step-back approach to integrating students' funds of knowledge into existing traditional practices.

However, just as literacy is a social phenomenon, so are assessment and policymaking. Although Sarroub and Pearson (1998) have characterized the reform of standardized reading assessment as "two steps forward, three steps back," the pressure to "teach to the test" is ultimately not an acceptable requirement that professional reading teachers readily embrace (p. 97). It may, indeed, be necessary for teachers and schools to ensure that students meet the requisite standards for high-stakes reading assessments. But that necessity must be understood for what it is, namely, a politicized marker supposedly indicating efficiency, not a pedagogically justifiable practice that helps children or even improves curriculum and instruction. As Johnston and Costello (2005) observe, "High stakes accountability testing has consistently been demonstrated to *undermine* teaching and learning" (p. 258). It sometimes forces teachers to simplify, drop, or simply ignore practices, texts, and knowledge about students that they would otherwise use to enhance instruction, motivation, and the learning environment. Most significantly, Johnston and Costello (2005) argue that it is "premature" to label any child as struggling "without first eliminating the possibility that the child's progress is a result of poorly configured instruction" (p. 263). When state departments and school districts use high-stakes tests at the expense of teacher decision making and local data, it "has everything to do with politics and relatively little to do with research" (p. 265).

Such conditions do more than make the labeling of some students as struggling readers premature; it makes such labeling unethical. While we acknowledge that political issues and the realities of standardized testing may impede teachers from using students' funds of knowledge as fully as possible to improve reading instruction, finding ways to blend our approach with existing practices is not only useful but essential to the well-being of youth, teachers, and schools in the 21st century. As standards for reading assessment emphasize, our job is to use assessment to meet the needs of our students—not just to label students with their reading difficulties.

> **The realities of standardized testing may prevent teachers from using students' funds of knowledge as fully as possible to improve reading instruction. However, as standards for reading assessment emphasize, our job is to use assessment to meet the needs of our students.**

Questions for Reflection

1. List what you know about the students in your classroom, school, and community. How much of what you know addresses the questions offered here about assessing students' own funds of knowledge?

2. Try asking your students about the ways they talk with adults and authority figures outside of school. Ask them why they communicate in those ways, and talk with them about what they think is the most appropriate and useful way for teachers to talk to students in English class. How does the information you get from these conversations affect your beliefs about teaching and managing in your classroom?

3. Today it is common for schools to utilize "common planning"—a practice in which teams or departments design curriculum and lessons so that each class is studying the same topics in the same ways while using the same texts at the same time. How could your department or team use students' funds of knowledge during common planning without sacrificing consistency in instruction?

4. Many schools simply don't have a sufficient budget to purchase new texts that address students' changing interests over time. How might knowing more about students' funds of knowledge help you connect the texts your school *does* have to students' real lives outside of school?

RECOMMENDED RESOURCES

Darling-Hammond, L. (2010). *The flat world and education: How America's commitment to equity will determine our future.* New York: Teachers College Press.

Gonzalez, N. E. (2005). *Funds of knowledge: Theorizing practices in households and classrooms.* Mahwah, NJ: Erlbaum.

Lewis, J. (Ed.) (2009). *Essential questions in adolescent literacy: Teachers and researchers describe what works in classrooms.* New York: Guilford Press.

6

Implementing Reading Comprehension Strategies

FOCAL POINTS

1. Struggling readers' decisions about whether and how to use reading comprehension strategies are tied to their understanding of what it means to read in school and what it means to be a good or poor reader.

2. Struggling readers need opportunities to observe their peers both having difficulties with texts and hearing what they did.

3. The social contexts of the classroom can influence if struggling readers will even try to use comprehension strategies.

"I use strategies all the time. I do things like reread or ask questions, and it really helps. I am learning a lot more now that I use them." —KATHERINE, a seventh-grade student

"I never use strategies. It's something you're supposed to use if you can't read. So, if someone saw me using a strategy, then they'd think I can't read. I don't want anyone knowing that!"—MARTIN, a seventh-grade student.

On the surface, Katherine and Martin's statements about reading comprehension strategies might indicate that they are two very different kinds of readers. Katherine appears to derive benefits from using comprehension strategies, as she has experienced firsthand how strategies can help her better understand texts. Martin's statement, on the other hand, makes it clear that he sees strategies as something to be used only by people who cannot read. He believes that if he uses strategies other people will identity him as a bad reader—something he clearly wishes to avoid.

Despite their different attitudes toward using comprehension strategies, neither Katherine nor Martin was actually meeting grade-level expectations in reading performance. Based on state and classroom reading assessments, Katherine read on a fifth-grade level while Martin read on a sixth-grade level. However, they were both in the same English language arts class, and they regularly received the same kinds of instruction on how to use comprehension strategies.

Helping students like Katherine and Martin learn how to use comprehension strategies is critical to their development as competent readers (Clark, 2009; Conley, 2008). Students who are adept at using such strategies are more likely to know how to respond to comprehension difficulties and thereby increase their understanding of texts (Kintsch & Kintsch, 2005; Pressley & Hilden, 2006). Additionally, students who can employ such strategies whenever they need to are much better able to explore complex ideas, develop new ways of seeing the world, and ultimately retain their understanding of what they have read far better than students who do not or cannot use comprehension strategies effectively (Keene, 2007).

What exactly are reading comprehension strategies? Reading comprehension strategies (and how they are used) are different from reading skills that typically support and promote understanding. Reading skills are used automatically and do not require students to make a conscious decision to apply them. By comparison comprehension strategies are "deliberate, goal-oriented attempts to control and modify the reader's efforts to decode text, understand words, and construct meanings of text" (Afflerbach, Pearson, & Paris, 2008, p. 368). Examples of commonly taught strategies include (1) making predictions, (2) activating prior knowledge, (3) paying attention to text structures, (4) creating visual representations of text, (5) summarizing text, and (6) rereading (Duke & Pearson, 2002; Keene & Zimmerman, 2007).

For example, while reading a student may come across a word that he or she does not understand. Rather than skipping over the word and moving forward with only limited comprehension, the student may decide to reread the sentence to see if he or she can determine its meaning. The student's decision to reread the sentence is an example of putting a comprehension strategy into action. However, the student's ability to decode words effortlessly and read fluently is a skill: the student does not need to think about what to do to say the words or how fast or slow to read—it is automatic.

A great deal of research has substantiated the benefits of providing explicit instruction to students on how and why to use reading comprehension strategies (Clark & Graves, 2005; Dymock, 2007). While such instruction can help all students, including marginalized readers, improve their understanding of these strategies, it is no guarantee they will use them. Regardless of the quality or amount of instruction they receive, the students themselves ultimately decide whether, when, and how they will use the strategies they learn (Hall, 2007; Moore & Cunningham, 2006).

Additionally, using comprehension strategies does not *necessarily* make one a better and more engaged reader. Such strategies are simply "a means to an end" (Keene & Zimmerman, 2007, p. 43), intended to help students engage thoughtfully with texts and serve as gateways to examining ideas from multiple perspectives. If students use the strategies merely to identify facts or locate "right" answers—or, worse, solely at the urging of the teacher—then they may not come to regard them as the invaluable tools that they are to help students engage deeply with texts and ideas.

In this chapter we explore the intersection between cognitive strategy instruction and the social landscape that students occupy in ELA classrooms. We examine the different ways in which students interact with comprehension strategies and discuss some of the rationales that guide their decisions. We consider how strategy instruction can be developed so that it responds to the social and cognitive goals of students who find themselves positioned as marginalized readers.

THE IMPORTANCE OF ONGOING COMPREHENSION STRATEGY INSTRUCTION

Most students likely receive basic instruction on comprehension strategies during their elementary school years. However, often these strategies are taught in a relative vacuum rather than hand in hand with the literacy practices that most require them (Beach & O'Brien, 2007). Instruction often focuses on teaching students how to apply comprehension strategies in hypothetical generic ways that will not necessarily be identified with reading texts in English (Dewitz, Jones, & Leahy, 2009). Thus, students might not initially appreciate the purposes that strategies have in helping them to better understand ELA texts.

For example, teachers might well provide students with instruction on how to make and check predictions and model how to use this strategy during reading. Students might then engage in guided practice on using this strategy and complete an assignment where they read text and chart their predictions. Thus, while students might learn how to make predictions, they did not necessarily learn how to use this strategy firsthand for gaining information or improving comprehension. Instead, use of the strategy in this context was something done at the request of a teacher to complete an assignment.

While marginalized readers have normally had some instruction on how to use comprehension strategies, they are unlikely to be able to use them effortlessly to comprehend texts in ELA classrooms. Throughout their elementary school career, marginalized readers likely received supplemental or remedial services to try to improve their reading comprehension abilities—including the use of comprehension strategies—through isolated skills-based instruction (Johannessen, 2004). This skills-based approach often results in marginalized readers having fewer opportunities to read challenging texts and to discuss them at great length (Johannessen & McCann, 2009). As a result, marginalized readers may have had relatively few opportunities to learn how to select and use text comprehension strategies in a purposeful manner for specific reading goals they have set.

> **Marginalized readers likely have had few opportunities to learn how to select and use text comprehension strategies in a purposeful manner for specific reading goals they have set.**

HOW DO STUDENTS
USE COMPREHENSION STRATEGIES?

Helping marginalized readers become more adept in using comprehension strategies requires understanding what guides their decisions about using them. When marginalized readers do not use comprehension strategies to make sense of texts, one might readily assume that they either need more instruction or are deliberately avoiding strategic approaches to reading. If they truly cared about learning, after all, it might be hard to believe that they could understand how to use them but elect not to!

However, Leigh's (Hall, 2009) yearlong study of a middle school struggling reader, Sarah, revealed that she actively chose not to employ comprehension strategies even when she understood them and knew that using them would increase her comprehension and allow her to become a better reader. Throughout the year, Sarah's teacher, Mrs. O'Reilly, provided the whole class with regular instruction on how to use a variety of comprehension strategies including setting a purpose, visualizing, and making connections. She often had students share how they used comprehension strategies during their reading and what they learned from using them.

In interviews, Sarah explained that ultimately her understanding of how and why to use comprehension strategies did not matter because she would never *choose* to use them. Much like Martin (in this chapter's introductory quotes), Sarah explained that using strategies would cause her to read at a slower pace and thus finish far behind the other students. As a result she believed she would be publicly recognized as a poor reader—a negative stigma that she sought at all costs to avoid. Sarah thus knowingly made decisions that compromised her abilities to read and learn and was saddened that she could not find a way to be a better reader and thereby maintain a positive social status in the classroom.

> Students may knowingly make decisions that compromise their abilities to read and learn and become saddened that they cannot find ways to be better readers and thereby maintain a positive social status in the classroom.

When struggling readers do use comprehension strategies, their decisions about which strategies to use and why may be closely connected to how they *see themselves* as readers. Although test scores may indicate that the students read one or more years below grade level, not all of them will classify themselves as being poor or struggling readers. Students who read below grade level may well see themselves as meeting or exceeding grade-level expectations during reading, which may influence how they use strategies during reading.

For example, Leigh surveyed 52 sixth-grade students by using the *Reader Self-Perception Scale* (RSPS; Henk & Melnick, 1995). The RSPS measures how students in grades 4–6 perceive their reading abilities. Based on their responses, students are classified as holding a high, average, or low self-perception about their reading abilities. The students who read below grade level and saw themselves as being poor or average readers were more likely to regard comprehension strategies as something separate from reading: strategies were something one did for the sake of doing them—because a teacher told you to—but not necessarily as a way to improve comprehension or to increase learning. When these students made decisions about which strategies to use, they were most likely to rely on one or two that they identified as being their favorite regardless of how appropriate that particular strategy may have been for the situation.

However, these patterns of use did not apply to struggling readers who identified themselves as being among the best readers in their classes. These students used comprehension strategies as a way to deepen their knowledge of content and to support their interpretations of texts. Rather than relying on a particular favorite strategy, they normally selected strategies they believed would best help them address the comprehension problem at hand and were more likely to try a different strategy if their first choice did not work out.

So, why do some struggling readers appear to use strategies in ways that benefit them while others use them in ways that are not always helpful—and some may not even use them at all? The key to understanding their decisions lies in understanding them—both as readers and as people. How struggling readers identify themselves as readers, and how they want to be identified by others, may largely determine how they use strategies during reading.

> **How struggling readers identify themselves as readers, and how they want to be identified by others, may largely determine how they use strategies during reading.**

READING IDENTITIES: WHAT THEY ARE AND HOW THEY INFLUENCE STRATEGY USE

The term *reading identity* refers to the value individuals place on reading, how capable they believe they are in understanding texts, and their interpretations of how people should interact with texts (Hall et al., 2010; McRae & Guthrie, 2009). Within school, the types of reading identities available to students (typically good, average, or poor/struggling reader) are deeply entrenched in social and cultural norms and serve as a framework for identifying and understanding people in particular ways (Wortham, 2006). Throughout their school careers, students have had many experiences with reading that allow them to understand what it means to be identified as a particular type of reader and where they fall within this continuum. The experiences they have can help them shift their identities as readers or serve to reinforce the identity they already embody (Holland & Lave, 2001; Wortham, 2004).

For example, Katherine, who expressed that she regularly used comprehension strategies, considered herself to be "a very good reader." She explained that she understood most of what she read and was able to get good grades on her assignments. She believed she recognized her comprehension difficulties when she experienced them and knew what to do to fix them. Martin, however, saw himself as a "bad reader" and one who rarely understood what he read. He said he often received low grades on his assignments and that he was not able to answer comprehension questions as quickly as most of the students in his class. He also explained that he never knew what to say when texts were discussed in any of his classes.

The reading identities Katherine and Martin adopted likely influenced how they engaged with classroom reading practices and more specifically how they used comprehension strategies. Students who self-identify as poor readers often choose to disengage from reading rather than publicly reveal their perceived weaknesses as readers (Hall & Nellebach, 2009; Smith & Wilhelm, 2004). Students who are struggling but who self-identify as good readers may still have difficulty in comprehending texts beyond the factual level, but because they associate themselves with a positive reading identity they may not believe they need to engage differently with texts or that they would benefit from further strategy instruction (Caldwell & Leslie, 2004; Ivey & Broaddus, 2000).

HOW TO ADDRESS READING IDENTITIES IN STRATEGY INSTRUCTION

Students' identities as readers can influence their decisions as they relate to not just strategy instruction but all classroom reading practices. The practices outlined below are meant to help you learn more about how your students see themselves as readers and how you can use this information to teach students about reading comprehension strategies. However, the ideas can be used to improve any aspect of literacy instruction implemented on a broader scale.

Finding a Way In: Understanding Your Students as Readers

One way to approach learning about your students' reading identities is to have a discussion about how they see themselves as readers and why. In having such a discussion, it is important to recognize that not all students will want to participate. Those who feel uncomfortable talking to you about how they identify themselves as readers normally do not want this information to be made public to their peers. Students who have had bad experiences while reading in school worry that sharing their experiences leads to public ridicule. Therefore you must honor students' right not to participate in this discussion.

However, having a discussion about reading identities can provide students a framework for talking about themselves as readers and for seeing how their classmates have made sense of their own experiences. Teachers can begin by posing questions and having students take time to reflect and compose a written response about how they identify themselves as readers. Examples of useful linked questions include:

"How would you describe yourself as a reader?"
"Why do you think this description fits you?"
"What would you like to change about yourself as a reader?"

Once students have answered these questions, teachers may choose to invite students to share their responses. The following conversation provides an example of how these discussions might be structured:

> MR. ALEXANDER: Let's talk for a minute about how we think of ourselves as readers. This is important because it's really connected to how we read in here. How would you describe yourself as a reader?
>
> JACOB: I'm good.
>
> MR. ALEXANDER: Why do you say that?
>
> JACOB: 'cause I read fast. I get almost all the words right when I read.
>
> MR. ALEXANDER: Okay. Who else would like to share?
>
> HALEY: I'm not very good at it.
>
> MR. ALEXANDER: Why's that?
>
> HALEY: I read slow. I don't always know what the words mean.

Jacob and Haley have offered information about how they see themselves as readers and have provided some evidence for their conclusions. While Jacob identifies himself as a good reader and Haley identifies herself as a poor one, the rationales they provide to support their conclusions provide important instructional insights. Jacob's understanding is that what makes someone a good reader is the ability to say words correctly and fast. His definition of what makes a good reader focuses very little on the meaning extracted from the words. Although we would want to gather more information about Jacob before firming up this conclusion, his initial response provides an important avenue to explore.

Haley may identify herself as a poor reader, but her rationale is much different from Jacob's. While she says she reads slowly, she also points out that she does not normally understand what the words mean. Her understanding of what makes someone a good or poor reader focuses on creating some meaning from the words read—something that was missing from Jacob's explanation.

Neither student contextualized the description of him- or herself. Haley believes she is not a good reader, but she does not specify whether there are certain academic disciplines, such as English, or certain text genres that she believes she is more or less successful with in reading. Both describe their abilities as readers, and what they think it means to read, in very generic and general terms.

In addition to considering what your students say during the discussion, it is also important to consider how you respond to them. While we might not agree with Jacob's or Haley's definition of what a good or poor reader is, the purpose of these initial discussions is not to correct or challenge their understanding but rather to learn what their understanding about reading is.

In this example, Mr. Alexander does not judge Jacob's and Haley's interpretations of themselves as readers or their rationales for their identities but simply allows them to share, asking only questions that are intended to clarify what they have said. Although Mr. Alexander may eventually want to ask Jacob if saying all the words correctly is the primary element of being a good reader, at this point the goal is to understand where students are coming from.

The information gathered from written responses and discussions can be used to plan instruction that helps students become better readers in ELA classrooms and targets how they use comprehension strategies to create meaning as they read. The remainder of this chapter focuses on how to use information about students' identities as readers to improve their comprehension abilities and how they employ strategies when reading. First, we look at how you can restructure strategies so that they are taught in service of the content being learned. Then we consider how to help all students make visible how and why they use strategies. Finally, we conclude by discussing how strategy instruction can be linked to helping students achieve their goals as readers.

Reading and Using Strategies in English: Putting the Discipline First

As noted earlier, most students have likely experienced reading comprehension instruction as a decontexualized process that does not help them understand how or why they should apply strategies independently or how or why strategies should be used when reading within a specific discipline such as English. Additionally, strategies are often presented under the guise of what "good readers do" or as ways to address comprehension difficulties (Hall et al., 2010). Students who self-identify as good readers might assume that strategies are for students who can't read well or something to be used when told to by their teachers. Students who self-identify as poor readers, such as Sarah or Martin, may reject comprehension strategies altogether for fear that using them will further expose their weaknesses.

> **Most students have likely experienced reading comprehension instruction as a decontexualized process that does not help them understand how or why they should apply strategies independently or how or why strategies should be used when reading within a specific discipline such as English.**

One way to help all students see the benefits of using comprehension strategies is to highlight not what *type* of reader uses them and why but how strategies can be used in the service of the discipline. Olson and Truxaw (2009) argue that teachers should make the content rather than the strategies the central focus of instruction. Putting the focus on the content places strategies in the background as support mechanisms to be used to gain deeper understanding or to clarifying uncertainties. This approach helps students focus on what it means to read and use strategies in English specifically and pushes them well beyond the simplistic conceptions of reading typified by Jacob and Haley's remarks earlier (Moje, 2008).

As texts are identified to support content knowledge, teachers should consider which comprehension strategies best support students' learning and then teach them how best to apply the strategies. For example, when reading texts in ELA classes, students generally need to use strategies to help them develop their own interpretations, understand what motivates different characters, consider how the actions of a character affect the outcome of events, and identify what the text is trying to persuade the reader to do or believe (Zwiers, 2008). Using the strategy of making predictions then takes on new meaning. Rather than telling students to read the section title or a segment of text and then consider what might happen next, teachers might instead ask students to predict how the decisions of one character could positively or negatively affect that character's life or the lives of others. In this instance, the prediction strategy takes on a specific use that is more relevant to the discipline.

Making the content central also changes the types of discussions students and teachers have about strategies. It shifts teachers from solely talking about "what good readers do" or how one "solves comprehension problems" and instead focuses the talk on how strategies are used by everyone at different times to develop a more thorough understanding of the text. For example, the following discussion shows how Ms. Winters talked to her eighth graders about how strategies can be used to better understand memoirs:

Ms. WINTERS: Let's take a look at "A Trip to the Doctor." What is the focus memory that the author is discussing here?

RACHEL: Going to the doctor.

Ms. WINTERS: Right. And what are some important details he shares about going to the doctor?

PATRICK: Something about how he got his adenoids taken out, and it was like all bloody and stuff—and I think it hurt.

Ms. WINTERS: How do you know it hurt, Patrick? What caused you to come to that conclusion?

PATRICK: It says right here [points to text] that he didn't get no anesthesia, but they cut stuff out of him. That would hurt.

MS. WINTERS: Right. He felt it. So, how did you come to that conclusion? You could have reread that part of the story where it explained he wasn't given any anesthesia, but you also had to make an inference. You used your background knowledge and concluded that having something cut out of you without any anesthesia would hurt.

In this example, Ms. Winters highlights three strategies students might have used, namely, rereading, making inferences, and using background knowledge. Rather than pointing out that Patrick employed the strategies because he was a good reader or because he didn't understand something, she showed how these strategies could be used to draw conclusions about the author and what he experienced by *anyone*. She also discussed how students might have used them to learn something relevant to English. By making content the central focus, Ms. Winters provided students the opportunity to learn how strategies are used in English rather than how strategies are used by certain types of readers.

The Benefits of Seeing Others Struggle

While situating strategies inside content can help students think about them differently, doing so is still no guarantee that students will use them. Students such as Martin and Sarah may hold a deep-seated conviction that strategies are used only by those who cannot read well. Therefore, part of helping marginalized readers recognize the value of reading comprehension strategies involves providing them opportunities to rethink their beliefs about who uses them and why.

One way to do this is to give students regular time to document and discuss their use of strategies. Discussions can then follow that highlight specifically which strategies students used, why, and what they learned from their experiences. By elevating discussions about comprehension strategies to the front and center in the classroom, students come to see that everyone uses a variety of strategies to achieve different purposes and goals. When strategies are seen as tools that everyone uses, they become something obviously helpful to all and thus not something used only by students who are less capable readers.

> Helping marginalized readers recognize the value of reading comprehension strategies means providing them opportunities to rethink their beliefs about who uses them and why.

Kelley and Clausen-Grace (2008) provide a framework that can help middle school students pay closer attention to both choosing the right comprehension strategy and observing how effectively they employ it. The framework has four stages. In the first stage, teachers define and explain the various strategies and model them for the class through a think-aloud. In the second stage, students consider which strategies are best to use when reading and receive extra support in whole-class and small-group instruction. In the third stage, students specify when and how they use strategies, sharing their own strategy use with the class. And in the final stage, students identify one or more strategies they need further help with.

By using this framework, students become more aware of what they are learning, become more confident in themselves as readers, and are better able to use comprehension strategies independently. The interactions that occur within this framework can also help reposition marginalized readers as primary knowers. When struggling readers have the opportunity to explain a strategy they used and how it helped them, they increasingly are seen as being knowledgeable and having something useful to offer the class. Additionally, marginalized readers can both readily identify with and learn from other students who struggled with comprehending texts and used strategies to help them better understand.

It is through these experiences that marginalized readers begin to see they have something to offer and that using strategies and engaging with their peers around written texts are worthwhile endeavors. These experiences also cause students to reconceptualize what it means to be a reader. Recently Dylan, a sixth grader, explained to Leigh how the practice of hearing the struggles his peers had with reading and how they worked to overcome them increased his own confidence as a reader:

> "I always thought I was one of the only ones who couldn't read. But now I see that everyone has problems. I like it when I can help someone else out. It's like I thought, hey, that person's a really good reader, but they needed some extra help. And I gave them that help!"

Connecting Strategies with the Person Students Want to Be as Readers: The Role of Cultural Artifacts

Helping struggling readers become more comfortable with, and adept at using, strategies means not only helping them see how strategies can improve their comprehension but ultimately helping them become the readers they want to be. Struggling readers often think that strategies, while helpful, will only keep them in their current position as struggling readers. Therefore, designing lessons and experiences that provide students the opportunity to see how their use of strategies helps them progress toward who they want to become as readers is significant.

What do such lessons look like? Bartlett (2005) argues that cultural artifacts play a central role in shaping students' literate identities. Cultural artifacts are symbols or objects that hold a collective, shared meaning within a specific context or for a community. In school, a cultural artifact can be a concrete object like a text or it can be label such as good/poor reader.

Artifacts have the power to help students rethink and develop new identities (Bartlett, 2007). They do not make students become better readers, but they can help students "seem and feel more literate" (p. 64) or reinforce students' current conceptualization of themselves as readers. For example, some students may see any text used in school as an artifact that represents their inability to read. Consider the following statement made by Michelle:

> "When I see a book [in school] I just think, ugh, we have to read *that*? 'Cause it's like always so hard, and I can never get it. I'd rather read one of my magazines. They're fun."

For Michelle, simply being told to read a text in school signified to her that she had limited reading abilities even before she opened the text and attempted to read it. Magazines, which she self-selected and read on her own, helped her see herself as literate.

Michelle's reaction to school-based texts does not have to remain fixed. Once we understand how and why Michelle views texts in the way that she does, and how these texts are tied to her identity as a reader, we can design lessons that enable her to have a positive experience with a school-based text and work on reshaping her identity.

For example, imagine that you are teaching the book *Catherine, Called Birdy* (Cushman, 1995), set in 13th-century England, which focuses on issues related to women's rights and marriage. In the book, Catherine's father spends his time trying to locate a suitor for his daughter—a practice that may seem highly remote to today's typical youth. Therefore, helping students make connections between the ideas in the text and everyday life will be essential to helping students get engaged with the reading assignment.

After students read a selection of text, you can review the ideas presented and ask them to consider how these ideas are represented in today's society. That evening, students should identify an artifact that symbolizes a personal connection to what they have read. The artifact could be anything—a novel, a video clip, a website, picture, or piece of jewelry or clothing. It could be something students used to better understand the reading—or it could be that the reading better helped them to understand the particular artifact they identified.

When students come to class the next day, they can share their artifact with a small group. One way to structure the discussion and presentation of artifacts is through an activity called the circle of objects (Brookfield & Preskill, 2005). This activity requires participants to focus on why they selected their object, what it helped them to learn, and how it plays a part in their developing identities as readers. In their groups, each student shares his or her artifact and reads a portion of the text aloud that the artifact best connects with. Each person then shares how connecting with this artifact has helped him or her work toward who they want to become as a reader. Others listen without talking or questioning, and this pattern of interaction continues around the circle.

Once everyone has had a chance to present his or her artifact, the floor is opened up. Students can now ask one another questions about the artifacts or who they are trying to become as readers. Students may also use this time to explore a central question, such as "How did this artifact help you better understand yourself as a reader?"

Cultural artifacts then take on several roles in classrooms. First, they stand to reinforce students' particular understanding of themselves as readers. For Michelle, if texts are continually assigned and used in the same manner as before, she will continue to see them as reminders that she cannot read very well.

However, having students identify artifacts that represent ideas and connect to texts can provide students like Michelle a new way to engage with texts and allow them to rethink how they view them. If students can be successful with texts, then texts start to serve as artifacts that represent positive aspects about them as readers. Thus, students begin to "seem and feel more literate" (Bartlett, 2007, p. 64), which in turn can change not just how they interact with texts but also how they self-identify as readers.

SUMMARY

Students positioned as struggling or marginalized readers do not necessarily resist using comprehension strategies because they are *uninterested* in reading or do not understand how to apply them. Instead, their decisions are often tied to their own notions about what it means to be a particular kind of reader and their desire to avoid being publicly identified as someone who cannot read well. Helping struggling readers feel confident in their abilities to use comprehension strategies means providing extra space where they can reexamine their understanding of reading identities and work toward becoming who they want to be as readers. Therefore, instruction needs to be mindful of not only the strategies students need to learn in order to comprehend text but also the social contexts that might support or constrain their use of them.

Questions for Reflection

1. Do your students use comprehension strategies? What guides their decisions?

2. How do your students identify themselves as readers? How do these understandings arise?

3. Examine one student who self-identifies as a good reader and one who self-identifies as a poor one. What similarities and differences do you notice about how they engage with classroom reading practices?

RECOMMENDED RESOURCES

Ganske, K., & Fisher, D. (2010). *Comprehension across the curriculum: Perspectives and practices K–12.* New York: Guilford Press.

Hiebert, E. H. (2009). *Reading more, reading better.* New York: Guilford Press.

Holland, D., & Lave, J. (2001). *History in person: Enduring struggles, contentious practice, intimate identities.* Santa Fe, NM: School of American Research Press.

7

Using Young Adult Literature to Promote Comprehension with Struggling Readers

Lisa Scherff

FOCAL POINTS

1. Using literary theory can help students become more critical readers and assist with comprehension.

2. When used with high-quality, engaging young adult literature, literary theory can provide a link to canonical works and help struggling readers to be more successful.

As noted earlier (in Chapter 1), very few U.S. eighth-grade students read at the advanced level, and about one-third of high school freshmen are 2 years or more below grade level in reading (Balfanz, McPartland, & Shaw, 2002; Peire, Grigg, & Donahue, 2005). As a result, there are a large number of students identified as struggling readers in English language arts classes. While reading and studying literature, especially canonical texts, is difficult for many students, it is particularly challenging for struggling readers. Although struggling readers may have been expected to read literature and canonical texts throughout school, they likely experienced insufficient support or instruction all along the way.

Lisa Scherff, PhD, is Associate Professor in the Department of Curriculum and Instruction at the University of Alabama.

As a classroom teacher, I faced numerous problems in teaching canonical works to my struggling readers. First and foremost, the literature (e.g., *A Separate Peace*, *Great Expectations*, *The Odyssey*, *Inherit the Wind*) I was mandated to teach was either too difficult for or not interesting to my students. Wanting and needing to use more than a group of "strategies" to address students' reading comprehension needs, I came up with a different approach to hook students, get them to read, and, more importantly, help them comprehend texts. After 4 years of frustration, I ended up deleting some of the traditional full-length works cited above (among the supplemental novels I had listed) and started using young adult literature instead as a way to better meet the required state standards. I searched the bookroom and found class sets of novels either no one was using or that were reserved for students in the honors classes. I chose novels like Rudolfo Anaya's *Bless Me, Ultima* (1999) and Robert Cormier's *I Am the Cheese* (2007) that have narrators that my students could relate to and that were easier for them to read.

Young adult literature is essentially literary works geared toward students ages 12–18 and written from their perspective. Adolescents like YA novels because unlike canonical works they have been written about adolescents, with adolescent readers in mind (Groenke & Scherff, in press). Moreover, YA novels are usually written in language that students, especially struggling readers, can understand and enjoy. And, high-quality YA literature abounds, meaning teachers have a multitude of titles to choose from.

Decades of classroom-based reading research show why YA literature is important and useful in middle and high school classrooms:

1. Engagement with reading and motivation to read increase when adolescents read YA novels, thus leading to more competent reading (e.g., Graves & Philippot, 2002; Ivey & Broaddus, 2001; McGill-Franzen & Allington, 2001).
2. Adolescent literature has the potential to broaden adolescents' vision of self and the world, providing an avenue for reflection (Landt, 2006).
3. Adolescents choose to read adolescent novels over more canonical works (Cole, 2008).

Just like canonical texts, YA literature provides the perfect opportunity to engage adolescents in reading and discussion that encourage critical thinking (Glenn, 2008). Young adult literature, according to Ted Hipple, "must be read with attention, not simply to its story lines, characters, or settings but also and very importantly to its themes" (2000, p. 2). Because of its focus on polemical issues as well as current problems and concerns meaningful to adolescents, YA literature is a natural scaffold to canonical texts (Probst, 2004, cited in Scherff & Wright, 2007).

To illustrate the difference between a canonical text and a young adult text, compare the two examples below, the opening to Jack London's *The Call of the Wild* (1903/2008), a "classic" title read in many eighth-grade classrooms, and Sherman Alexie's *The Absolutely True Diary of a Part-Time Indian,* a YA novel published in 2007.

The Call of the Wild

"Old longings nomadic leap,
Chafing at custom's chain;
Again from its brumal sleep
Wakens the ferine strain."

Buck did not read the newspapers, or he would have known that trouble was brewing, not alone for himself, but for every tide-water dog, strong of muscle and with warm, long hair, from Puget Sound to San Diego. Because men, groping in the Arctic darkness, had found a yellow metal, and because steamship and transportation companies were booming the find, thousands of men were rushing into the Northland. These men wanted dogs, and the dogs they wanted were heavy dogs, with strong muscles by which to toil, and furry coats to protect them from the frost.

Buck lived at a big house in the sun-kissed Santa Clara Valley. Judge Miller's place, it was called. It stood back from the road, half hidden among the trees, through which glimpses could be caught of the wide cool veranda that ran around its four sides. The house was approached by gravelled driveways which wound about through wide-spreading lawns and under the interlacing boughs of tall poplars. At the rear things were on even a more spacious scale than at the front. There were great stables, where a dozen grooms and boys held forth, rows of vine-clad servants' cottages, an endless and orderly array of outhouses, long grape arbors, green pastures, orchards, and berry patches. Then there was the pumping plant for the artesian well, and the big cement tank where Judge Miller's boys took their morning plunge and kept cool in the hot afternoon.

The Absolutely True Diary of a Part-Time Indian

I was born with water on the brain.

Okay, so that's not exactly true. I was actually born with too much cerebral spinal fluid inside my skull. But cerebral spinal fluid is just the doctors' fancy way of saying brain grease. And brain grease works inside the lobes like car grease works inside an engine. It keeps things running smooth and fast. But weirdo me, I was born with too much grease inside my skull, and it got all thick and muddy and disgusting, and it only mucked up the works.

My brain was drowning in grease.

But that makes the whole thing sound weirdo and funny, like my brain was a giant French fry ...

But jeez, did my mother and father and big sister and grandma and cousins and aunts and uncles think it was funny when the doctors cut open my little skull and sucked out all that extra water with some tiny vacuum?

I was only six months old and I was supposed to croak during the surgery. And even if I somehow survived the mini-Hoover, I was supposed to suffer serious brain damage and live the rest of my life as a vegetable.

Do you comprehend what the authors are saying? (I had to read the London passage three times to get the gist of what he was saying.) What aspects of the two passages might impact students' understanding? In terms of vocabulary, many of the terms (brumal and ferine, for example) in the London text are archaic and beyond most students' reach. In comparison, Alexie takes what could be a lot of technical terminology related to hydrocephaly and frames it in an interesting and understandable way ("water on the brain").

In terms of syntax, Alexie writes in a way that teenagers would understand, that is, with informal language and a conversational tone. This style doubtless would assist struggling readers. Syntax in *The Call of the Wild*, on the contrary, would definitely cause some problems. While the London text may have been understandable to readers of his time, today's teenage readers would struggle with the long sentences with their many clauses. How would you help students read and comprehend these passages? What text features might assist with comprehension (personally, I like Alexie's use of similes)?

INCREASING COMPREHENSION: INSTRUCTIONAL APPROACHES

One approach to dealing with more demanding texts like London's is to have students answer discussion questions or to teach them the difficult vocabulary words in an attempt to help them better understand what they are reading. Another approach is to have students build a KWL chart ("what we know, what we want to know, what we learned"—to build background) or engage in a think-aloud exercise, hoping they will recognize where they are having comprehension difficulties and helping them to address them. While all of these practices can be helpful, they are still not enough to enable numerous students to comprehend fully what they read, especially when the subject matter is far removed from their lives or when the vocabulary is particularly abstruse.

Students need purposeful, well-thought-out instruction that is parceled out "*over an* extended time frame" (Underwood & Pearson, 2004, p. 141, emphasis added) in order to attain higher levels of comprehension and understanding. As Keene (2007) points out, it is a mistake to assume that students really understand what they read simply because they can answer questions, restate, retell, or summarize text, and learn vocabulary. Many of our students, including struggling readers, can comprehend at the literal level. However, in order to reach higher levels of comprehension—and be able to interpret, evaluate, and apply what they read—students need scaffolding experiences that encourage them to critically question and discuss texts and make them active meaning makers (Fisher, 2008).

Students also need to be able to make connections between their experiences and lives and the texts they read in order to aid comprehension, and YA literature meets that need well. But simply reading YA literature is not enough. Struggling readers need instructional experiences that make them dig and think more deeply about what they read, which is why I turn to literary theory.

What is literary theory? In *Critical Encounters in High School English* (2000), Deborah Appleman describes it as follows:

> Literary theory ... provides lenses designed to bring out what is already there but what we often miss with unaided vision.... [They] bring into relief things we fail to notice. Literary theories recontextualize the familiar and comfortable, making us reappraise it. They make the strange seem oddly familiar.... Literary theories can become critical lenses to guide, inform, and instruct us. (pp. xvi, 2)

In this chapter, I argue that using literary theory can help students become more critical readers and assist with comprehension. Because text study, both print and nonprint, is the heart of English language arts classes, literary theory is not something that has to be *added* to an already full curriculum, but rather it is already a standard part of teaching. In particular, when used with high-quality, engaging YA literature, literary theory can provide a link to the more canonical works that struggling readers will be reading in middle and high school English classes.

HOW YOUNG ADULT LITERATURE AND LITERARY THEORY CAN HELP WITH COMPREHENSION

Using literary theory helps students "understand that there are many ways to know texts, to read and interpret them" (Moore, 1997, p. 4). Knowing, reading, and interpreting are synonymous with research-based practices teachers already know and use—questioning, inferring, evaluating, synthesizing, and using graphic and semantic organizers.

Literary theory asks students to question texts, look for bias, and use their firsthand experiences in the reading process.

Literary theory asks students to question texts, look for bias, and use their firsthand experiences in the reading process.

There are many literary theories that can be brought into the middle school classroom, and students will likely have firsthand experience with the ideas behind many of them. For example, many students have experienced prejudice (race theory) or have felt powerless or the effects of the powerful (Marxist theory); similarly, female students have been told they can't do math as well as boys, and boys are socialized to not play with dolls (feminist/gender theory). As such, literary theory is not just for "advanced" students, but *all* students. And, when used with high-quality YA literature that engages even the most reluctant reader, literary theory can foster critical thinking and increase comprehension. In short,

> literary theory can and should be used with secondary students. Using literary theory as they read texts enables students to become theoried and skilled readers with a variety of interpretive strategies and theoretical approaches. As they become constructors of meaning, with multiple literary visions of their own, they become adept at reading the world around them. (Appleman, 2000, p. 11)

However, the relative accessibility of YA novels to struggling readers should not be misinterpreted as necessarily implying "easier" teaching.

Literary theory is not just for "advanced" students, but for *all* students. When used with high-quality YA literature that engages even the most reluctant reader, literary theory can foster critical thinking and increase comprehension.

Using YA literature to teach literary theory is no different than teaching other types of literacy in our classes; instruction must be rigorous, and teachers must be prepared to teach ideas and concepts explicitly.

In the sections that follow, I show how teachers can teach two award-winning young adult novels to struggling readers through a combination of comprehension instruction and literary theory instruction. For each novel, I provide an outline of a literary theory that works particularly well, a short plot summary, a "traditional" comprehension tool, and an updated version that incorporates the literary theory.

BORDER STUDIES WITH *THE ABSOLUTELY TRUE DIARY OF A PART-TIME INDIAN*

In their article "Standing on the Border: Issues of Identity and Border Crossings in Young Adult Literature," Niday and Allender (2000) show how border studies theory can be used to help students explore both characters' identities and their own self-identities. Adding literary theory to novel study also helps students make connections between their lives and the text while making more easily understood the symbols and themes found in texts (Frye, 2001). As Niday and Allender (2000) explain, border studies theory first originated amid the cultural exchanges occurring along the U.S.–Mexican border. Anzaldua (1987) coined the term "border crossings" to refer to how individuals moved across such diverse borders as those defined by race, gender, or geography. Root (1996, pp. xxi–xxii, cited in Niday & Allender, 2000) further clarifies four ways of looking at border crossings:

1. Individuals can bridge borders by having both feet in two groups; they are entirely immersed, respected, and accepted by two cultures at the same time.
2. Individuals can shift foreground and background identities to cross borders delineated by race and ethnicity; for example, someone with a bicultural or multicultural identity or background might want to momentarily emphasize one background while de-emphasizing another.
3. Individuals might sit decisively on a border, experiencing it as the central reference point; in some cases, individuals might create a new or modified category.
4. Individuals might "camp" in one cultural group for a long period of time and make trips into other camps periodically in order to have their needs met.

The reason why border studies work so well with adolescents is because the latter often experience border crossings in and outside of school. For example, many students cross a "bridge" each day by leaving home and coming to school. Some are able to bridge both worlds with ease, while others are more at ease at home. Likewise, students are often more comfortable with one group (teammates from sports, for example) but branch out from this group to socialize periodically with others (e.g., students from another school).

Sherman Alexie's *The Absolutely True Diary of a Part-Time Indian* (2007), which won the National Book Award for Young People's Literature in 2007, is a book that not only appeals to struggling middle school readers, especially males, but also is highly appropriate for using border studies theory to increase understanding about its themes, characters, and structure. The protagonist is 14-year-old Arnold Spirit ("Junior"), who decides to switch from attending the high school on his reservation to attend Reardon, a high school in a nearby rich white town, in order to "find hope." This fateful decision causes Junior to be treated as a pariah among his own people. For those on the reservation, he cannot both be an Indian and attend a white high school. Thus, Arnold lives in two disparate worlds: in his new school, he faces racism daily for being an Indian, and out of school (on the reservation), he is hated by his own people for wanting to improve his education. This dual existence of Arnold's makes border studies a perfect literary theory to use with this novel.

While students can rather easily make connections between theory and their lives, teaching literary theory to struggling readers, especially those who have experienced a more rigid curriculum or who have not had practice with this type of analysis, needs to be scaffolded and done very deliberately, just as with other components of the discipline. One way to do this is to turn to existing instructional models that work and add the theoretical component. In the sections that follow, I show how I adapted the *literature response model* (found in Brown & Stephens, 1995 and later adapted by Kraver, 2007), originally designed to assist with comprehension instruction, by combining it with border studies in order to help students make longer-lasting connections with Alexie's book.

> Teaching literary theory to struggling readers, especially those who have experienced a more rigid curriculum or who have not had practice with this type of analysis, needs to be scaffolded and done very deliberately, just as with other components of the discipline.

The Literature Response Model

Wanting her students to read more critically, Kraver (2007) adapted Brown's (1995) literature response model and came up with a five-level approach, around which she organizes students' responses to literature. The lessons and activities start at level 1 and move up to level 5. The model is flexible, allowing teachers to raise issues and ideas that relate more specifically to their students and what they are studying. As students work through each level, their understanding and comprehension of the text grows. Kraver (2007) writes:

> Informed by the work of Rosenblatt, Brown's model ... encourages students to express their content-based thoughts about and their personal and emotional responses to the texts they encounter. As well, there is a compelling logic to the order of the five-step model, beginning with the assumption that students cannot engage a text until they have read and, preliminarily at least, understood the essentials of what they have read, and ending with a critical assessment of the text. (p. 68)

At the factual level, the focus is on surface-level content and getting facts from the story. At level 2, the empathetic level, the goal is a personal connection between reader and text, with students placing themselves in a story or relating the story to their lives. Critical analysis is the goal of the analytical level. Kraver's fourth state, the applicative level, focuses on examining the themes or issues gleaned from their reading (e.g., whether relating to class, race, gender, ethnicity, etc.) and applying them across time. Finally, at the critical level, students bring it all together by assessing what they have been reading and bringing closure to their reading.

I adapted Kraver's model, using it to create questions rather than fully-eveloped lessons. Generic questions/prompts for each level might look like this:

- *Factual:* Describe what _____ looks like; describe _____'s personality.
- *Empathetic:* What do you think of _____ [insert issue, cause, social problem]?
- *Analytical:* What is the importance of _____ as a symbol in the novel? What is the author's tone toward _____?
- *Applicative:* Compare and contrast the treatment of women in the novel with how they are treated by present-day American society.
- *Critical:* How do you feel about the novel now that you have finished reading it? What do you think happens to the characters now that _____?

Since I believe students get enough factual-level questions in today's test-driven culture, in Table 7.1 I present some ideas for discussion questions based on Kraver's *last four* levels (omitting the factual level) and Root's four ways of looking at border crossings. Because the levels of response get more complex, it is a natural scaffold for students.

As stated earlier, by incorporating literary theory (in this case border studies), the probability that students will remember and understand what they have read is increased because the questions go beyond incidents in the story; students have a new way to "crack the code" of the story and look more deeply without additional effort. Moreover, by making all of the questions relate to border studies rather than shifting topics randomly, I link them in a consistent way. All of the sample questions in Table 7.1 relate to border studies because they ask that students consider Junior in relation to one of the four positions outlined by Root (1996). This template also provides a way to differentiate the process of instruction while making that sure all students are provided an opportunity to take part in a critical discussion about the novel. Even if some students are only able to work at the empathetic level, they can have conversations with classmates working at higher levels because all of the questions relate to border studies. These conversations, in turn, can lead to deeper connections with the text for all students.

TABLE 7.1. Literature Response Model (with Cultural Studies Approach, as Applied to *Alexie's Absolutely True Diary*)

Root's four ways of looking at border crossings	One can bridge the border by having both feet in both groups.	One crosses between and among social contexts defined by race and ethnicity, highlighting the shifting of foreground and background.	One decisively sits on the border, experiencing it as the central reference point.	One creates a home in one "camp" for an extended period of time and makes forays into other camps from time to time.
Empathetic	"Can a person fit equally well in two groups?"	"Has anyone ever been upset with you for hanging out with a new or different group of friends?"	"Like Junior in Chapter 2 (p. 11), relate a time when you were caught between being mad at and loving your parents at the same time?"	"If you were Junior, would you hide or promote your Indian identity at Reardon?"
Analytical	"Based on the book's title, how might someone be a 'part-time Indian'?"	"What is the symbolism of Junior dressing as a homeless person for Halloween?"	"What is the symbolism of the drawing on page 43?"	"Why is Rowdy so mad that Junior wants to go to a different high school?"
Applicative	"Does Junior successfully navigate between the two worlds of the reservation and Reardon? Explain."	"If Junior were poor but white, do you think the Reardon students would have treated him better?"	"Does Junior's sister really change her life by getting married and moving? Explain your answer in relation to this third border crossing category."	"How does Junior's house serve as a different 'camp' for Rowdy?"
Critical	"Do you think Alexie feels that people can exist equally in two groups? Why or why not?"	"Why does Alexie make Junior and Roger 'friends' in the story, especially after knowing that Roger is a racist?"	"Do you think it is better for someone like Junior to be a 'part-time' Indian, or should he choose one side, the other, or a new identity? Explain."	"Which 'camp' do you think Junior will spend more time in, the white world or the reservation? Why?"

Note. Based on Kraver (2007) and Root (1996).

As an extension activity, or as students become more confident, students can learn how to write their own questions for each level (with or without theory). This assignment was something we undertook in my classroom, producing wonderful results—not only in terms of achievement but in students' levels of self-assurance. To hear students debating the correct level of a question and providing a justification shows that they understand what they are reading and that they are highly engaged with the text as well.

The Seven *C*'s of Comprehension

Are you not quite ready to try the literature response model? Another comprehension-building strategy that works well with literary theory is Farmer and Soden's (2005) "seven C's of comprehension." The seven C's framework was developed to help students deepen their knowledge about a topic of study. Although originally designed to be used with the teaching of a new concept or as part of an inquiry project, the model can easily be used during the study of novels as a continual process throughout students' reading. This strategy is very similar to the KWL process (know–want to know–learned; Ogle, 1986) except that it includes more opportunities for students to speak, listen, and write.

In Table 7.2, I outline one way a modified version of the seven C's (using a literary theory focus) could be used with the first few chapters of *The Absolutely True Diary of a Part-Time Indian*. I provide information about how I would complete the first four steps; the final three steps need little explanation. As in the sample for the literature response model (Table 7.1), all of the questions/prompts relate to border studies.

At the connect stage I ask students to consider the relevance of the title ("Part-Time Indian"); then to clarify I would have them research Alexie's life, Indian reservations, reservation schools, and border studies itself—which further links the title of the book to the idea of borders and the next levels of comprehension. The consider stage requires students to pose their own questions about what they will read; I would encourage students to write questions that examine the concept of borders. These questions are then used to guide their reading of the novel. The final three steps are cyclical in nature in that students revisit their original questions and, therefore, border studies as they discuss, summarize, and predict.

This seven C's process can be repeated throughout the course of studying the novel. As students get further into the reading, the questions posed to them can become more strategic (i.e., relate specifically to concepts, events, and people in upcoming chapters) in the Connect phase. As students enter the consider phase, they can begin to write their own questions exploring border study or any other theory they may be engaging with.

TABLE 7.2. Seven *C*'s of Comprehension

Connect. In this prereading stage, teachers introduce the novel to students; a number of reading strategies could be used (brainstorming, anticipation guide, etc.)

Pose questions to the class before reading the novel (make sure they incorporate ideas from border studies).
- "Based on the title, what do you think this book is going to be about?"
- "What do you think of when you hear the word *Indian*?"
- "What do you know about Indian reservations?"
- "How do you think someone can be a 'part-time' Indian?"

Clarify. Teachers work to confirm or challenge students' prior knowledge.

Discuss students' answers to the questions posed, using information about Alexie's background, photos of and facts about reservations/reservation schools, and border studies.

Consider. Students write three questions that they will consider throughout their reading; these should be relevant and detailed.

After the discussion, each student writes three questions that they will think about as they read (encourage them to focus on the notion of "part-time").

Collect. Students try to find answers to their questions (from the novel).

Read a sample number of chapters (I would read them aloud to students); students follow along with their three questions in mind.

Converse. In pairs, one student shares knowledge learned with his or her partner while that person writes a summary of what is said; then the writer reads the summary back to the speaker.

Conclude. Students use the written summary in the converse step to write a more lengthy summary in their own words.

Calculate. Students add to their summaries by predicting what will happen in the next stage of reading.

Note. Based on Farmer and Soden (2005).

STUDYING BLACK FEMINIST THEORY WITH *COPPER SUN*

While its name may sound intimidating, black feminist theory is rather easy to introduce and try out with students. At its most basic level, this theory involves a careful analysis of marginalized groups (Hinton, 2004).

Although there are multiple ways to study literature through use of a black feminist viewpoint (for a thorough discussion, see Hinton-Johnson, 2003), the core idea of emphasizing the intersection of race, class, and gender (e.g., Collins, 1990; Hinton, 2004) is the most straightforward approach for middle school students. Many will have had some negative life experiences relating to race, class, and/or gender, thereby making this theory relatively easy to relate to personally. Hinton (2004, p. 63) provides a list of questions to use when discussing texts from a black feminist perspective:

1. How are the interlocking oppressions of race, class, and gender at work in the lives of the characters?
2. How do characters resist race, class, and gender oppression?
3. How do characters express a philosophy of liberation by assisting and encouraging themselves and others in efforts to prevail over multiple oppressions (racism, classism, sexism, heterosexism, and so forth)?

Sharon Draper's *Copper Sun* (2008), one of IRA's "Notable Books for a Global Society," is a perfect novel to introduce the theory to students because, although it is easy to read (5th-grade reading level), it is also a complex story in terms of its treatment of race, class, and gender. In the novel Amari is a 15-year-old girl living in African village. One day, a group of white slave traders comes to their village. Initially feigning kindness, they end up killing many villagers and kidnap the rest to be sold into slavery, including Amari. She survives the voyage to the Carolinas, only to be sold to a cruel plantation owner. Amari eventually escapes with Polly, a white indentured servant, and Tidbit, the young son of a slave woman. The three set out to try to reach Fort Mose, a safe haven for runaway slaves in Florida.

Reading-Level Inventories

Hinton's three questions, while easy perhaps for high school students to answer, might well be too open-ended for middle school students to successfully deal with. However, there is a way that the questions could be scaffolded and differentiated so that all students could understand and answer them according to their individual skill and comprehension level. While reading *English Journal* last year I came across an article by Declan FitzPatrick (2008) in which he modified Hillocks's (1980) reading-level inventories in order to increase comprehension and support higher-order thinking skills among his students. FitzPatrick found that his students encountered problems in discussing complex texts such as Edgar Allan Poe's "The Cask of Amontillado" because they needed support at "lower levels of comprehension" (FitzPatrick, 2008, p. 57). He turned to Hillocks's reading-level inventories, which were originally designed to determine "students' ability to make increasingly complex inferences about fiction" (p. 57).

Because Hillocks's (1980) questions increase in sophistication, FitzPatrick (2008) suggested that teachers use the inventory to better gauge their students' comprehension levels. If students struggle with higher levels of questioning, then teachers have more insight for planning and scaffolding literature instruction and discussion. The levels start with the most basic information—the stated characters and settings—and increase in complexity, moving on to a simple inference (level 4) and ending with questions that ask readers to pull everything together (level 7). Table 7.3 summarizes Hillocks's and FitzPatrick's reading levels.

As with my example for the Alexie novel, I believe that by incorporating literary theory with differentiated comprehension questions students will remember and understand what they have read because the questions go beyond the general incidents in the story; all of the questions, regardless of level, are centered on the same theoretical ideas. What might these look like when combined with literary theory? In Table 7.4 I provide sample discussion questions and prompts for *Copper Sun* based on reading levels and black feminist theory (BFT). Questions in the left column concern general aspects of the novel, while those in the right column include the influence and intersection of race, class, and gender. Again, the purpose of creating questions with literary theory is "to bring out what is already there but what we often miss with unaided vision" (Appleman, 2000, p. xvi).

As Table 7.4 shows, as the level of questions builds in complexity, they all still relate to black feminist theory. At the most basic level (e.g., Why isn't Amari allowed to weave the yarn?), students think more critically about the text in terms of race, class, and/or gender. And, because this level 1 question relates to why Amari is not allowed to do man's work, it can provide a nice discussion point for students to contrast that against the efforts it takes to get to Fort Mose (i.e., difficult for anyone, even a man).

Teachers can create the questions to be posed out loud during reading or to be handed out for students to work on in class (either in groups or individually) or for homework. All students are provided with the opportunity to take part in a deep discussion about the novel. Even if students are only able to work at the empathetic level, they can have conversations with classmates working at higher levels because all of the questions relate to black feminist theory. These conversations, in turn, can lead to deeper connections with the text. As with the literature response

TABLE 7.3. Reading-Level Inventories

	Hillocks (1980)	FitzPatrick (2008)
Level 1	*Basic stated information:* Questions about literal information that is prominent and repeated and important to high levels of understanding; without this information students cannot understand the text in a meaningful way.	*People, location, action:* Basics of who is in the story, what people are doing, where they are; restating important information; identifying major revelations.
Level 2	*Key details:* Questions about details that are important to the twists and turns of the plot; details so important that they are likely only to be mentioned once.	*Turning points, key details:* Determining which events change the course of the story; distinguishing between important and irrelevant information; identifying facts that have the greatest impact on the plot.
Level 3	*Stated relationships:* Questions that require readers to locate and repeat a relationship that is stated in the text.	*Reasons and explanations, cause and effect:* Reexplaining a connection stated in the text.
Level 4	*Simple implied relationships:* Questions that require readers to make a single inference by dealing with denotative and connotative clues and relating the information to personal experience and prior knowledge.	Inference: Explaining the implication of a particular statement in the text.
Level 5	*Complex implied relationships:* Questions that require readers to discern a pattern among a variety of inferences and draw an appropriate conclusion.	*Generalization and evaluation:* Demonstrating the implied connection between several details from various places; generalizing about a major change in a character; generalizing about implied comparisons or contrasts.
Level 6	*Author's generalization:* Questions that require readers to propose a generalization about the nature of the human condition that may be inferred from this text.	*Application of generalization:* Supporting a generalization about the world, using evidence from the text; applying the generalizations suggested in the text to the world; demonstrating the implications of the author's representation of the world.
Level 7	*Structural generalization:* Questions that require readers to articulate how the parts of the work function together to generate certain effects.	*Structural generalization:* Supporting a generalization about the purpose of literary elements used in the story; explaining how the author's generalization is supported by the structure of the story; connecting literary techniques to a generalization about human experience.

TABLE 7.4. Reading Levels and Reading Levels plus Black Feminist Theory for Sharon Draper's *Copper Sun*

	Reading levels	Reading levels + black feminist theory
Level 1	"Who is telling the story?"	• "Why isn't Amari allowed to weave the yarn?" • "Why doesn't Clay or his stepmother speak up and stop Amari's whipping earlier?"
Level 2	"Who are the strange people Besa sees in the forest?"	• "How can 'playing dumb' (p. 96) help Amari?" • "Who is in more 'trouble' because of Mrs. Derby's mixed-race child?"
Level 3	"Why does Tybee only speak Ashanti when the white men are not around?"	• "Why does Polly, an indentured servant, call herself 'regular' in comparison to the slaves?"
Level 4	"Why did Bill teach Amari English?"	• "What does Isabelle Derby mean when she says she has very little power over what goes on?" (p. 123) • "Explain what Polly means when she says, 'What is the advantage of being white if I have to work like I'm black every day?'" (p. 130). • "On page 159, we encounter the first use of the word *nigger*—why now?"
Level 5	"On page 141 we learn that Clay seems to dislike his stepmother; from evidence in the text, what seem to be the reasons?"	• "Chapter 15, 'Polly and Clay' is an important chapter. Through Polly's eyes, we see ironic views about race, class, and gender. Compare and contrast them." • "In the novel, what do we learn about how women treat other women?"
Level 6	"What do you think Isabelle Derby means by 'I pray for this child, Teenie'?" (p. 121)	• "Polly can read and Amari understands English; yet, women are not supposed to possess such skills. What does that say about literacy and race, class, and gender back then?" • "Do those same attitudes apply today? Explain."
Level 7	"Why does the author use many colloquialisms throughout the novel (such as 'just 'cause a chicken got wings don't mean it oughta fly' and 'love don't mean pig spit around here')?"	• "How does the phrase 'you must learn to make music once more' (p. 25) apply to the women in *Copper Sun*?" • "How did race, class, and gender affect each of the following characters: Amari, Polly, Tidbit, and Mrs. Derby?"

model, teachers can have the students write their own questions for each level (with or without theory).

SUMMARY

Middle school students not only appreciate literature activities and discussions incorporating literary theories, but they can also participate with skill and insight—even those students who have not been exposed to theory before. More importantly, students will attest that such discussions help them to remember what they read. Here's proof.

Preservice teachers in my young adult literature course taught the young adult novels *Copper Sun* (Draper, 2008) and *Sold* (McCormick, 2006) as part of a summer enrichment program for teenagers, many of them struggling readers, transitioning from middle to high school. The preservice teachers used black feminist theory (along with cultural studies, feminist theory, and critical race theory) to frame their class discussions of the novels. The soon-to-be ninth grade students made multiple connections between their life experiences and knowledge ("it's like being in jail"; "it's like with Martin Luther King, Jr.") and other readings (e.g., *To Kill a Mockingbird*) they had done in school. When the future teachers competed against the teens in a question–answer contest, the adolescents won (and I don't think the preservice teachers let them). Audiotaping the last day of the program, my university students asked the teenagers what they thought about how the books were discussed, and more than one student said that *they never got to talk about books that way in the past* and that *it will help us remember what we read.*

> **Middle school students not only appreciate literature activities and discussions incorporating literary theories, but they can also participate with skill and insight—even those students who have not been exposed to theory before.**

Questions for Reflection

1. Do you or does your school include YA literature as part of its English language arts curriculum? If not, what obstacles prevent its inclusion?

2. What theories do you think your students could most closely relate to? How might you find the answer to this question?

3. Do you see any barriers to incorporating literary theory in your study of novels? If so, what are they?

RECOMMENDED RESOURCES

For Incorporating Literary Theory

Eckert, L. S. (2006). *How does it mean?: Engaging reluctant readers through literary theory.* Portsmouth, NH: Heinemann.

Latrobe, K. H., & Drury, J. (2009). *Critical approaches to young adult literature.* New York: Neal-Schuman.

For Teaching Adolescent Literature

Herz, S. K., & Gallo, D. R. (2005). *From Hinton to Hamlet: Building bridges between young adult literature and the classics* (2nd ed.). Westport, CT: Greenwood Press.

Groenke, S. L., & Scherff, L. (in press). *Teaching young adult literature through differentiated instruction.* Urbana, IL: National Council of Teachers of English.

8

Culturally Grounded
Vocabulary Instruction

When you explain any word ... you put in its place another
equally incomprehensible word, or a whole series of words,
with the connection between them as incomprehensible as
the word itself. [But] ... when [a student] has heard or read
an unknown word in an otherwise comprehensible sentence,
and another time in another sentence, he begins to have a
hazy idea of the new concept; sooner or later he will ... feel
the need to use that word—and once he has used it, the word
and the concept is his.

—TOLSTOY (1903, p. 143)

FOCAL POINTS

1. An effective framework for teaching vocabulary consists of four parts: providing frequent, varied, and extensive language experiences; teaching individual words; teaching word-learning strategies; and fostering word consciousness.

2. Cultural theorists have identified several key principles that underlie a productive learning environment for nonmainstream students to learn language, namely, valuing and celebrating language diversity, code switching (i.e., changing languages) for various purposes, and critiquing the typical power dynamics of ELA classes.

3. By combining this four-part vocabulary program with these culturally grounded principles, teachers can design a more productive environment for students to better learn vocabulary.

For over a century researchers have consistently confirmed that vocabulary knowledge is the best predictor of reading comprehension (Daneman, 1991). Stahl and Nagy (2006) correctly observe that "if the reader does not know the meanings of a sufficient proportion of the words in the text, comprehension is impossible" (p. 4). For marginalized middle school readers, vocabulary knowledge is often problematic since their understanding of word meanings lags behind that of their typical peers (Baker, Simmons, & Kame'enui, 1995). To add to the challenge of reading, vocabulary grows more complex in academic texts during the middle grades (Stahl & Nagy, 2006). Therefore, it is crucial for ELA middle school teachers to make systematic vocabulary instruction a central focus of daily classroom work.

To increase marginalized readers' engagement and enjoyment while learning vocabulary, we advocate teaching them *culturally grounded vocabulary* that draws on students' own funds of knowledge. In this way, as students learn new words, they do so in the context of language and experiences that are already familiar to them. This approach also incorporates principles thought to enhance learning about language, including (1) valuing and celebrating the home languages of students (Delpit & Dowdy, 2008; Ladson-Billings, 1994); (2) highlighting different ways of speaking strategically, depending on the social context (Gee, 1996; Purcell-Gates, 2006); and (3) creating an environment in which students feel free to critique language uses and situations as they learn new words (Fecho, 2004).

> **Culturally grounded vocabulary instruction draws on students' own funds of knowledge to help them learn academic vocabulary. As students learn new words, they do so in the context of language and experiences that are already familiar to them.**

Additionally, culturally grounded vocabulary instruction is built on components considered essential by middle grade students. Research indicates that students acquire word meanings from diverse sources (Nagy, 2005) and deeper-level vocabulary knowledge through multifaceted classroom experiences (Hiebert & Kamil, 2005). The way to accomplish this process best is through comprehensive vocabulary instruction, which has been shown to increase the working vocabulary of *all* students, including marginalized readers (Baumann, Ware, & Edwards, 2007).

There are numerous ways to structure culturally grounded vocabulary instruction, including (1) immersion in rich language sources through wide-ranging reading and writing (primarily through self-selected reading and teacher-read alouds, examining specific word choices through writing exercises), (2) teaching individual words (through semantic associations, definitions, web browsing), (3) teaching word-learning strategies (through morphemic and contextual analysis and direct use of the dictionary and thesaurus), and (4) fostering word consciousness (through metaphorical use of language, figurative language, word etymology, and reflective or metacognitive thinking). Although these components are listed separately, they work best in combination, each influencing the others.

By coupling these four vocabulary-building components with culturally grounded pedagogical practices teachers create a "third space," where students can learn new words in the context of language and experiences that are already familiar to them. Learning new vocabulary in this way affords marginalized readers opportunities to be positioned as primary knowers, which invariably increases their engagement and enjoyment in learning vocabulary. Students' vocabularies then gradually grow over time, helping them to better comprehend the texts they read.

In the remainder of this chapter we take you inside an eighth-grade ELA class in which culturally grounded vocabulary instruction was undertaken (Edwards, 2006). We start by introducing the teacher, Ms. Franklin, as well as three students from one of her ELA classes. To help you understand what culturally grounded vocabulary instruction looks like in practice, we have organized this discussion into four sections, each corresponding in turn to the essential vocabulary components listed above. Within these four sections we provide detailed examples of how Ms. Franklin was able to culturally ground these vocabulary practices.

MEET MS. FRANKLIN AND THREE OF HER STUDENTS

Ms. Franklin is an African American teacher with over 14 years of experience who centered her instruction on issues of race, class, gender, and social justice. Ms. Franklin believes that her students are more willing to accept and engage in what she is teaching if she provides a bridge from academic reading and learning to students' personal funds of knowledge. She explained:

> "I feel that if I don't know them, I cannot reach them. And if you want to get to know a child better, talk about their families. And then I can reach that inner person and go where I need to go to reach them so they embrace *me* and accept what *I* am giving them. It goes back to respect. If I respect that family and who they are, then they will respect what I am trying to teach them."

Ms. Franklin held high expectations of her students, and students respected her because, as Abraham put it, "Ms. Franklin really cares about you, and she wants you to do your best." Lemarcus commented, "You can tell I'm her favorite because she's always gettin' on me. She doesn't let me get away with nothin'!"

Lemarcus, Tenisha, and Abraham were placed in Ms. Franklin's supplemental ELA class because they had not scored sufficiently high on the state ELA minimum competency test taken at the end of the preceding school year. Although they were enrolled in a regular ELA class, the school district required "at-risk students" to take an additional ELA course that was referred to as a "supplemental" course. The district administrators believed that increasing these students' ELA instructional time would give them a better chance of passing state reading and writing tests.

According to state assessments and the accelerated reader (AR) program, Tenisha, Abraham, and Lemarcus read nearly 2 years below grade level at the beginning of the school year. However, each engaged with reading in his or her own way. Tenisha avidly read fashion and music magazines, kept a journal, and wrote many notes to friends. She stated that she did not read books unless they were specifically assigned for class. Lemarcus read 12 self-selected novels on his own before winter break, something he had never done before. Abraham merely said that he sometimes read for fun, but not all the time.

COMPONENT 1: IMMERSION IN RICH LANGUAGE SOURCES THROUGH WIDE-RANGING READING AND WRITING

Ms. Franklin knew that struggling middle school readers can substantially increase their vocabularies by immersing themselves in texts rich in new and varied language and by closely examining their word choices through intensive writing activities. On average, she directly taught 10–12 new word meanings each week, that is, 400–500 words over the course of the school year. However, she was committed to identifying other ways of developing new vocabulary that went beyond her own teaching.

Accordingly, Ms. Franklin exposed her students to a wide variety of texts and writing experiences. She had her student read from both fiction and nonfiction books, literary anthologies, magazines and newspapers as well as such sources as the Internet, various song lyrics, and poetry. To culturally ground her instruction, Ms. Franklin used texts that connected to students' funds of knowledge, prose about topics to which they were emotionally tied. She also allowed students to make choices about which texts they read together and which ones they read independently. As the students read, Ms. Franklin tailored her vocabulary instruction to language encountered within the readings.

Students sampled a wide range of genres, including persuasive essays, poetry, narratives, business letters, and mysteries. As students read these different genres, Ms. Franklin had them carefully consider word choices as they created similar text themselves. Writing exercises thus provided students opportunities to demonstrate intertextual links in their word choices; that is, they were able to use new vocabulary they had just learned while reading immediately in their own writing.

An example of students reading widely and then composing similar prose occurred when Ms. Franklin focused on one of the state's grade 8 ELA performance standards, in which students were required to produce a multiparagraph persuasive essay. The text that the school district supplied to Ms. Franklin as an example of persuasive writing was "To Thomas Lincoln and John P. Johnston" by Abraham Lincoln (1848). While Ms. Franklin considered this essay an important academic text, it did not suit her as the best way to begin her students' introduction to persuasive reading. She found certain language—"idler," "vastly," "tooth and nail"—for example likely to be too arcance or stilted to grab her students' attention for learning how persuasion works. Also, she was concerned that her marginalized readers might find this essay to be too difficult to tackle as the first example of persuasive prose.

Therefore, Ms. Franklin first turned to persuasive writings that related to topics she knew interested her students and about which they were already knowledgeable. Some of the choices included "Should Schools Provide Vending Machines?," "Global Warming?," and "Best TV Shows for Middle School Students." Her students also read an example of persuasive writing from one of Ms. Franklin's former students. With each of these reading experiences, Ms. Franklin consciously focused on word choices that worked to persuade the reader, having students pick out and share words they found to be colorful or ones that drew them into the piece.

After her students had read a wide selection of persuasive texts, Ms. Franklin believed they were ready to compose their own. To culturally ground the assignment, she connected it to a topic the students were interested in and had a lot of knowledge of, namely, their families. As a class, her students voted to make the topic of the persuasive essay to be which household chore was the worst to have to do. Each student also had the option to pick a different topic if this one did not suit him or her, although no students opted for the alternative. As the students engaged in conversations about which chore was the worst, they laughed and playfully argued about who "had it the worst." The enthusiasm was evident.

For Tenisha, Abraham, and Lemarcus, reading widely within a particular genre and writing simi-
lar compositions afforded them
opportunities to be positioned for
academic success. As these students engaged in conversations
with their peers about words,
they co-constructed vocabulary
knowledge through student-to-
student interactions. In talking
together, Tenisha, Abraham, and Lemarcus became primary knowers,
learning from one another as they pooled their ideas and knowledge.

> **As students engage in conversations with their peers about words, they co-construct vocabulary knowledge through student-to-student interactions, learning from one another as they pool their ideas and knowledge.**

For example, Tenisha taught the meaning of the word *saunter* to the
class during a discussion about interesting words students found over the
course of a week while reading independently. Tenisha read the word in
the context of the passage, explained its meaning, and then demonstrated
what sauntering looked like—immediately setting off a gale of laughter
in the room.

To further culturally ground this lesson, Ms. Franklin had students
consider the context in which such words as "saunter" would work strategically for them, with many expressing that this would be a word they
would not likely use frequently in their conversations with friends. Lemarcus commented, "Your friends would be like 'What's wrong with you?' "
Abraham agreed with him, adding, "Right, 'cause 'saunter' doesn't fit
into an everyday conversation.... But you could use it in a story to be
more descriptive about how a particular person was walking." Many
students nodded in agreement.

A couple of days after discussion of the word *saunter*, as Abraham worked on his introduction to his persuasive essay, "The Worst
Chore Ever," he wrote, " 'I want it squeaky clean when I get back!'
my mother exclaimed as she ... " Abraham paused, turned to Tenisha, who had originally presented the word, and asked, "You know
that word *saunter* you talked about? How do you spell it?" After the
word was spelled, Abraham continued writing: " 'I want it squeaky
clean when I get back!' my mother exclaimed as she sauntered out of
the room." Upon receiving praise for including the word, Abraham
responded, "Yeah. It's a good word because it shows that my mother
can just leave any way she wants, and I'm stuck cleaning the whole
house all by myself."

With Tenisha being positioned as a primary knower who had worthwhile vocabulary words to offer, Abraham learned the meaning of a new
word that made its way into his persuasive essay. Obviously, as Tolstoy
(1903) had put it, "The word and the concept is his" (p. 143). Now,

whenever Abraham reads the word *saunter* in texts, he will understand its meaning and better comprehend what he reads.

Not only did Ms. Franklin include experiences where students read widely and had opportunities to write, but also she made sure that she provided some time in every class period for students to read independently from self-selected texts. This opportunity usually occurred during the first 10 minutes of class, with the routine being that as soon as students walked in, they were to start reading.

As students read independently, Ms. Franklin searched for ways that would engage them in vocabulary learning. One way was to have students keep a journal of interesting words they found while reading. As they read, students marked words that caught their attention or words whose meaning they were unsure of. In their journal they would include the word, source, its use in context, and a definition. Sometimes they would write a sentence using the word. Lemarcus collected such words as *frayed*, *painstakingly*, and *indignantly* from Steven Schnur's *The Shadow Children* (1994) and *beneficial*, *pessimism*, and *annihilate* from Darren Shan's *Cirque Du Freak: The Lake of Souls* (2005).

TEACHING SPECIFIC WORDS

Words that are identified as being difficult in upcoming texts should have their meanings taught and analyzed only if not knowing the meaning would affect students' comprehension of the reading passage (Graves, 2006). If the goal is for students to know what a particular word means, "Explaining it is unquestionably more effective than waiting for the student to encounter it numerous times in context" (Nagy & Scott, 2000, p. 277). However, if the goal is for students to take true ownership of words and use them freely, then instruction must go beyond merely defining them in class.

There are numerous ways to structure instruction that can help students take ownership of words. In this chapter, we cover two: (1) including definitional information and contextual information about each word's meaning and (2) involving students more actively in word learning (Stahl & Nagy, 2006). Unfortunately, the richly textured instruction that students need to truly own a word—that is, to readily recognize it while reading and to be able to use it in written prose—comes with a cost, usually measured in time. However, if knowing the meaning is really essential, sufficient time should be devoted to teaching it.

Ms. Franklin usually strove to accomplish all three goals with the words she taught. This perseverance resulted in her students being actively involved, processing information about words at deeper levels, and automatically connecting new information with previously known information. For example, in teaching students about the genre of mysteries, Ms. Franklin directly taught vocabulary words that were often found in them, such as *deduce, purloin, sleuth,* and *alibi.* To teach *deduce,* Ms. Franklin first had students self assess their knowledge of the meaning by using a graphic organizer, rating how well they knew the meaning of the word— very well, somewhat, or not at all.

Tenisha indicated that she knew it "somewhat" and that she thought it meant "you reduce something, like you make it littler." Lemarcus and Abraham did not know the meaning at all. As students in the class offered their opinions, Ms. Franklin wrote their responses on the board.

Next Ms. Franklin presented both definitional and contextual information about the word. To provide definitional information teachers can include synonyms or antonyms, elaborate on the definitions or provide examples or nonexamples. They can also initiate discussions about the differences between the new word and related words (Stahl & Nagy, 2006).

For *deduce* Ms. Franklin displayed the definition: "to infer from a general rule or principle; reach a conclusion by reasoning." A discussion of *infer* occurred when Lemarcus stated that his dictionary included that word as a synonym. This exchange led students to look up *infer.* They found the definition: "to find out by reasoning; conclude." From these two words, students then discussed how this word would relate to mysteries. Tenisha ventured that "the story could be about how someone solves a crime, and they have to figure it out from all the evidence. They *deduce* it."

To provide contextual information, teachers can have students create sentences using the word, discuss the meaning of the word in various sentences, create a story that includes several targeted words, or create silly questions that involve pairing words and creating a question out of each pair (e.g., "Can a *villain* be a *sleuth?,* Would you rather be *filthy* or *dirty?*"). For *deduce* Ms. Franklin displayed the sentence "Because the safe was too heavy for one man to move, the detective deduced that there were at least two thieves." When students discussed how *deduced* was used in this sentence, Lemarcus surmised, "So, if you deduce something, you figure it out from the clues."

Ms. Franklin confirmed Lemarcus's statement and asked him whether there was something in his life that he could deduce. Lemarcus looked at Abraham, who sat across from him, and in a jocular tone but with a deadpan expression he responded, "I can deduce that Abraham takes my pens 'cause he never has one and he's the only one around!" When Ms. Franklin asked if others had a sentence to offer, Tenisha volunteered:

"The police on *Bad Boys* deduced it was really the old man who killed the lady after they found his gun."

As Ms. Franklin presented definitional and contextual information in this example, it is important to note how she actively involved students in constructing links between new information and previously known information. Actively involving students is the second principle of effective vocabulary instruction in teaching specific words (Stahl & Nagy, 2006). Lemarcus stated the definition in his own words and came up with a sentence that involved how *deduce* might be used in his life. Tenisha connected the word to a TV show as she created her own sentence. When students participate fully in these cognitive exercises, they retain the information learned far better (Stahl & Nagy, 2006).

The next principle of effective instruction as it relates to specific vocabulary words is to actively involve students in word learning (Stahl & Nagy, 2006). One way to do this is through discussions. When students do not know anything about a word, they seem to learn a great deal from their peers. Often students are collectively able to come up with a word's *full* meaning from the *partial* meanings contributed by several individuals.

For Tenisha, Abraham, and Lemarcus, class discussions about words allowed them to be repositioned as primary knowers. For example, Lemarcus helped another student understand the meaning of *purloin* when Ms. Franklin taught specific words. During a class discussion a student indicated that he was having a difficult time remembering what *purloin* meant—that he "just didn't get it." Lemarcus jumped into the conversation, exclaiming, "I got it—let me set you straight! You heard of sirloin?" The student responded, "Yeah, that's steak—what you eat." Then Lemarcus said in a sing-song rhythm, "Yeah. Now, if you ain't careful, I'm goin' to purloin your sirloin! I'm going to steal your steak!" The class erupted with laughter, and the student repeated in the same rhythmic tone, "Purloin the sirloin! Steal the steak!" A few days later, the student was asked if he remembered what *purloin* meant. He immediately responded: "Steal. Purloin the sirloin. Steal the steak. If you purloin it, you steal it."

TEACHING INDEPENDENT
WORD-LEARNING STRATEGIES

Ms. Franklin wanted her students to be equipped with word-learning strategies such as contextual analysis and morphemic analysis that could be applied to unknown words when reading independently. Ms. Franklin said she found that her students—both those struggling and those not—

were more likely to use context than to stop during the middle of reading and look the word up in the dictionary.

Contextual analysis involves inferring the meaning of a word by scrutinizing surrounding text, which includes syntactic, semantic, and linguistic cues in preceding and succeeding words, phrases, and sentences. The goal of using contextual analysis should not be to get a perfect definition but rather to try to get enough information to comprehend the basic story (Stahl & Nagy, 2006). Contextual analysis is important since most vocabulary knowledge is gained as students hear and read words in multiple contexts. However, students should understand that sometimes it takes 20 encounters to understand fully a word learned from context and that a lot of text does not contain clues (Stahl, 1999).

Morphemic analysis involves deriving the meaning of a word by examining its meaningful parts (morphemes), such as prefixes, suffixes, and word roots. It is important to teach morphemic analysis because breaking words down into their morphemic parts often yields a definition instantly—for example, knowing *hemi-* (half) and *sphere* (an object shaped like a ball) makes learning the word "hemisphere" quite simple and straightforward (Stahl & Nagy, 2006). In addition, as students learn the meanings of morphemic parts—prefixes, suffixes, and roots—they are able to apply this knowledge to previously unknown words they encounter (Baumann, Edwards, Boland, Olejnik, & Kame'enui, 2003).

To teach morphemic analysis Ms. Franklin provided introductory lessons that showed how certain words were composed of recurrent elements—various prefixes, suffixes, and roots—and the key thing was to know how the parts functioned together to make up the word's meaning. For example, she taught the most common prefixes, grouping them into prefix families (e.g., placing *mis-* and *mal-* together because they both meant "bad").

An example of Ms. Franklin teaching contextual analysis in culturally grounded ways occurred during the reading of the novel *Homecoming* by Cynthia Voigt (2003). From experience, Ms. Franklin found that *Homecoming* was a popular well-written novel that touched on such significant universal themes such as child abandonment, verbal abuse, and racism. To focus on contextual analysis Ms. Franklin had students examine excerpts such as the one below, using context clues to figure out the word in italics.

> Aunt Cilla sent Christmas cards year after year with pictures of baby Jesus on them and long notes inside, on paper so thin it could have been tissue paper. Only Momma could *decipher* the lacy handwriting with its long, tall letters all bunched together and the lines running into one another because of the long-tailed, fancy z's and f's and g's.

First, students worked independently, writing down what they thought the word meant, marking words that helped them to figure out the meaning, and wrote where they might have encountered the word before. They then discussed their ideas in small groups and then in a whole-class setting.

Abraham checked on his sheet that he had heard of *decipher* before and "somewhat" knew its meaning. He underlined the words *Only Mamma*, *handwriting*, and *all bunched together* as context clues, and he wrote on his paper that the word meant "You figure it out." During small-group discussion Abraham told others that his "grandma always does the Celebrity Cipher in the paper," and he quickly explained how letters represent other letters and that you have to "break the code" to solve the Celebrity Cipher. After Abraham offered his ideas, another student in the group added that Abraham's definition seemed right because the text indicated that "their momma could read that fancy writing that the aunt did."

During whole-group discussion, Ms. Franklin asked if there were any morphemic elements to aid in understanding the meaning. One student noted the prefix *de-*, and as they referred to the meaning of the prefix *de-* ("something derived from a specified object") they made the connection that the aunt was able to figure out what the words in the letter were by decoding the fancy writing.

To encourage students to apply morphemic and contextual analysis skills as they read independently, Ms. Franklin used an article in *Jet* magazine about Fantasia, a past winner on the reality television show *American Idol*. Ms. Franklin chose this text because she knew students were very interested in Fantasia after having heard them discussing the release of her new album.

During the reading of the article, students focused on inferring the meanings of the unknown words. Ms. Franklin coached students to look for morphemic elements and context clues. When Tenisha read the sentence "After [Fantasia] won the reality show's grand prize of a $1-million recording contract, she *catapulted* into instant stardom and capped off a year full of accomplishments," she inferred that the word *catapulted* meant "that Fantasia was *thrown into* being a star right away."

WORD CONSCIOUSNESS

The phrase *word consciousness* is used to describe an interest in and awareness of words (Scott & Nagy, 2004). Motivation plays a key role in capturing students' interest and their desire to learn new words. Graves (2006) describes students who are word-conscious in the following way:

> Students who are word-conscious ... are interested in words, and they gain enjoyment and satisfaction from using them well and from seeing or hearing them used well by others. They find words intriguing, recognize adroit word usage when they encounter it, use words skillfully themselves, and are on the lookout for new and precise words, and are responsive to the nuances of word meanings. They are also well aware of the power of words and realize that they can be used to foster clarity and understanding or to obscure and obfuscate matters. (pp. 127–128)

To help students become aware of the power of words, Ms. Franklin emphasized the different ways of speaking, depending on the social context (Fecho, 2004; Gee, 1996). For example, she had students read and discuss Eloise Greenfield's (1972) poem "Honey, I Love." The first part of this poem reads "I love / I love a lot of things, a whole lot of things / Like / My cousin comes to visit and you know he's from the South / 'Cause every word he says just kind of slides out of his mouth. / I like the way he whistles and I like the way he walks / But honey, let me tell you that I LOVE the way he talks" (p. 4).

After this poem was read, Tenisha excitedly told the class how she felt about it: "Now, *that* poem is real! I like *that* one!" When asked why she liked it, Tenisha responded:

> "The way it is written is how someone would actually speak—like ghetto. Like this word here—*'cause*. If you were writing, usually you would have to write *because*, but she doesn't. She writes it the way you would really say it—*'cause*. And I like this little phrase here— 'but Honey, let me tell you that I love the way he talks.' But she has the *s* on *talks*. I wouldn't add the *s* to that though because that's not how you would say it for real. Will you read it again?"

Another specific activity Ms. Franklin used to foster word consciousness was having students collect in a journal phrases and sentences from their reading that stood out as effective uses of words—metaphors, striking figurative language, concrete descriptions, plays on words, or any other use of words that stood out to them.

Martin Luther King, Jr.'s "I Have a Dream" speech served as a text for students to find analogies, symbolism, personification, metaphors, repetition, and other literary elements. Year after year, Ms. Franklin found that her students enjoyed reading this speech and considered it to be one of the best speeches they had ever read. Ms. Franklin played a tape of the speech so that students could hear Dr. King's voice, and they jotted down words that stood out for them. During a class discussion, Abraham said, "His voice sings. That right there gets you to hear his words. And these words like *discord*, that makes it serious.... He wants black people treated fair, so he says it with strong words, so it's powerful."

Abraham said that "it was cool" and "motivating" to learn words the way they did from Dr. King's speech. He stated:

> "When you've got things like Dr. King's speech to inspire you, that will motivate you to try to understand those words, 'cause there are some tough words in that speech. But that's way better than getting a list of words. And it's our culture. I mean, that would be embarrassing if you didn't know what he was saying 'cause you didn't take the time or pay attention in class when we talked about what those words meant. You know?"

Ms. Franklin wanted her students to be able to make the connections between the vocabulary learned in school and how that knowledge could help them as individuals beyond the confines of the classroom (Fecho, 2004; Ladson-Billings, 1994). Therefore, to develop students' word consciousness, Ms. Franklin had them examine the question "How does learning about language and vocabulary connect you to your world?"

> "When you've got things like Dr. King's speech to inspire you, that will motivate you to try to understand those words, 'cause there are some tough words in that speech. But that's way better than getting a list of words. And it's our culture."
> —Abraham, eighth-grade student

Ms. Franklin also had students consider "the Discourses they belonged to" (i.e., language in relation to other social practices) and the language style of each using the terms *Discourses* (Gee, 1996) and *code switching* (Delpit & Dowdy, 2008), words that the students eventually came to comprehend and even use in their own vocabulary. In a class discussion, Lemarcus said, "If you can switch your words up—like that code switching you talked about—so that you can talk to people on the street corner, your friends or your teachers, or just anybody, really; well, that's like being able to speak another language. It's like you got power."

Since Ms. Franklin showed openness to various ways of using words—not just standardized English—for all school writing, Lemarcus, Tenisha, and Abraham were never positioned to feel inferior about their home languages. They were taught that there are different ways of communicating, depending on the situation, and thus they became more willing to consider deeply their vocabulary choices when writing. Ms. Franklin did not forbid students' use of their home vocabularies when writing. Instead, she set up situations in which students discussed various styles of writing and why those styles worked *for strategic purposes*. She did not impose a certain style without helping students understand why it might work to their advantage. For Lemarcus, through these discussions and examinations of word choices, he began to become more conscious about his word choices. As he put it:

> "We talked about how that girl used detailed words, how you got to pick words that really tell what's happening, so you see it. You know? That's what I tried to do with mine. I tried to use different kinds of vocabulary words that I don't use when I talk. Now, that's a big change in me."

Tenisha also became more word-conscious expressing it as follows:

> "Sometimes you need to take the slang out, but sometimes the slang might be what you need. Now, that's where Ms. Franklin is *different* than my other teachers, 'cause all they care about is correct grammar."

SUMMARY

Words are strongly connected to our lives and our cultures. When teachers acknowledge this close connection and teach vocabulary in culturally grounded ways, they set up an environment that increases marginalized readers' engagement, sensitivity, and enjoyment in learning new vocabulary. Furthermore, they take the learning of word meanings to a deeper level where students thoroughly consider where and for what purposes the words they learn in school would be used and what that means for them as individuals in their everyday lives. By combining widely researched methods of vocabulary instruction with culturally aware pedagogical practices, teachers can help reposition marginalized readers as primary knowers, where they can experience greater academic success.

Questions for Reflection

1. How do you currently engage your students in the four vocabulary components, namely, immersion in rich language sources through wide-ranging reading and writing, teaching individual words, teaching word-learning strategies, and fostering word consciousness?

2. How can you connect students' funds of knowledge with the task of learning new vocabulary?

3. How can you expand or change what you currently do to teach vocabulary in culturally grounded ways?

4. What challenges do you face in implementing culturally grounded vocabulary instruction?

RECOMMENDED RESOURCES

Beck, I. L., McKeown, M. G., & Kucan, L. (2002). *Bringing words to life: Robust vocabulary instruction.* New York: Guilford Press.

Blachowicz, C., & Fisher, P. J. (2010). *Teaching vocabulary in all classrooms.* Boston: Allyn & Bacon.

Delpit, D., & Dowdy, J. K. (Eds.). (2008). *The skin that we speak: Thoughts on language and culture in the classroom.* New York: New Press.

Graves, M. F. (2006). *The vocabulary book: Learning and instruction.* New York: Teachers College Press.

Johnson, D. D. (2001). *Vocabulary in the elementary and middle school.* Boston: Allyn & Bacon.

9

Fostering Discussions about Texts

In order to enable middle level students to answer factual, analytical, and imaginative questions about the texts they read, they need to be given a way to enter inside of them, as well as a way of thinking about analyzing, and questioning them from the outside.

—MINNICK AND MERGIL (2008, p. 37)

FOCAL POINTS

1. Struggling readers typically wish to be more involved in discussions about texts than they are.

2. Discussions can enable struggling readers to become primary knowers by sharing their own interpretations of texts.

3. Struggling readers may find discussions either empowering or too dangerous or risky to participate in, depending on how they are structured.

As the cited quote from Minnick and Mergil (2008) suggests, discussions consist of more than simply answering a set of predetermined questions in order to obtain the "right answers." Rather, they should also provide ample opportunities for students to advance *multiple* interpretations of texts and explore interpretations very different from their own. Through talking about texts, struggling readers can begin to better understand their world, how they engage with it, and how they are shaped by it (Knickerbocker & Rycik, 2006). Discussions can help students take

132

greater control of their learning by providing opportunities for them to offer their interpretations, ask questions central to their concerns, and develop their reading comprehension abilities (Applebee, Langer, Nystrand, & Gamoran, 2003; Evans, 2002).

Discussions can help students take greater control of their learning by providing opportunities for them to offer their interpretations, ask questions central to their concerns, and develop their reading comprehension abilities.

Marginalized readers, though, may have limited experiences with text-based discussions. Rather than being full participants in them, they often are likely to find themselves being called from the classroom to receive additional skills-based instruction (Moller, 2004–2005). These experiences often result in marginalized readers being further isolated from their peers and having fewer opportunities to engage with texts in critical and thoughtful ways.

When marginalized readers do get the opportunity to participate in discussions, they can find them both empowering and dangerous. Discussions serve as one way of positioning students as certain types of people and readers (Wortham, 2004). For marginalized readers who have continually been positioned as secondary knowers, discussions may be one more event where they are seen as less knowledgeable and capable than their peers. However, it is also through discussions that spaces can open up that enable these students to create new identities and to reshape their social relationships and positions in classrooms.

Through discussions, spaces can open up that enable students to create new identities and to reshape their social relationships and status in classrooms.

It is in creating such spaces that discussions become transformative in terms of what students learn and how they develop as readers.

This chapter focuses on how discussions can be structured to allow full participation from marginalized readers. We consider full participation to mean that all students feel comfortable sharing their interpretations and questions about texts regardless of how well formulated these are. Students also feel comfortable responding to the ideas of others and using the questions and interpretations generated by their peers to inform and potentially reshape their initial understanding.

In considering how to help marginalized or struggling readers become full participants, we explore how to structure discussions so that marginalized readers' ideas are valued and encouraged. Rather than considering how to structure discussions in ways that are "easier" for marginalized readers, we examine how discussions can be used to further their understanding of complex texts and push them forward in their development as academic readers. In doing so, we look at how discussions can help marginalized readers gain a way into texts and provide them and their peers a way to understand and value multiple perspectives.

THE BENEFITS OF DISCUSSIONS

Engaging marginalized readers in discussions provides an opportunity to connect them with more challenging and complex texts than they may be used to reading. Throughout their school careers, marginalized readers are likely used to being assigned texts written below their grade level and considered easier to read. However, having discussions about texts that are difficult and challenging for all readers will not necessarily put marginalized readers at a disadvantage. When presented with challenging texts, marginalized readers are likely to be highly responsive and to end up *improving* their comprehension abilities (Gamoran, 1993). While using challenging texts requires teachers to think through the kinds of support and instruction students will need, such texts also provide a way to help marginalized readers become a larger part of classroom life and engage with texts in a more critical and thoughtful manner (see Chapter 7 for a full discussion).

Discussions also enable students to hear divergent interpretations while interacting with students from diverse backgrounds (Eeds & Wells, 1989). Students' experiences both in and outside of school provide them with a framework for understanding and responding to texts. Putting students in small groups and asking them to share their questions and answers allows them to hear a variety of ideas. When students are facilitated in being perceived as primary knowers (Aukerman, 2007), each perspective is more seriously considered and examined. Thus, students potentially leave the discussions after having deepened or reconstructed the understanding they began with.

Finally, discussions allow students to reexamine their roles as readers. It is through discussions that students can start to see their role as readers as "puzzle solvers, text and genre investigators, and potential authors" (Damico, 2005, p. 644). As students start to expand their understanding of what it means to read, they may become more critical consumers of texts. Rather than focusing on finding the one "correct" answer, students begin focusing on the ideas and beliefs that are or are not promoted in texts and how these ideas or beliefs influence their daily lives and the interpretation of texts (Hall & Piazza, 2008; Smiles, 2008).

STUDENTS' PERSPECTIVES ON DISCUSSIONS

Some students who are positioned as struggling readers may enjoy participating in discussions, seeing them as opportunities to learn from their peers. For example, when asked what she thought about small-group text-based discussions, Emma, a sixth grader and struggling reader, said:

> **Some students positioned as struggling readers may enjoy participating in discussions, seeing them as opportunities to learn from their peers.**

> "I actually learned something. I learned something about what they [the group members] thought about the stuff we read. My group liked to *argue* about stuff. They like to make you understand what they think about something. If you said something, they would be like 'Why do you think that?' And you have to *explain* it to them, and it helps you understand it better. The more we talked, the more I understood."

Emma's explanation of her experiences with small-group discussions can provide a counterexample to what might normally be seen in classrooms. It is common to see struggling readers sitting in silence during discussions, which suggests they may not be participating (Hall, 2010). However, there are many ways to view participation—particularly from the perspective of a struggling reader. Consider the statements these struggling readers made when asked how they felt about participating in text-based discussions:

> "In front of the whole class? That's scary 'cause you don't want to be seen getting an answer wrong. I just listen and learn that way."
> "I listen real hard to what my group members say. That helps me learn."
> "I wish I understood this stuff better so I could say more."

The examples provided here suggest that struggling readers see discussions as occasions that can be scary but also helpful. As noted throughout this text, struggling readers generally gauge whether to participate based on how they believe they are going to be perceived as readers. Although speaking may be considered a central part of discussions, not all struggling readers believe they can or should offer their questions or ideas, given their common self-image as inadequate.

However, marginalized readers definitely believe that small-group discussions heighten their interest in texts and encourage them to strive for improvement in their reading abilities (Blum, Lipsett, & Yocom, 2002). Evans (2002) concluded that students need to believe their ideas will be respected and that their peers will listen open-mindedly to what they have to say. She also learned that students sometimes experienced special problems in work with members of the opposite gender and in some cases even attributed their inability to participate in discussions to that single factor.

The findings presented here suggest that discussions can be a highly contentious space for marginalized readers. Some, like Emma, are able to find success and fully participate and share their ideas, while others find them to be frightening activities that threaten to expose their weaknesses as readers. Structuring discussions so that marginalized readers are more willing to share their ideas is not about finding easier reading texts or having them work with students of like abilities. Rather, *all* students, not just struggling readers, need more help in learning how to work with one another and respond to one another in ways that are tolerant and that demonstrate that everyone's ideas and questions are important and therefore deserve respect.

> **Structuring discussions so that marginalized readers are more willing to share their ideas is not about finding easier reading texts or having them work with students of like abilities but, rather, more about tolerance and mutual respect of diverse viewpoints.**

THEORETICAL PERSPECTIVES ON DISCUSSIONS

While discussions generally help students in numerous ways, many questions remain about how best to structure them and the specific benefits and limitations each approach affords. Before we consider what, specifically, discussions should look like in practice, let us consider various theoretical perspectives in approaching the issue. These perspectives broadly illuminate how students learn from discussing texts.

For most of the 20th century, "new criticism" dominated the way discussions were structured in ELA classrooms (Thomas, 2008). New criticism views texts as being neutral self-contained documents that present specific facts or ideas to readers. Under new criticism, the goal of the reader is to identify literary structures, examine how these structures are used within the text, and then use them to understand and explain the text. New criticism does not consider how readers' cultural and social backgrounds shape their interpretations of texts—or even consider such experiences as relevant to properly understanding the texts. Under the new criticism rubric, the meaning of the text resides within the text itself and is not open to multiple subjective interpretations based on the reader's personal history or unique point of view.

Unfortunately, as O'Flavan and Wallis (2005, p. 32) point out, structuring discussions solely under a new criticism framework results in students spending the bulk of their time trying to figure out what interpretations their teacher has arrived at:

> We were raised to believe that texts contained particular meanings and that our job was to seek those text-bound truths. Of course, what we were really in search of was our teachers' interpretations of the text. So, as *teachers*, we were often frustrated as to why our well-intentioned analyses and syntheses of what an author meant or what a text implied received only cursory attention from our students. Consequently, we were compelled to tell our students what texts meant. There was little room in our class discussions for variant readings.

Other theoretical positions provide a different way to approach discussions so that students' background and interpretations of text are honored and have space to be explored and refined. Rosenblatt's (1978) reader response theory stresses that it is what the individual reader brings to bear on the text that will ultimately influence his or her interpretation or response to it. According to Rosenblatt (2004), texts are not neutral self-contained documents that are waiting for readers to uncover and identify a singular fixed meaning. Meaning also does not lie solely within the reader. Instead, meaning is created when readers *transact* with the text. Readers bring their prior knowledge and personal histories to texts, and those shape and influence how they engage with and make sense of the ideas that texts present.

As students read, they assume a stance, or purpose, for engaging with the text. The two stances noted by Rosenblatt (2004) are the efferent and the aesthetic. In an efferent stance, readers are focusing on identifying specific pieces of information that are relevant to them. This information may be related to questions formulated by either the teacher or the students. In an aesthetic stance, readers focus on how they are feeling, their emotions, and pictures that enter their mind and are living in the moment as they read. Rosenblatt argues that these stances are placed on a continuum and that readers can move up and down the continuum and in and out of either stance as they read. Thus, reading is not an either–or phenomenon, and students can shift from one stance to the next as they wish.

We agree that engaging with texts is not a neutral process and that texts do not possess a set of absolute truths that are waiting to be uncovered by readers. Additionally, we agree with Rosenblatt (1978, 2004) that readers' personal histories, prior knowledge, and purposes or stances for reading transact with texts in order to create meaning. However, we also see literature discussions as a sociocultural activity where students' interactions with texts, their peers, and their teachers contribute to their interpretations. As such, discussions involve more than just an individual reader transacting with texts but rather a community of readers who transact with texts and one another in a variety of ways.

Literature discussions, then, reflect the context and cultural norms of the class as a whole. Within the classroom, students react to others' interpretations and use this information to create new understandings or to confirm what they already think. Students can use language to position themselves (for example, being the leader of a group) or to position others. As students react to one another, they determine which texts are valued, how they can be used, and how they should be discussed (Bloome & Egan-Robertson, 1993; Galda & Beach, 2004). Discussions, then, are not merely occasions for sharing the right answers or one's interpretations but rather opportunities for students to begin transforming themselves as readers and thinkers or, alternatively, be further marginalized and shut down.

For marginalized readers, this view of discussion as a sociocultural activity is key. Marginalized readers who believe they have little of worth to contribute or believe their ideas are not valued may limit their participation because they think it is not wanted or useful. Additionally, students who believe that there are single fixed interpretations of texts may crowd out those who offer alternative perspectives, making it more difficult for struggling readers to have their say. Therefore, understanding the social and cultural norms students have long experienced in literature discussions can provide important information about how they generally approach discussions. Talking to students frankly about what free-flowing discussion really looks like in practice from a sociocultural perspective, and helping them understand how to better implement it, provides one way to fully engage struggling readers in text-based discussions.

THE TEACHER'S ROLE IN DISCUSSIONS

As we have already seen, how teachers structure discussions can shape the ways in which students talk about and interact with texts (Basmadjian, 2008; Hill, 2008). In a traditional discussion format, the teacher prepares questions for students to answer. The teacher then evaluates students' responses and provides feedback whenever necessary. This particular structure, often referred to as IRE (interrogate, respond, and evaluate), places the emphasis on what the teacher values and on identifying the teacher's interpretation of the text.

The following example demonstrates what an IRE format looks like. Students are reading the book *Selkie Girl* (Brooks, 2008; see review by Jung, 2009). The text draws on a Scottish mythical seal, called a selkie, that can take on a human form and interact with other humans who are not selkies. Brooks uses this myth as a way of exploring how individuals are accepted, rejected, and marginalized within society. In the example below, the teacher has created questions about the text that she wants students to discuss:

TEACHER: What is a selkie?

AMANDA: Seals!

TEACHER: Right. Sort of. They are seals, but what else can you say about them?

AMANDA: They live in the ocean.

TEACHER: Yes, sometimes. Let's go back to what a selkie is. Amanda says they are seals, but what else can we add to that?

SAM: They can become human and go on land.

TEACHER: Yes? But how do they become human?

SAM: They lose their skin and shape-shift.

In this example, the teacher selected the question to be explored and structured the discussion so that students were forced to consider the definition of a selkie. The teacher evaluated each response and then responded with questions or statements that led the discussion in the direction the teacher wanted to pursue. While this particular format gives little control to the students, and little if any opportunity for them to debate and explore their own questions and responses, there can be times when such a framework is useful. Spiegel (2005) has noted that the IRE structure is most helpful when teachers want to assess what students have learned from texts or see how well they understand specific concepts.

Multiple researchers though have argued for peer-led discussions as opposed to teacher-centered, or teacher-led, discussions that use a traditional IRE structure (Almasi, 1995; Berne & Clark, 2006; Carico, 2001). In peer-led discussions, students bring their own questions and ideas to the table and discuss what they see as being important and central to the text. Peer-led discussions can help students become more responsible for their participation and learning as well as construct more complex understandings about texts (Berne & Clark, 2005; Evans, 2002).

Wilson and Laman (2007) showed how a peer-led discussion by

middle school students provided opportunities for them to better understand themselves and one another while simultaneously allowing them to explore how they get positioned in school. In their study, students discussed a picture book titled *I Hate English* (Levine & Bjorkman, 1995) in which the main character moves from China to America and has to learn English. One Chinese student, Qing, shared information with his small group about the Chinese language but also discussed how difficult it had been for him to learn English. The ideas and questions Qing presented to his group resulted in their positioning him as being knowledgeable about Chinese culture and having valuable insights that could further their understanding of the text. Rather than being seen solely as an English language learner (and potentially a secondary knower), Qing used the peer-led discussions to shift his position into that of a possible knower or even primary knower.

Peer-led discussions can also create spaces for struggling readers to make regular and substantive contributions (Evans, 2002). Discussions can be structured so that struggling readers can shift their roles from those who are less capable and must rely on the support of students who are seen as better readers, to those who can challenge and help their peers make sense of text (Moller, 2004–2005). However, shifting from a position of a less capable to a more capable reader can seem risky for struggling readers who may not believe they belong in such a position. The next sections explore different ways to structure discussions so that struggling readers can begin to make this shift and so that their peers will welcome them into this new role.

DEVELOPING STUDENTS' AGENCY IN DISCUSSIONS

An important factor in creating spaces for struggling readers to be fully involved with discussions is developing their agency in ways that support deep discussions of text. "Agency" refers to an individual's freedom to interact with the world in ways that support his or her goals and purposes (Moore & Cunningham, 2006). Individuals' decisions about how to act are often influenced by a number of elements such as their prior experiences, the current environments they reside in, and their social, cultural, and linguistic circumstances, or background. However, it is often how individuals relate to these various elements that largely determines their relative latitude in making decisions about what they want to do and who they want to be.

Struggling readers' past experiences with text-based discussion—and more importantly how they regard them retrospectively—likely contribute most to deciding how to engage with discussions in the future. If struggling readers have accepted being positioned as persons who have little to offer in the way of interesting ideas and questions, they may enact their agency by choosing to remain silent and say little. That is, they may speak only when asked fact-based questions that have definitely "right" answers and pose little risk to their being further positioned in a negative light.

Language plays a critical role in structuring discussions in ways that enable struggling readers to feel more comfortable in talking about text. Carico (2001) has found that when students talk about texts in peer-led discussions they sometimes use language that may unintentionally (or occasionally intentionally) exclude others from participating. Students sometimes emphasize issues that are gender specific and that may be offensive. Such types of talk can end up excluding peers who do not have the background knowledge or experiences to understand and respond to it. Additionally, some people may make inconsiderate remarks or use language that is considered inappropriate in school.

On the other hand, allowing students to be more open in their language use can provide an empowering way for students to explore their life experiences and to speak more than they may have before. Carico points out that in ELA classrooms we often privilege "the language of eloquence" and expect students to speak fluidly and clearly about their ideas. If all ideas must be presented as polished, many (chiefly economically disadvantaged) students may limit their participation as they may not believe their relatively "unpolished" ideas are ready to share. The challenge then becomes helping students learn how to be mindful of what they say while also providing them the freedom and space to fully explore their ideas.

Helping struggling readers develop and enact their agency in ways that enable them to be full participants in text-based discussions means taking into account what kind of talk gets privileged in discussions. As was noted in Chapter 3, how teachers and students talk about texts with one another shapes students' understanding of how they should participate and whether they are capable of doing so in the traditionally valued ways. If speaking eloquently, *only* is privileged, then struggling read-

> **Helping struggling readers develop and enact their agency in ways that enable them to be full participants in text-based discussions means taking a much more tolerant attitude toward home-based or informal language being used in discussions.**

ers may end up speaking only when they are confident they are offering up "acceptable" ideas. However, structuring discussions so that they are places for diverse ideas to be expressed, questioned, and further explored enable all students to see them as special sanctuaries for the continual reconstruction of one's understanding. When discussions are no longer fixated on finding the "right" answer, they can create spaces for struggling readers to share their insights without fear of peer rejection.

DISCUSSIONS AS A WAY
TO UNDERSTAND DIVERSE POPULATIONS

Discussions can provide a forum for helping students better understand individuals from diverse groups and see them as more than a predictable collection of stereotypes (Athanases, 1998). Such discussions are about more than just having students read multicultural texts and say what they think or understand about the texts. Rather, students should draw widely on their sociocultural background as a mere prelude to considering how and why they interpret texts in the ways that they do (Rice, 2005). While students' gender, race or ethnicity, and socioeconomic status inevitably influence how they view and understand literature, their diverse backgrounds as reflected in their personalities and opinions can also serve as a real-life diorama challenging fellow students to expand their understanding of others (and of literature).

The selection of texts is the first step to helping students to explore different backgrounds. Figure 9.1 contains suggestions for books that could be helpful in getting students to explore the perspectives of students from diverse backgrounds. Montgomery (2000) recommends that texts should contain "culturally significant themes" and provoke a reaction from students. Texts should also serve as both a window and mirror allowing students to look into the lives of people they would not normally experience and as a way to understand themselves and how their views influence their understanding of texts and interactions with the world (Brooks, Browne, & Hampton, 2008). Selecting texts that can work toward these goals means understanding your students and the issues that are important and significant to them. Students should also have a say in what texts are selected for reading, based on issues that they would most like to explore. By involving students directly in their selection, texts can be linked to students' lives beyond school, thereby creating a more authentic purpose for reading them.

For example, *To Kill a Mockingbird* (Lee, 2002) is a text that can serve as both a window and a mirror (Brooks et al., 2008). Its focus on racism in the 1930s can provide a window for viewing racism from a historical perspective and understanding how it has long been a part of our society. It can also serve as a mirror by providing a way for students to look at how they have experienced and dealt with racism as it is enacted

Almond, D. (2006). *Clay.* New York: Random House/Delacorte Publishers.

Bartoletti, S. C. (2008). *The boy who dared.* New York: Scholastic.

Booth, C. (2008) *Kendra.* New York: Scholastic.

Bowman, R. (2007). *It's complicated: The American teenager.* Brooklyn, NY: Umbrage Editions.

Budhos, M. (2006). *Ask me no questions.* New York: Simon & Schuster.

Dessen, S. (2006). *Just listen.* New York: Penguin Group USA/Viking.

Geerling, M. (2008). *Fancy white trash.* New York: Penguin/Viking.

Gratz, A. (2006). *Samurai shortstop.* New York: Penguin Group USA/Dial.

Hijuelos, O. (2008). *Dark dude.* New York: Simon & Schuster.

Lansens, L. (2006). *The girls.* New York: Little, Brown.

Marillier, J. (2008). *Cybele's secret.* New York: Random House/Knopf.

Menzel, P., & D'Aluisio, F. (2008). *What the world eats.* Berkeley, CA: Ten Speed Press.

Pratchett, T. (2008). *Nation.* New York: HarperCollins.

Sheth, K. (2007). *Keeping corner.* New York: Hyperion.

Shields, C. J. (2008). *I am Scout: The biography of Harper Lee.* New York: Henry Holt.

Valentine, J. (2008). *Me, the missing, and the dead.* New York: HarperCollins/HarperTeen.

FIGURE 9.1. Books for exploring diverse perspectives.

in their own lives. The text can provide students who have experienced racism a way to connect with the story and a way to help their classmates understand how racism looks today and how it affects them.

Discussions that ask students to consider different perspectives are asking them to reconsider the beliefs and values they currently hold. Such discussions can be threatening to students. It is often common for students to privilege their own interpretations and not examine the sociocultural factors that shape their beliefs and understanding of the world (Rice, 2005). When this potential for self-examination arises, students are more likely to shut down alternative ways of thinking or to view them as lesser than their own approaches (Hall & Piazza, 2008).

While disagreements issue may be difficult to avoid in discussions, it is possible to respond to them in ways that move students forward. Hall and Piazza (2008) identified two ways to work toward common ground. One way is to first understand our own beliefs and biases as teachers and to be honest about those with students as much as possible. For example, sharing our own experiences with racism, how we responded to it, and what we learned from our actions can help students see that we are open to other perspectives and that we reconsider and even reconstruct our own beliefs—just as we are constantly asking them to do.

Second, we can make explicit that not everyone shares the same belief systems. By being open and up front that we do not all see the world in the same way, students can begin to feel that it is okay to voice ideas different from their peers. Discussions then become spaces where students can test out new ideas and get feedback. Because all students have experiences, questions, and ideas related to central concepts such as racism struggling readers have a natural entryway into discussions.

ENGAGING STUDENTS
IN MULTIMODAL DISCUSSIONS

Multimodal discussions allow students to make meaning and respond to texts through a variety of media including but not limited to writing and speaking (Jewitt, 2008). Multimodality refers to drawing on a variety of sources, including traditional printed texts as well as visual images and music, to make sense of what has been read and to communicate that information to others (Walsh, 2008). Discussions that utilize a multimodal approach recognize that reading and discussing texts involves considering not just what to say but how to say it and what format might best represent that information (Doering, Beach, & O'Brien, 2007).

Engaging students in multimodal discussions enables them to develop and refine the more traditional reading skills and strategies that have historically been taught throughout school while also allowing them to draw on and continue to develop the other forms of literacy they have significant experience with. When students are afforded other forms of sharing ideas and information, space opens up for struggling readers to fully participate. As noted throughout this text, struggling readers are often positioned as having limited reading abilities *in school* but often engage in a variety of sophisticated literacy activities *outside of school*. Allowing them to participate in discussions that use a multimodal format gives them the opportunity to bring their diverse literacy abilities into school while also positioning them as possible or even primary knowers.

What might a multimodal literature discussion look like in practice? First, students still read texts and are expected to respond to them and discuss them in small groups or within the whole class. While students may sometimes compose a traditional written response to their readings, they are asked to consider other modes of responding.

For example, students reading Sherman Alexie's book *The Absolutely True Diary of a Part-Time Indian* (described in Chapter 7) could bring in a photograph of an Indian reservation—perhaps one they found online or one they took while on vacation—and use it as a way to discuss the text. Another student might speak with a Native American about the text and share the information learned with his or her group. These ideas can be extended further by having students create short video clips or a podcast about their impressions and understanding of the text.

Additionally, students do not always have to produce or identify multimodal artifacts (e.g., photo, video, text) that represent their interpretations of or conclusions about the text. The role of the artifact can be reversed in that students can identify an artifact that helped them better understand a particular aspect of the text. However, allowing students to bring in various artifacts does not mean that they will critically engage with them. Students may accept the artifact at face value and not attempt to either critically analyze its source or use the text/artifact as a way to critically analyze or interpret the piece of literature you have assigned. Additionally, students may view their artifacts as more authoritative than the assigned text and may use them to shut down and silence other points of view.

However, it is possible to help students become more critical of outside texts while using them to engage critically with classroom texts. Stevens and Bean (2007) recommend having students examine texts by considering (1) what information is or is not being presented; (2) what is missing from the text; (3) who the text is intended for; (4) who is being silenced or left out of the text; and (5) what the text wants from its readers. By posing such questions, students are put in the position of more readily seeing that the text is trying to persuade them or present them with a new idea to consider. Such questions also assist students in recognizing that texts are not neutral and can do more than merely entertain or present facts.

Having students participate in multimodal discussions and helping them think critically about the artifacts they identify or create will likely be a new practice. Although students may engage with other forms of media outside of school, they may not be used to using those forms in school as a way to understand and discuss literature. In many ways, this emerging practice can help to level the playing field for struggling readers. As they see their peers who are typically positioned as good readers struggle to engage with texts in new ways, they have the opportunity to see that *we all* have difficulties engaging with texts as we learn and grow as readers.

SUMMARY

Discussions about texts can serve as a powerful way to reposition struggling readers and can help them become full participants in classroom reading practices. In structuring multiple ways to understand and implement discussions, we are not suggesting that one approach is necessarily better than another or that a particular one should be used exclusively. Each has both benefits and limitations, and many can be used to further students' reading abilities and their understanding of texts. Perhaps the most useful way to consider how best to structure discussions is to assess whether the intended structure advantages struggling readers, encouraging their maximum participation. Ultimately, discussion that recognizes the potential for *everyone* to contribute insights and participate actively will likely be the most beneficial.

Questions for Reflection

1. To what extent do your reading discussions recognize and value diverse views and experiences?

2. Do your discussions typically follow an IRE (interrogate, respond, evaluate) format, or are they more student-centered, allowing students opportunities to explore ideas and questions that are central to both the text and their lives in a more open-ended way?

3. How often do students positioned as struggling readers take a leadership role in your small-group or whole-class discussions? What could be done to increase their involvement and active participation?

RECOMMENDED RESOURCES

Copeland, M. (2005). *Socratic circles: Fostering critical and creative thinking in middle and high school.* Portland, ME: Stenhouse.

Schoch, K. (2010). *How to teach a novel.* Retrieved March 5, 2010, from *howtoteachanovel.blogspot.com*

Vandergrift, K. E. (2010). *Young adult literature: Vandergrift's young adult literature page.* Retrieved March 5, 2010, from *comminfo.rutgers.edu/professional-development/childlit/YoungAdult/index.html*

10

Reading Texts
on the Internet

FOCAL POINTS

1. Reading online requires all students to learn new skills and strategies.

2. How well students read printed academic texts is not always an indicator of how well they can read online texts.

3. Some struggling readers may be better at comprehending online texts.

The ability to locate, comprehend, and apply information found on the Internet has become a central part of our everyday lives. The Internet can be used to locate information needed immediately such as what time a movie starts, the menu at a new restaurant, or directions to a friend's home. The Internet also provides ways for us to get up-to-the minute information about current events, solve problems, or share information about our lives with others.

Students who are positioned as struggling readers however are likely to have limited access to Internet texts in school (Karchmer, 2004). In some cases, these limited opportunities can be due to the technology that is available to all students in school. However, students who are positioned as struggling readers are often seen as not possessing the skills needed to successfully engage with online reading tasks. Rather than use the Internet to help students develop their reading comprehension abilities, they may spend a disproportionate amount of their time completing drills in classrooms and engaging in multiple-choice reading assessments.

147

Even when classrooms have adequate technology, teachers tend to engage most with students characterized as good readers rather than struggling ones (Wilder & Dressman, 2006). Likewise, students who identify themselves as struggling readers often limit their involvement in classroom reading practices even when these practices are altered and even if they have extensive experience in using Internet texts at home. Their decision for doing so is likely grounded in their understanding of what it means to be a struggling reader, their belief that they have little to offer, and their attitudes about how struggling readers should participate in school. Therefore, simply increasing the amount of technology available to students, and providing them time to use it, is unlikely to create significant change for those students.

Although struggling readers may be seen as lacking the abilities to comprehend traditional print-based texts in school, this does not mean they have limited abilities to comprehend and even create online texts (Alvermann & McLean, 2007). Students who have grown up using the Internet as a way of learning information and networking with others have a remarkable range of skills and experiences that may go unrecognized in school. In short, being positioned as a struggling reader of traditional print-based texts does not necessarily make one a poor reader of online texts (Coiro, 2009). Similarly, being seen as a good reader of traditional print-based texts does not automatically make someone a good reader of online texts.

Engaging students with Internet texts requires more than simply providing them with a computer and getting them on a search engine. To read and use these texts effectively, students must learn how to apply skills previously used with traditional texts to an online format as well as develop new ones. This chapter explores how to help struggling readers gain greater access to Internet texts in ways that will foster their online reading comprehension abilities. We explore the challenges of helping students comprehend online texts and develop the skills they need to succeed.

STEPPING INTO THE WORLD OF NEW LITERACIES

The integration of the Internet into our society requires all of us to read, think, and interact with text in new ways. Reading is no longer limited to opening a book and reading text in a linear fashion. As the Internet has developed, reading has become a nonlinear and highly interactive experience that has required the development of new literacies.

The term *new literacies* refers to "the skills, strategies, and dispositions necessary to successfully use and adapt to the rapidly changing information and communication technologies and contexts that continuously emerge in our world and influence all areas of our personal and professional lives" (Leu, Kinzer, Coiro, & Cammack, 2004, p. 1571). While communication technologies such

> **The integration of the Internet into our society requires all of us to read, think, and interact with text in new ways. Reading is no longer limited to opening a book and reading text in a linear fashion.**

as the Internet require students to engage with print-based texts, the ways in which they interact with these texts is much different than how they would approach a traditional print-based volume. On the Internet, students have a complex range of texts and genres they can utilize almost simultaneously in order to explore and debate ideas, all while having the opportunity to access a variety of perspectives (Tierney, 2007).

Stepping into this world of new literacies, helping students access it, and designing instruction that utilizes it can be challenging. As teachers, most of us are considered to be digital immigrants. The term *digital immigrant* (Prensky, 2001) refers to those of us who did not grow up in a digital society but instead had to learn how to engage with it and develop new literacies much later in life. As such, digital technologies are something we have had to adapt to rather than something that has been an integral part of our lives since birth.

"Digital natives," however, have grown up with the Internet and other forms of technology. According to Prensky (2001), they are accustomed to multitasking, such as viewing the graphics on a topic before they read about it, finding needed information almost instantly, and being able to connect from one text to another quickly and efficiently. The literacies most often valued and demanded by schools, in contrast, can seem almost foreign to digital natives, to whom that type of learning often strikes them as needlessly protracted, passive, and even isolating.

The position of students as digital natives, and our positions as digital immigrants, highlights an important point about students who are also positioned as struggling readers. Burns (2008) argues that students who are highly literate in the new literacies—digital natives—tend to be labeled as struggling readers in school based solely on their "seemingly inability to learn print-centered academic literacies" (p. 8). He challenges us to consider whether students who are positioned as struggling readers are really *poor* readers or whether they are sim-

> **The label of "struggling reader" may well be a false one that exists only to capture those students who are not successful—or have disengaged from participating—in the literacy practices championed by "digital immigrants."**

ply *different* readers. In considering this question, he states: "If youth read differently, then the institutionally imposed 'struggling reader' label puts them in an untenable position with regard to academic engagement. In their out of school lives they may experience themselves as competent, but in school they consistently hear they are failing" (p. 8). According to Burns, the label of "struggling reader" is a false one that exists only to capture those students who are not successful—or have disengaged from participating—in the literacy practices championed by "digital immigrants." What results is a cultural divide where, in effect, students and teachers do not speak the same language or value the same types of literacy practices. In such a divide, a student's "success" often means sacrificing his or her own ideals and cultural practices toward literacy and adopting or appearing to adopt what is valued and practiced in school.

UNDERSTANDING AND RESPONDING
TO THE CULTURAL DIVIDE

Understanding and responding to the cultural divide that can exist between digital natives and digital immigrants requires some work on the part of the immigrants. However, it does not mean reworking instruction so that it panders to what adolescents want to do and simply think is fun. Viewing differences in approaches to literacy and technology in an "us-versus-them" mindset creates a false dichotomy that will do little to help teachers and students succeed (Alvermann & McLean, 2007). A more productive approach is to consider how we, as teachers, understand and use new literacies and the similarities and differences in how our students engage in them.

One important aspect of understanding different approaches to literacy is how digital natives respond to online texts versus traditional print-based texts. Adolescents who have grown up with the Internet and are used to reading multimodal texts expect that texts will require them to navigate different forms of media, some of which—but not all—include print. They are not used to paying attention to texts that contain only words—and no other forms of media—for extended periods of time (Lankshear & Knobel, 2003). The result is not that adolescents *cannot read* print-based texts or *are too lazy* to read them, but that these texts are *not part of their social world*—a stark contrast for those of us who have grown up with them and now find ourselves adapting to multimodal online texts (Burns, 2008).

However, not all adolescents are equally savvy at reading online texts. Lei (2009) notes that, even if students regularly use technology, not all of them engage with it "critically, wisely, or meaningfully" (p. 88). In fact, some adolescents do not know how to fully use the technology they are engaging with, often using it in ways that are superficial.

Providing instruction that engages students with both online and print-based texts means understanding how they have and continue to engage with both types of texts. It also means considering your own experiences with reading both on and offline and evaluating the ways you engage students in both types of reading in your classroom. Thus helping your students learn to read texts, both online and off-line, is in part about understanding your own abilities and involvement with these different types of text. This undertaking requires us to consider what types of text we privilege, how we incorporate them into our classrooms, and the types of instruction and opportunities students are afforded with each. It also means being open to our own limitations and, in part, willing to be students ourselves. As we seek to help our students become better readers of online and off-line texts, we are also in part working at becoming better readers ourselves and crafting a new understanding of what it means to be a reader and what new literacies look like in practice.

DIFFERENCES BETWEEN INTERNET
AND TRADITIONAL TEXTS

A first step toward understanding how to address new literacies and online reading in ELA classrooms centers on knowing the structural differences and demands that exist in reading online and print-based texts. Reading Internet texts is not the same as reading the texts typically assigned in schools, such as textbooks, trade books, or novels. Online texts are also different from texts that students might read at home, such as magazine articles, graphic novels, or video game manuals. These have their own unique features and structures that students must learn to understand and navigate in order to successfully comprehend them.

Coiro (2003) has observed that Internet texts are complex documents that create unique reading experiences for each individual. Internet texts are not bound together like traditional books with a clear beginning and end. Instead, they often have multiple links within them that allow readers to travel to different pages within the same website or that can connect them to information on different websites created by different authors (Lawless, Schrader, & Mayall, 2007). Thus, the reading experience becomes different for each person, with no two people likely to experience it in the same way.

Additionally, online texts often contain multiple forms of media such as videos, music or sound, and cartoons. All of these forms can be on a single page or connected by links. Additionally, some websites offer a comment or forum area where readers can share their thoughts and respond to what others have said. This feature makes reading online a more interactive process where individuals can shape their learning not just through multiple texts and media forms but through direct discussion with people all around the world.

Finally, the enormous quantity of information available to students through online texts is not always readily apparent. Accessing information through online texts requires students to recognize that some information is "hidden" and requires clicking on links to connect with additional texts or media (Coiro & Dobler, 2007). This type of reading requires a great deal of self-direction and focus on the part of the student. As students navigate the Internet, they must pay attention to what they have and have not learned, what they still need to find, and have specific ideas for how to go about finding the still needed information.

SKILLS AND STRATEGIES REQUIRED
FOR ONLINE READING

Reading online texts also requires students to use a broad range of skills. Some skills such as identifying facts or synthesizing information are the same ones students use when reading print-based texts (Wilder & Dressman, 2006). Other skills, such as conducting a search and identifying appropriate websites, are more specific to reading online texts and may be new to many students.

Coiro (2003) noted four critical skills that adolescents need to be successful in reading online. First, they need to consider how to identify a website that meets their needs. Identifying an appropriate web page requires students to use a search engine. As in looking in an index or table of contents, students have to know one or more key words in order to locate information about their topic. However, unlike traditional print-based texts, a search engine provides students with an enormous array of results listing sources simply too numerous to evaluate (Eliopoulos & Gotlieb, 2003). Rather than have to review a short number of pages, students may find themselves with literally hundreds or thousands of websites being suggested to them for possible review. Even when students identify the best keywords and search for a topic, they do not necessarily know how to interpret the returned results or focus on the most relevant websites listed (Henry, 2006).

Second, students need to know how to navigate within a website in order to find the information they need. While this process requires scrolling up and down to read a page, it also means students have to determine which links within the page, if any, they should select. In traditional texts, students can skim headings and read the index to identify places that will likely be most helpful. In an online environment, however, students must recognize that the information they seek may well be "hidden" and require clicking on links within the website to access additional forms of text (Coiro & Dobler, 2007). This more convoluted process may require students to make a large number of predictions and a greater number of inferences than when reading traditional texts.

Third, students must be able to distinguish information that is indisputably factually accurate from an author's personal opinions and theories. As a result, they must take precautions to assure that the information presented to them is truthful and accurate. In the process, they must consider how reputable and reliable each important online source really is (Coiro, 2003). Students—particularly those who have spent only a limited amount of time reading online—may not be able to recognize advertisements on the web or may not take into account who wrote a particular text and their purposes for doing so. Therefore, just as with traditional texts, students need to be able to analyze, assess, and critically review the information that is presented.

Finally, students need to be able to synthesize what they have learned. This task often requires students to put together ideas across multiple documents. Given that these documents can take on multiple forms and have varying purposes, students will need to be able to do more than communicate a list of facts. Thus, a more critical approach to reading is demanded in the online realm.

THE ROLE OF PRIOR KNOWLEDGE IN STUDENTS' COMPREHENSION OF ONLINE TEXTS

Having students read online texts requires an understanding of their prior knowledge and their experience with online texts. Prior knowledge refers to what students already know about a topic. As students read a piece of text, they have to be able to connect that information to their prior understanding about a topic. Students' prior knowledge will differ on any given topic. For example, a student who lives on a farm will have a much different kind of knowledge about animals than a student who owns a dog or who has never had a pet. These differing degrees of prior knowledge can influence students' interactions with and comprehension of online texts.

Reading online texts adds a whole new dimension to prior knowledge and comprehension. In addition to what students know about a particular topic, their prior knowledge of and experience with online texts also come into play. Students who are more successful in comprehending online texts are better able to draw on their prior knowledge about a topic when searching for or reading more online texts (Coiro & Dobler, 2007).

There is conflicting information regarding the role of prior knowledge and its relationship to comprehending online texts. Cromley and Azevdo (2009) found that middle school students with more prior knowledge about a topic were better able to locate relevant websites more quickly than students with limited prior knowledge. However, Coiro (2009) found that students' ability to comprehend online texts may be connected to how successfully they can apply the skills mentioned earlier in this discussion. Coiro's study of middle school students showed that students who possessed little prior knowledge and had only limited online reading skills had the greatest difficulty in comprehending online texts. When students had little prior knowledge but strong online reading skills, the relative lack of prior knowledge did not have a negative effect on how well they could comprehend online texts.

Coiro's (2009) study showed that students with only limited online reading skills often read online texts at a slower rate than students with average or better online reading skills. The former also had difficulty in focusing their attention on the many details and images presented to them in online texts. Rather than type keywords into search engines, students with limited online reading abilities might type keywords directly into the URL box followed by ".com" to see if they can find the texts they need.

> All students, not just those positioned as struggling readers, can experience difficulties in comprehending online texts just as easily as they can experience success.

The research conducted by Coiro (2009) and Cromley and Azevdo (2009) found that all students, not just those positioned as struggling readers, can experience difficulties in comprehending online texts just as easily as they can experience success. In developing lessons that use online texts, teachers should try to be well informed about students' prior knowledge of the given subject matter as well as their skills in engaging with the online environment. Although marginalized readers may possess limited prior knowledge on many school topics, they are no more likely than good readers to have inferior online skills—particularly if they have had extensive online experience either at school or at home. Therefore, how students get positioned as readers based on print-based texts has little to no bearing on how well they can read texts online.

TEACHERS' EXPERIENCES IN USING ONLINE TEXTS AND DEVELOPING NEW LITERACIES

Part of helping students develop new literacies and become better readers of online texts requires examining your own experiences with these texts, thinking about the value you place on them, and looking at how your instruction does or does not support students' reading development in this area. While you personally might feel comfortable getting online, finding the information you need, and applying what you find in your life, how comfortable are you in helping students engage in these practices? To what extent do you already engage students in reading online texts and for what purposes?

Middle grade teachers tend to focus on helping students acquire basic literacy skills and often believe that such instruction is more important than helping students develop new literacies that are connected to reading Internet texts (Mallette, Henk, Waggoner, & DeLaney, 2005). Acquiring an understanding of comprehension strategies, text structure, and the ability to analyze information is often viewed as a skill set that must be learned separately from online reading. This attitude can result in a stultifying perspective where one comes to view print-based and online texts as so divergent that they must be used independently of each other.

Of course, from the viewpoint of literacy as a social practice, texts are used interchangeably as needed to fit specific requirements, and students must be encouraged to seek out knowledge in a variety of communications media, writing genres, and text types. While students need instruction that teaches them how to engage with both online and print-based texts, how texts are selected and used should also be based on the intended object or purpose of the lesson (McVee, Bailey, & Shanahan, 2008). However, most teachers lack sufficient information to competently design reading activities that engage students productively in online reading (Lei, 2009). When teachers do receive such instruction themselves, it often focuses more on understanding technology and how to use specific programs rather than on the different skills that students need to successfully engage with these technologies and how to develop them.

Additionally, schools often serve as institutions whose primary goal is to indoctrinate students into a "singular, accepted school-based literacy, which is an academic Discourse controlled by teacher instruction and based on a particular curriculum" (Hagood, 2000). This singular form of literacy may not always value new literacy practices or may not value them in the ways that students use them in their lives. Having spent a significant amount of time in schools themselves teachers may have special difficulty facing the dilemma of what types of literacy to encourage or value.

Helping students develop their abilities to read online requires that you be aware of their prior knowledge as well as your own prior knowledge and experience with new literacies and online reading. It also means fairly evaluating your own instruction and curriculum, that is, considering how online reading is integrated alongside print-based texts, how often students are expected to engage with these texts, the purposes they are expected to use them for, and the ways they are expected to read, write, and discuss them. While doing this type of evaluation is highly personal, it can open up windows for seeing what literacy practices are privileged or marginalized in your classroom and create spaces for struggling readers to become full participants.

USING THE INTERNET IN ELA CLASSES

There are multiple approaches to using the Internet in ELA classes. In the sections that follow we look at three approaches that provide you with a diverse set of strategies that can help struggling readers improve their reading of a variety of texts. First, we explore how to connect online reading with students' funds of knowledge. Next, we look at how to develop and use online discussions to engage students in talking about texts. Finally, we discuss how to use online texts to deepen and expand students' knowledge about issues discussed in print-based texts.

Using the Internet to Connect Reading Practices to Everyday Life and Student Interests

Given that struggling readers often feel disconnected from classroom reading practices, finding ways to connect their interests to the curriculum can motivate them to become more engaged (Margolis & McCabe, 2006). When struggling readers believe that a reading task can help them achieve a *personal* goal, they may be more willing to participate despite the difficulty of the task. Internet texts can help students connect the reading practices of the ELA discipline with their experiences and interests outside of school, resulting in the creation of a third space.

As was noted in Chapter 2, third-space reading practices help students apply what they know and do outside of school to the academic literacies they are developing in school. As a result, students are more likely to see the relevance of what they are being taught to their everyday lives. Engaging in third-space reading practices does not mean removing academic literacies and curriculum topics from your classroom. Rather, it means finding ways to use the Internet that capitalize on students' interests while helping them learn traditional curriculum and develop their reading abilities.

For example, Eagleton, Guinee, and Langlais (2003) studied eighth graders in an ELA class who were given the assignment to use print and Internet texts to research someone who was a hero to them. The students initially discussed what it meant to be a hero but were individually free to create their own definition of the term. They were then provided instructions on how to conduct an effective search for their hero, including how to identify relevant keywords and find the most useful websites.

Eagleton et al. (2003) noted that students were motivated and engaged with the hero project, since it allowed them to utilize online texts and connected them with a hero they were interested in learning more about. However, some students also encountered difficulties in completing the project. Many began the project having difficulty selecting keywords for their hero and needed consistent help in analyzing their search engine results. These difficulties were not limited to struggling readers, as the authors noting that "the Internet inquiry process is a challenging task for all middle school learners" (p. 28).

A different way to connect literacy practices to the lives of struggling middle school readers was explored by O'Brien et al. (2007). In their 2-year study, they focused on engaging struggling readers in practices that were intended to "explore ideas, construct community, and develop agency in meeting personally relevant goals—practices *other than* reading and writing activities geared toward meeting standards, improving test performance, and meeting specific pre-targeted curricular outcomes" (p. 55). They found that many of the students entered the study with a low self-concept and sense of agency. However, over time many students began to feel better about themselves as readers and take charge of their learning and involvement with classroom reading practices. Because the students typically found their involvement with Internet texts and other new literacy practices to be motivating factors, many of them likely participated more than they normally would.

Despite the success both of these studies showed, O'Brien et al. (2007) highlighted a critical tension that exists in working with struggling readers. While third-space reading practices can help struggling readers find ways to participate more actively, they do not automatically change their

While third-space reading practices can help struggling readers find ways to participate more actively, they do not automatically change their status as struggling readers in school.

status as struggling readers in school. Not only do struggling readers bring with them the negative messages many of them have received about themselves as readers, but also they likely continue to receive those messages, both implicitly and explicitly, throughout the school day. Until such messages cease to exist, students will likely experience tension over the issue of how much to engage in classroom reading practices and what they think they are capable of doing.

Using the Internet to Respond to Texts

Having students read and respond to texts is a central component of the ELA curriculum. The Internet provides a different medium for students to read, reflect on, and discuss texts that they may be assigned to read. By using the Internet, students have the opportunity to be more reflective and to locate and evaluate supporting information for their interpretations (Black, 2005).

As students read a text, they can use the Internet to post their reactions or insights in a variety of ways. One way is to engage in an asynchronous discussion by using an online discussion board. Discussion threads allow for teachers to post specific questions that all students must respond to as well as provide space for students to begin their own threads that focus on questions that are central to them. Students can also maintain blogs and use them as vehicles for commenting on texts. Blogs can sometimes be challenging, as they require students to navigate to different websites to read what their peers have posted. Some students may get more traffic and responses to their blog than others, resulting in some students feeling more isolated.

Engaging students in online responses to texts, particularly through an asynchronous discussion format, can have multiple benefits. First, students must write out their thoughts. This process can help students become more critical and reflective on what they are saying. Second, writing online is also highly interactive (Grabill & Hicks, 2005). As soon as students post a response, they can get feedback almost instantly from their peers or teachers. Students can participate more often and at a higher volume than they can in a traditional face-to-face discussion. Rather than waiting to be called on, students can begin to participate immediately. Finally, students' written responses serve as a record that they can revisit and draw on as their interpretations develop further.

Responding to texts online can take on a dimension that more traditional written responses do not usually allow for. Rather than compose a short written response, students can insert links to other online texts or include videos and other sources of media that can support their interpretations of a text, present other points of view, or raise questions. Having students create multimodal responses requires them to engage in many of the skills discussed earlier, including evaluating the source of a text and its author and considering the degree of authority that the text brings to bear on other arguments or interpretations (Swenson, Young, McGrail, Rozema, & Whitin, 2006).

Connecting Literature-Based Projects with Internet Texts

Students can also engage with online reading to deepen their knowledge about the ideas presented in novels and young adult literature as well as learn about the authors who have written them. O'Brien et al. (2009) argue that students need to be able to analyze and respond to what characters say and do in literature by understanding the larger sociocultural and historical framework those characters operate in. Engaging in such interpretations, in their view, requires students not only to empathize with what characters experience but also to "critically reflect on characters' experiences in different and social political worlds, which force them to grapple with the dialogic tensions constituted by conflicting cultural perspectives" (p. 91).

Students can use the Internet to identify and read texts that give them a broader perspective on the social and cultural influences that shape what happens in a text. For example, when reading the historical fiction book *Catherine, Called Birdy* (Cushman, 1995), students might benefit from learning more about the era in which the book took place and what life was like in England at that time. Students' first reaction might be to do a search using the keywords "1290" and "England," which would return thousands or even millions of results.

However, understanding the actions the characters in Cushman's text engage in requires more than understanding basic historical facts. Students need to understand the role of women during that time, the history of classism, and how these beliefs shaped what was considered right and normal. As students learn more about the major issues that are central to the book, they can also consider how these issues are present in their own lives today.

SUMMARY

Using Internet texts in ELA classrooms has great potential for all students, particularly struggling readers. First, students who are labeled as struggling readers often acquired that label based on how they engaged with print-based texts. If students positioned as struggling readers in school regularly read online texts, they may develop higher levels of comprehension than might normally be expected. Additionally, reading online may be difficult for most students. The majority of middle school students will likely need significant help in acquiring the skills needed to locate, analyze, and evaluate content on the Internet.

By connecting online texts to common ELA practices, such as reading, responding, and discussing print-based texts, students can develop their online reading comprehension abilities while furthering their academic content knowledge. The practices outlined in this chapter show how print-based and online texts can constructively be used in conjunction with each other. Using both types of texts simultaneously enables students to draw on multiple texts to create interpretations and arguments while applying what they learn to their everyday lives.

Questions for Reflection

1. In what ways do you engage students in reading online texts and for what purposes?

2. What literacy practices are privileged in your classroom or school? How do these privileged practices support or marginalize new literacies?

3. How do your students use the Internet in and outside of school? How can you capitalize on their experiences and knowledge to teach ELA content better?

RECOMMENDED RESOURCES

College of Education at North Carolina State University. (2010). *New Literacies Collaborative.* Retrieved March 9, 2010, from *newlitcollaborative.ning. com*

Lankshear, C., & Knobel, M. (2006). *New literacies: Everyday practices and classroom learning.* Philadelphia: Open University Press.

Leu, D. (2010). *The New Literacies Research Team.* Retrieved March 9, 2010, from *www.newliteracies.uconn.edu*

11

Using Nonprint Media and Texts to Support Marginalized Readers

Stergios G. Botzakis

FOCAL POINTS

1. Reading is performed not just with books, poems, and short stories but also with such other texts and media as graphic novels, movies, television programs, and the Internet.

2. Critically reading varied texts and media can help struggling students to develop the requisite skills typically taught in ELA classes, such as making inferences, analyzing texts and social situations, and making informed decisions with the information that they gather.

More so than ever, students need to be able to read, examine, and respond to texts in diverse media formats. They watch television programs and decide to what extent they wish to emulate the characters and events they view or to buy the products advertised. They go online and read movie reviews to decide whether they want to see a film. They text one another various messages, create videos to post on YouTube, and take part in digital communities like Facebook and MySpace. Some play video games that allow them to interact with people around the world to complete missions or just be sociable.

Stergios G. Botzakis, PhD, is Assistant Professor of Adolescent Literacy in the Department of Theory and Practice in Teacher Education at the University of Tennessee, Knoxville.

Students use diverse technologies on a daily basis, and part of teaching them to participate in the contemporary world includes teaching them to be literate and how to deal successfully with the various texts they encounter.

Students use diverse technologies on a daily basis, and part of teaching them to participate in the contemporary world includes teaching them to be literate and how to deal successfully with the various texts they encounter. This undertaking can range from observing simple courtesies, such as not talking on one's cell phone while ordering at a restaurant (Frey & Fisher, 2008), to harnessing digital technologies to read and create audio, video, and images to communicate and demonstrate learning.

The purpose of this chapter is to show how teachers can help marginalized readers learn to read critically a wide variety of texts and media sources. Print texts in particular have long been accepted in ELA classrooms, but the newer media are often seen as distractions or obstacles to students' proper education. One can easily find articles about how video games cause violence, cartoons and TV shows make minds dull, and music lyrics present racy and inappropriate messages youth should not hear. However, a reality that ELA educators have to deal with is that print is no longer the only *or even the primary* source of information and entertainment for 21st-century youth, as there are televisions, radios, computers, video games, and other technologies conveying texts people interact with daily. Multimedia texts are so pervasive that they "no longer just shape our culture—they are our culture" (Thoman & Jolls, 2004, p. 18).

Critical media literacy is a hybrid of critical literacy and new technologies. Critical literacy involves using language (reading, writing, thinking, listening, and speaking) to discuss "how power is used in texts and by individuals to privilege one group over another" (Johnson & Freedman, 2005, p. 2). It has long been embedded in a part of such ELA activities as reading multicultural literature, examining language use, eliciting reader responses, and engaging in classroom dialogue to think about and comprehend academic texts and content (Fecho, 2004). The media portion of critical media literacy comes from the new technologies and media that make up our world in the 21st century and beyond. Critical media literacy entails using critical literacy skills to examine and respond to media texts.

As was noted in Chapter 2, print-based literature has dominated the ELA discipline as a result of its unique history, even today when such texts are not always central to people's primary literacy experiences. Educators should keep in mind that the texts themselves are not always so central to ELA education as are the thinking, reasoning skills, and appreciation invested in them. Moreover, creating a relevant curriculum and supportive environment for marginalized readers in ELA classrooms (as discussed in Chapter 3) where they may be possible or even primary knowers (Auckerman, 2007) requires that teachers acknowledge and include diverse media, but educators must also ensure that these media are read critically, as with any traditional print texts.

HOW TEACHING CRITICAL MEDIA LITERACY HELPS MARGINALIZED READERS

Not being able to control the direction of a discussion completely or teach a specific curriculum topic as planned may seem like a drawback associated with incorporating a critical media literacy approach in ELA classrooms. Some teachers believe that taking time to discuss students' own views and opinions takes away time better spent in covering such traditional curricular standbys as literary devices, symbolism, or analysis. Others do not like the loss of control that can accompany unfettered critical discussion in class (Fecho & Botzakis, 2007).

However, developing one's critical media literacy has significant rewards for marginalized readers. First, using critical media literacy to frame discussions about texts encourages *all* students to participate (Johnson & Freedman, 2005). In creating a learning environment where all students can be primary or at least possible knowers, critical media literacy activities key in on one area that many marginalized students are expert, namely, power relations. As they have long struggled with reading academic texts by the time they reach middle school, they know what it's like to be positioned as undesirable and feel powerless. They have serious thoughts and feelings about such situations, and the insights that marginalized readers can provide in critical responses to texts can help peers better relate to the issues and content of texts they are reading.

Second, exploring critical media literacy more fully brings texts into the ELA classroom that students use in their daily lives. Because of the personal funds of knowledge (Moll & Gonzalez, 2001) that students bring to these nonprint and media texts, there is a reduced cognitive load for marginalized readers. With little need to learn or decipher background or contextual knowledge because it is already familiar to them, marginalized readers can focus more on immediate comprehension and act as primary knowers. Being such experts lends a level of comfort and engagement that may be a new and positive experience for these students (Alvermann, 2001a; O'Brien, 2006).

When marginalized readers are able to actively employ their funds of knowledge, it enables them to demonstrate expertise that, in turn, can transform what and how teachers teach. Students who engage in critical

When marginalized readers are able to actively employ their funds of knowledge, it enables them to demonstrate expertise that, in turn, can transform what and how teachers teach.

media literacy are more likely to draw on their background knowledge to help them comprehend texts (Hobbs, 2007). Instead of focusing simply on such straightforward details as ones relating to plot and character, discussions can branch out to more complex ideas relating to conflict, symbolism, or other analyses. When critical media literacy is the key focus, students can draw on and critique a wider range of textual sources enabling even marginalized readers to find real value and engagement in ELA education.

Bringing media into the ELA classroom is not about "dumbing things down" but rather about creating learning situations where marginalized readers can use their background knowledge to maximum advantage. The nonprint and multiple media texts they consume every day can be used for teaching academic reading skills and strategies, and teachers can heighten students' participation by allowing them to learn and apply literacy skills by using texts in formats they know and feel comfortable with. Used in conjunction with traditional print texts in English, newer media emphatically support rather than hinder higher motivation, engagement, and achievement. In what follows, I specifically address how such connections can be made in practice, using media to inculcate the reading skills most needed in ELA classes.

WHAT'S A TEXT? WHAT IS READING?

ELA education has been influenced by "cross-disciplinary fertilization" (Hobbs, 2007, p. 6) among literary, cultural, media, and communication studies, which results in a broad and more encompassing definition of what constitutes a text and what it means to read one. Texts here are defined as "all forms of symbolic expression that convey meaning from authors to readers" (Hobbs, 2007, p. 7), including words but also images, colors, sounds, patterns, movements, or other things that can be interpreted to "make meaning" (or read).

Historically speaking, the concept of "reading" has applied more broadly to a number of different communication acts, including body language, identifying emotion based a person's facial expressions, clues from clothing and lifestyle attributes, indications of animals' passage from their tracks, and the "reading" of future events from tea leaves and of past calamities from the patterns of rock strata in canyons (Manguel, 1997). Currently, people read a great number of things in online contexts, on television, and in video games utilizing various combinations of texts, images, sounds, and movements. However, still there is an overwhelming inclination in ELA classes to focus almost exclusively on printed texts, despite marginalized readers' special difficulties in reading print in isolation.

When it comes to reading in traditional ELA classes, reading comprehension is important but often taken for granted as only the first stop on the way to explicating more literary analysis. In this rarified atmosphere, marginalized readers often find it difficult to contribute meaningfully, as they are much more familiar with concrete activities designed to assist in raising their reading scores or building their basic reading skills (Meier & Wood, 2004). The more abstract tasks demanded of them in middle school may not be so familiar to them, but critical media activities could well prove helpful in making connections with these students so that they get at least a glimpse of the ultimate intended goals of such instruction. Students' close familiarity with various media sources could well provide them a headstart in undertaking certain literary analyses, as their diverse and esoteric reading habits might well counteract a number of the typical reading comprehension problems that normally disincentivize their reading of print texts.

In this chapter, texts to be examined are not simply limited to books, essays, short stories, and poems but also extend to television commercials, movies, songs, websites, and almost any other item that falls under the umbrella term of *text*. In order to develop a greater understanding of these more nontraditional texts, first let us take a look at how they are typically constructed. Then I present activities that cross over a number of media—from television to literature to film—that can help readers of all kinds to develop the ability to critically read texts and media.

Grammars

All texts—not just print-based genres—have sets of rules that make them work. ELA educators are probably most familiar with the traditional grammar of literature, including conventional spelling, sentence construction, semantics, tone, plot structure, and symbolism, for example. Other media and technologies also use their own particular grammars to convey meaning (New London Group. 1996), whether the grammars seem obvious or even invisible. Since a central goal of reading in ELA is to analyze texts, it is important that teachers examine, break down, and teach these grammars in their classes. It can be difficult, though, to identify which features should be focused on, taught, and used for reading. Below I include synopses of the grammars of some multimedia texts that should be used in ELA class to help all students read well.

Literature

Literature is probably the most familiar genre to ELA educators, so I will not go into much detail here. Plot and character are what many people attend to when reading, but analyses of narrative structure, figurative language, conflicts, symbolism, and themes are also part of the grammar of literature.

For the purposes of this chapter, I use John Knowles's novel *A Separate Peace* (1960) as the example of a literature text. In my experience, this novel about boys attending a New England prep school during the 1940s elicits varied responses from students and teachers, depending on where it was assigned. When I taught at an all-boys prep school, it was relatively well received because students could readily relate to the setting and social situations. The antagonism between the two main characters, Gene, the narrator, a southerner who is somewhat of an outsider at the school, and Finny, his roommate who is an excellent athlete but somewhat pushy, is something they can understand and talk about. In an urban middle school context, however, I got a much different response, with many students wanting to know why we were even reading a book about rich white kids who had no real problems. Of course, in both environments the novel lived up to its potential for involving students in multiple aspects of literary grammar, as defined above.

Film/Television

To begin to speak about such visual media as film or television, teachers and students should become familiar with the terms associated with each medium. Doing so builds a vocabulary and establishes a framework to which even marginalized readers can readily relate, just as one seeks to do in teaching vocabulary associated with the traditional elements of literature (Kist, 2005). Helping students learn to read visual media requires knowledge of specific types of shots, such as long shots or close-ups; transitions, such as pans or jump cuts; and camera angles, framing, and pacing. Additionally, blocking, lighting, music, and costuming also come into play.

Some of these visual characteristics are genre-related. For instance, if someone knows he or she is watching a romantic comedy, there is the expectation that two people will fall in love, face complications, and then eventually reunite for a happy ending. In the course of the story, one would expect to find lots of visual shorthand, such as a closeup shot of hand-holding or a kiss to communicate the couple's love for each other, or a shot of someone slamming a door and walking away at a point of conflict. When the couple is apart, sad music might be included in the soundtrack. If there is a wedding at the end, a montage of various characters' faces to show their emotions at how the tale concludes or perhaps a group shot might suggest the idea of a new, larger family.

These types of common conversations are used strategically by filmmakers to help people make sense of film, just as their word choices are crafted by authors to create certain literary effects and tones. The visual aspects of film also are analogous to the types of devices and figurative language that many fact-oriented learners sometimes struggle with in academic reading. Films also use symbolism, for example, but in ways that marginalized readers are far more familiar with than in their reading of print-only texts. Space does not allow for delineating all the grammatical features of film here, or their analogues in print-based literature, but a good reference for ELA teachers on film and television is John Golden's (2001) *Reading in the Dark*.

Graphic Novels

Just as with film, graphic novels have their own system of symbols that teachers can use to teach literary devices. The grammar of graphic novels is based on features that create meaning, such as the panels, angles, facial expressions, motion lines, or thought balloons used in illustrations (Jacobs, 2007; McCloud, 1993). Panels are the squares that contain the action; motion lines usually depict someone running or falling down, and thought balloons allow the reader to see a character's inner dialogue, operating much like a soliloquy in a play.

Graphic novels also use what Yang (2008) calls "visual permanence," the idea that a comic image may give the illusion of motion and time passing while yet remaining static. Visual permanence can work well in helping marginalized readers understand the idea of figurative language in academic print-based texts. For example, it can be used to speak about how one can tell a graphic novel image is supposed to be set in a sinister, scary place (based on interpreting its series of dark, increasingly smaller panels) and can be compared to how an author like Edgar Allan Poe could produce the same effect with words. Using visual cues might be extended to help marginalized readers appreciate how figurative or symbolic language works. In other words, by helping marginalized readers see how graphic novels work, teachers can also help them realize how essentially the same effects are achieved in traditional academic texts.

Mass Media

Mass media cover a wide range of texts, from print to electronic to audio. A great number of features can be included in such a grammar, and these vary by the specific medium being discussed. Mainly, the mass media are focused on the amount of attention they can grab and sustainably hold onto (Lanham, 2001). The features that are manipulated in order to attract that attention should be the subject of detailed analysis in ELA classes.

In the case of magazine advertisements and newspapers, font types, size, color, and layout figure greatly into how meaning is successfully conveyed. Take, for instance, how the front page of a newspaper attempts to draw the reader's eyes to particular headlines or photos. In television commercials, imagery, the soundtrack, tone, and movement are the chief tools used to send the viewer a message. They often include peppy or sentimental jingles and feature bright colors so as to instantly stimulate feelings of ease, cleanliness, desire, and happiness on the part of viewers. In video games, camera angles, jump cuts, motion, music, color, text scrolling, and sound effects combine to create the typically exciting "reading" experience. Although a player is normally sitting in a static position, on screen it may appear that his or her character is traversing a perilous landscape, constantly battling enemies and celebrating victories or completed tasks. In point of fact, the relatively motionless video game player is highly active cognitively when immersed in the typical gaming environment.

Reflecting the foregoing descriptions, it is clear that there are myriad types of texts, and there is not space enough here to describe them all. But for teachers who understand the need to use these types of texts to support marginalized readers, the raw materials that can be used for thought, appreciation, and analyses in English classrooms are not only available but rich and plentiful in 21st-century multimedia texts. In the section that follows I describe activities that draw upon these various texts and their grammars to teach marginalized readers in ELA classrooms.

HAVING CONVERSATIONS ABOUT
CRITICAL MEDIA LITERACY

The questions often asked in critical media literacy activities provide a framework for comprehension of a great number of texts, whether fictional, informational, or some other variety. For example, the Center for Media Literacy (2004) provides the following five questions for critical media study:

1. Who created the message?
2. What creative techniques are used to attract my attention?

3. How might other people understand this message differently from me?
4. What lifestyles, values, and points of view are represented in—or omitted from—this message?
5. Why is this message being sent?

These five questions get at both concrete and abstract ideas simultaneously and provide a platform for critical thought and discussion. I have used these questions with my middle school teacher education classes to analyze text and examine how different media portray the same kinds of things. In order to examine and juxtapose media images, I make a chart using the five Center for Media Literacy questions above and make three other columns for comparing different types of media that share a similar topic. I do this after I have taught about the different types of grammars that media types use, because the grammar of each text figures strongly in questions 2 and 4.

One of the most popular activities in my middle school and teacher education classes is comparing how chickens are portrayed in a variety of sources. I include a variety of texts to analyze, including a Purdue chicken magazine ad, a PETA comic book titled *A Chick's Life,* and a Burger King commercial for the "tendercrisp" chicken sandwich. Such comparisons have always generated talk of authors' intentions and also great discussions about animal rights, agriculture, where our food comes from, and vegetarianism—all in the context of learning how texts are structured in different ways to convey meaning and influence interpretation.

The following responses come from doing this activity with the Burger King advertisement (available for viewing at *www.youtube.com/watch?v=eQENCnAhEXk*):

> "The music made it interesting. Also that it sounds like they're saying a swear word."
> "They made the sandwich look huge. It took up the whole screen! The real sandwich isn't that big."
> "I think that this sandwich is meant for boys. It looks like it's for cowboys. Girls would like diet food, healthier food."

Even though these comments come from prospective middle school teachers, I can easily imagine a middle schooler making similar statements.

While these sample reactions do not capture the full range of their responses, they do convey the idea that critical media literacy connections were being made. Teachers were discussing how advertising works and how it is structured to influence consumers of text. They were also getting at gender differences and how things could be pitched and structured variously to communicate with boys versus girls. Finally, they were also drawing connections between textual modes so that this activity was not presumed to be relevant to only one medium or another.

Although I might not always rely specifically on these questions, they are a great starting point for marginalized readers as analytical tools for increasing the relevance of academic work and supporting both response and comprehension. They are the starting point for our reading activities and discussion, providing a framework for marginalized readers to at least partially ground their understanding.

CONTINUING THE CONVERSATION: CRITICAL MEDIA LITERACY AND RHETORICAL TECHNIQUES

Research has shown that critical media literacy is good for more than generating discussions (Hobbs, 2007; Morrell, 2004). Engaging students in critical media literacy has produced improvement of reading comprehension in 11th-grade ELA students, particularly in identifying and summarizing the main idea of a news article and identifying details of what they read. Although these results were with high school students, similar activities are being encouraged with students in upper elementary school (e.g., Botzakis, 2007, 2009) and by many states' middle grade ELA standards in the area of propaganda (e.g., Tennessee Department of Education, 2009).

Another area where a media literacy activity can be useful is in delineating rhetorical strategies that can be used in persuasive writing. Commercial directors use a great number of persuasive techniques in their work, and being able to identify and describe them is one of the first steps to critical response and a helpful tool for students creating their own persuasive works—core goals of the ELA curriculum. Once the class creates its list of rhetorical techniques, members could be assigned to create an opinion piece, with students either selecting a favorite technique or being assigned a specific one to use.

Even the timeworn topic of whether or not school uniforms should be mandated in every district might take on refreshingly new trappings if the assignment were to produce a video on the subject. Instead of students writing a persuasive essay, they would have to create an opinion piece that would be scripted, recorded, and shared in class or with an administrator. The persuasive writing would be done for a specific audience and in a manner relevant to students' lives, and it would capitalize on students' interest in and enjoyment of video technology.

Any videos produced could easily be uploaded to YouTube or another such website, for more people to enjoy watching as well. The presentation could also be done by using PowerPoint, as a skit, or as a full-page ad for a newspaper. Having an audience and a practical purpose will likely motivate students to create a maximally persuasive and polished new-media product. As a bonus to both teachers *and* students, this type of activity familiarizes students with alternative media fulfilling state educational requirements.

> **Having an audience and a practical purpose motivates students to create maximally persuasive and polished new-media products. As a bonus for both teachers** *and* **students, this type of activity familiarizes students with alternative media while simultaneously fulfilling state educational requirements.**

Reading Pictures: Making Inferences and Summaries

Making inferences from a text can be difficult for marginalized readers, but many can more readily make inferences from graphic novel images in an almost unconscious manner (Frey & Fisher, 2004). Marginalized readers may struggle with making inferences from texts because of their reading comprehension and vocabulary difficulties, but they may feel more at ease making predictions and observations from pictures. Students can make quite complex, informed, and insightful comments about even a small set of pictures, and this ability can then be extrapolated into the world of more traditional texts. The use of a comic or graphic novel format here provides a more comfortable nonthreatening entry into more complex thinking and learning.

Many students struggle with summarizing what they have read almost as much as they struggle with inference making. I have used graphic novels to cover this skill as well. I do a critical reading exercise with my classes by using a page-long cartoon from *Will Eisner's New York: Life in the Big City* (Eisner, 2006, p. 101) called "Prisons." There are no other words on the page. On this page are four small vignettes: a young boy with a baseball glove looking out of his snow covered window and standing in front of a table full of medicines; an apparently well-off woman standing small and alone, looking out of her huge penthouse window; a homeless person looking in on a butler; and two men eating sandwiches at work, one in an office with a phone to his ear, the other outside on a scaffold for washing windows.

I cover the title of the cartoon and ask my students what they think it might be. I get numerous kinds of responses, such as "Windows," "Sorrow," "Trapped," or "Waiting." I have the students individually explain why they chose the title they did and how the title applies to all four scenes. In the course of this discussion students have to flesh out the inferences they have made from each vignette in the picture. These details are then collected into a main point that embodies their title.

Afterward I tell my students what title Eisner used, we discuss how well that title applies, and then finally we compare and contrast his choice to theirs. During the course of the discussion, I also pose a few other questions, such as "Who do you think is the most free?" or "Who has it the worst?" I really enjoy hearing the long, detailed reasons students share in their responses. When I conduct the "Prisons" cartoon activity, I find that I get participation from almost all corners of the classroom, with students who typically remain quiet contributing and marginalized readers acting as primary knowers.

> The "Prisons" cartoon activity can stimulate participation from almost all corners of the classroom, with students who typically remain quiet contributing and marginalized readers acting as primary knowers.

Video Games and Narrative Structure

Sometimes dealing with text details and the making of inferences needs to be scaffolded, as many marginalized readers have difficulty in seeing "the big picture" while reading. In those cases, teachers might scaffold their reading by first teaching students plot structure and sequence and only then teaching them to summarize what they were reading. Video games offer complex plots, often broken down into episodes, that are highly relatable to story-mapping activities typically used in schools to help students learn and understand common academic text structures.

Even games as simple as Pac-Man have a plot, and more contemporary ones such as Halo or the Star Wars: Knights of the Old Republic have sophisticated, layered storylines. In Knights of the Old Republic, for example, the protagonist begins the game as a Jedi who has had his memory completely wiped out. He must escape from the devious actions of a Sith lord bent on destroying all Jedi. The player creates a new identity for the character, leads him through adventures where he accomplishes tasks, amasses artifacts, and makes allies. At the end of the game, the player learns he is actually Revan, the mentor of the Sith adversary he has been fleeing, and a confrontation between the mentor and his treacherous student then ensues.

Having students who are familiar with this game—or ones like it—stop to record what occurs at each level of play is the same task as summarizing what happens in a typical chapter from a novel. Students need to be able to determine which details to include and to provide reasons for why certain actions or objects are important in the grand scheme of the story. In short, they must make connections between the details and overall plot structure of the narrative, a task long associated with ELA instruction and frequently a source of frustration among marginalized readers. Video games can provide a background where marginalized readers—perhaps already familiar with the plot, characters, and settings—can focus more on the work of analyzing the text rather than having to learn about it for the first time.

LITERARY ANALYSES WITH MEDIA

When using nonprint texts in ELA classes, one is not confined solely to discussing such concrete tasks as making inferences, producing summaries, and developing reading comprehension but also can launch discussions into more abstract literary concerns. The complexities of images and narratives in these texts lend themselves well to commonly taught and assessed areas of ELA such as character development, close reading, genre comparisons, and connections across texts. I detail a few activities that address these areas below by touching on a variety of texts, including reality television shows, films, and literature.

Exploring Characterization Using Reality Television

Just as novels provide certain details about characters from which readers draw conclusions, so do the directors and stars of reality television programs. Even though they are ostensibly not scripted (and while many would not be appropriate for teaching in middle school classrooms), these shows are presented in a manner that conveys a narrative progression, and students consume them voraciously. Taking a cue from an activity developed by Howley (2007), ELA teachers could use short clips from reality TV shows to explore character development, one of the traditionally studied elements of literary studies.

On *American Idol*, for instance, viewers come to know the various contestants over a period of time. At first, there are many hopefuls who audition. As time progresses, the producers present the background circumstances of some of the contestants, introduce their particular styles and interests, and establish their personalities for the purposes of the program. In the competition that follows viewers see how the various contestants adapt to different song genres, different types of performances, and the pressures of competition. A narrative progression follows each contestant's growth and abilities in the competition, from baby-faced beginner to eventual polished performer.

Working with *American Idol*, teachers can show students clips of one of the singers and then have them write about what each performance says about the artist. The students can report their opinions and include details to support what they feel. Potential areas of discussion about reading and textual grammar come from students' analyses of the program's direction: the lighting choices, the camera angles, any special effects, and the choreography. Students could also discuss the choices made by the singer: the choice of song, the clothes he or she wore, whether or not the contestant played an instrument, and how the contestant presented him- or herself to the audience.

In this activity, character study can be done in a medium that many marginalized readers are quite comfortable with. Many people, including students, watch these programs and have their preferences and tastes already formed. Taking an opportunity to break down and expand on how those choices have been made can help students become more aware of how they interact with media. By writing over the course of several episodes, students can explore how each artist tries to create a narrative and an image to sell to the viewing public to attract votes. Developing a unique personality is just as important as talent in such a competition, and in effect the singers are all creating characters to promote themselves as much as possible.

Comparing Alternate Media Versions

The purpose for viewing any particular media source in ELA class is not simply to watch the movie, say, for its own sake but also to make critical analyses. This process entails simply examining a single scene, comparing two different film versions, or making connections between different types of text, such as the original book compared to the movie. One of the most thoughtful discussions I ever saw about *A Separate Peace* involved an eighth-grade class where the teacher compared the passage in the novel where Finny falls out of the tree with the same scene as enacted in a 5-minute clip from the 1972 movie version of the movie.

The class began to discuss the event by referencing first how it was depicted in the film. One student commented on how dark the whole scene was shot in the film. This statement led the teacher to ask why the students thought the director might have chosen to deliberately obscure one of the most pivotal scenes in the story. Students responded that the director probably wanted to create a sense of mystery about what Gene had done. Some said that the ambient light was so insufficient that Gene likely could not see well and that his actions therefore were accidental. Others suggested that the scene was shot darkly because compositionally the director wanted to adumbrate in this fashion the evil intentions Gene had for his friend. No definitive answer was offered to this question, but the directorial decisions—the "grammar" of the film—made for great springboards for discussions of the director's intentions.

The class next turned to discussion of how the same scene was originally represented in the novel, focusing on the following text (which reflected Gene's perspective):

> Holding firmly to the trunk, I took a step toward him, and then my knees bent and I jounced the limb. Finny, his balance gone, swung his head around to look at me for an instant with extreme interest, and then he tumbled sideways, broke through the little branches below and hit the bank with a sickening, unnatural thud. It was the first clumsy physical action I had ever seen him make. With unthinking sureness I moved out on the limb and jumped into the river, every trace of my fear of this forgotten. (Knowles, 1960, pp. 59–60)

Probably the most important word in the passage is *jounce,* and this passage offered a great opportunity to explore how word choice affects meaning. Students shared what they thought the word meant. Then, the class looked up *jounce* and discovered that it meant "to move in an up-and-down manner."

After seeing the film clip and then reading the short passage, students took sides on whether or not Gene's jouncing of the tree limb was intended to bring harm to Finny. Some students felt that Gene was acting out of jealousy or anger to shake his friend out of the tree. They could say from his facial expression in the film that it appeared he had acted in anger. Others thought that Gene was afraid, unsure, and clumsy at the moment and that his shaking the tree was not malicious in intent. Discussing why someone might shake a tree limb provides marginalized readers the opportunity to express what they think happened in this key moment, and this discussion becomes colored by their views on friendship and jealousy.

This discussion gave the class a question that lingered through their analysis of the rest of the story. In analyzing just this passage, they also looked at why Gene, "with unthinking sureness," leapt into the river, which colored the discussion differently and provided evidence for the debate over his intentions. As we read on, students looked for further evidence about whether Gene would try intentionally to harm Finny. This thought became a driving question that came up again and again as they saw how the plot unfolded. It provided purpose that helped some marginalized readers make more sense of what they were reading. And the presence of both versions allowed readers to draw on evidence from diverse materials and interpretations for their arguments.

SUMMARY

This chapter presented a number of scenarios and activities in which new-media bridges could be constructed to traditional ELA curricula via nonprint texts, including television programs, graphic novel images, TV commercials, and films. Incorporating texts familiar to students into critical media literacy activities can assist them in accomplishing a great number of ELA tasks. These activities also introduce students to diverse content knowledge, including reading comprehension, plot structure, rhetorical devices, characterization, and literary analyses.

However, greater access to technology and the mass media does not necessarily improve students' performance and even magnify the effects teachers have on their lives. Building constructively on students' self-chosen interests may prove beneficial in instructional contexts but does not guarantee student success academically without complementary instruction (Kamil, 2008; Krashen, 2001). Using computers and other types of technology is no guarantee of success or even improvement since they do not automatically create an "even playing field" where students might be motivated to strive harder (Wilder & Dressman, 2006). Mindful, attentive, and effective teachers need to ask challenging questions and create more media-aware instruction to better address the needs of marginalized readers (NCTE, 2004a). But new educational resources alone—however media aware—are not sufficient in themselves to involve marginalized readers without imaginative teachers to share them.

> New educational resources alone—however media-aware—are not sufficient in themselves to successfully involve marginalized readers without imaginative teachers to share them.

Questions for Reflection

1. Which types of texts matter most to you? Are they books, movies, cartoons, websites, television shows, songs, or something else?

2. Which types of texts matter most to your students?

3. Can you see other connections between traditional ELA texts or curriculum and newer types of technology and texts that would work well in your classroom? What are they?

RECOMMENDED RESOURCES

Christel, M. T., & Sullivan, S. (Eds.). (2007). *Lesson plans for creating media-rich classrooms*. Urbana, IL: National Council of Teachers of English.

Golden, J. (2001). *Reading in the dark: Using film as a toll in the English classroom*. Urbana, IL: National Council of Teachers of English.

Morrell, E. (2004). *Linking literacy and popular culture: Finding connections for lifelong learning*. Norwood, MA: Christopher-Gordon.

Xu, S. H., Perkins, R. S., & Zunich, L. O. (2005). *Trading cards to comic strips: Popular culture texts and literacy learning in grades K–8*. Newark, DE: International Reading Association.

12

Relevant Curriculum and Policy for Middle School Struggling Readers

Patience is a virtue, but persistence to the point of success is
a blessing.

—DIAMANDIS (1989)

FOCAL POINTS

1. We have developed considerable knowledge about the conditions and environments needed to support marginalized readers.

2. Current state-mandated curricula and testing systems often prevent teachers from creating the conditions and environments needed to support marginalized readers.

3. Teachers can and should act locally and strategically to enact reform in ways that will help so-called struggling readers.

The approach to reading instruction that we advocate in this volume is relatively straightforward in its conception, but it is neither simple nor easy to implement, given the current state of accountability in 21st-century schools. In order to learn to read and understand the disciplinary literacy they need to participate in English language arts, formerly marginalized readers (and indeed all readers) need teachers who can provide them with goal-oriented explicit instruction, modeling, and practice with a variety of both disciplinary and general texts. They benefit from warm, highly participatory classes in which they have a voice and some choice in both the kinds of material they read and the kinds of tasks they complete to demonstrate learning. They develop confidence when their teachers are demonstrably warm and positive as well as enthusiastic about believing that they can succeed. They are more motivated to learn when they are allowed to read about topics that relate to their everyday lives and interests, and they engage even more when they can strengthen their most valued personal attributes through academic study. They benefit when *all* students are treated as developing readers in a learning community and when labels like "struggling reader" are absent from all conversations about teaching and learning.

However, while these conditions for successful reading instruction are straightforward enough, teachers don't always have the freedom to implement the approaches and instructional practices we know marginalized readers need in order for them to succeed. We know teachers don't always have the autonomy to modify curriculum or to choose when to teach certain concepts that depend on the needs of particular students in different classes. In a system that uses high-stakes standardized tests to evaluate teaching and learning, it's difficult to ignore demands to remediate students who don't meet state standards and are therefore labeled as "struggling." However, researchers are repeatedly finding that "struggling readers" don't necessarily struggle because they are deficient, unintelligent, lazy, or incapable. Rather, they often struggle because the ways in which reading is taught and assessed in school *position them to fail*. Because children are expected to adapt to school instead of the other way around, they are taught using a curriculum that systematically and methodically *decreases* their motivation, comprehension, and opportunities to the point that there is no realistic chance they can improve. In very real ways, the current state of reading instruction *prevents* some middle schoolers from learning to read (Allington, 2007; Franzak, 2006).

> **Researchers find that "struggling readers" don't necessarily struggle because they are deficient, unintelligent, lazy, or incapable. Rather, they often struggle because the ways in which reading is taught and assessed in school *position them to fail*.**

Teachers' abilities to implement good practices for reading instruction are also affected by how school is organized. Even in highly collaborative team-teaching settings, it's still difficult to reach every student. Teachers may be obligated to use certain kinds of text instead of others as a result of district-level mandates or simple lack of resources and time. They are often expected to teach certain titles, authors, and genres as a matter of tradition rather than focus on teaching reading skills and disciplinary concepts using texts kids will find interesting and relevant. They may be forced to deal with large classes that contain students with highly varied reading experiences, abilities, and even languages. They are also often obliged to teach regimented curricula that don't reflect what we know to be healthy instruction—namely, using students' own unique funds of knowledge, providing all students with equitable access to a variety of texts, providing children with extended time and regular opportunities to practice reading, and helping them apply their academic learning to their daily lives and personal identities. Teaching middle grade English is by no means an easy job when standardized testing and rigid curricula limit students' opportunities to learn (Scherff & Piazza, 2008).

Time is precious in middle grades classrooms, and we acknowledge that teachers are primarily responsible—as they should be—for teaching core content in their subject areas. We also acknowledge that while students should be active participants in their own education, sometimes there is little a teacher can accomplish when a child doesn't cooperate or resists instruction for any reason. State benchmarks for student performance on standardized tests put immense pressure on teachers and administrators, and that pressure often leads to educators' narrowing the curriculum to include *only* those skills and concepts needed to pass the tests. However, as we discuss in this chapter, such "drill and kill" orientations are not healthy for children or professional educators (Guthrie, 2002).

Whatever the constraints, even in schools where the curriculum is narrowed owing to the pressures of testing, the approach we recommend in this book is at least as effective as any prepackaged reading program designed to increase test performance (Guthrie, 2002). In fact, even where our approach may result only in equivalent or modest gains relative to preprogrammed designs, gains in students' reading efficacy, motivation, and engagement are likely to far outpace any gains from traditional approaches. Would you rather have students who did well on a test but feared reading and hated school, *or* would you prefer students who scored at least as high on the tests but still engaged in classroom activities with enthusiasm and pleasure that continued beyond graduation? The choice is obvious. Ohanian (2009) argues passionately for teachers to "return to pride in our profession" (p. 380) by doing what we know is right for our students even in the face of political pressures to meet standards and "teach to the tests." As teachers, sometimes we may have to go beyond our classroom work and take local action to ensure that we meet the needs of all students, including marginalized readers. Ohanian writes:

> We must throw out the federally sanctioned absentee owners, the absentee experts, the profiteers and their lackeys.... Instead, we must look to the particular knowledge, fidelity, and care of local remedies. Speaking at the NCTE Annual Convention in Nashville, 2006, Richard Allington offered a brilliant strategy of resistance, recommending

that every teacher examine the state code of ethics for teachers. Then, when ordered to read a script or to stop reading aloud or to commit some other abusive practice [that violates principles of good teaching], teachers should say, "Please put in writing that you want me to violate the state code of professional ethics." (p. 380)

But how can teachers afford to buck the systems that employ them? Today, administrative policies such as common planning, lockstep pacing guides, and standardized examinations give teachers little room to innovate or individualize instruction, and they leave little or no time to do the things we know will benefit middle school readers most. In this chapter, we discuss the current state of reading instruction in secondary schools, explore how current policies get in the way of helping marginalized readers, and suggest ways in which teachers can adapt their instruction productively and in alignment with state and local mandates even as they educate administrators, parents, school board members, and policymakers about how to position young adult readers (and their teachers!) for success.

POLICY AND COMMON SENSE

For most people—including educators—the traditional ways school is taught now seem like common sense. For example, research has thoroughly demonstrated that most English teachers teach as they were taught—not because it's the best way but because it feels familiar and comfortable (Grossman, 1990; Lortie, 1975; Marshall et al., 1997). The teacher assigns students to read a text (usually literary) and next offers lectures and discussions of the content. He or she then assigns students exercises related to that content, and finally the teacher tests students for understanding before moving on to the next topic or work of literature. We must be teaching this way for good reasons, right?

Sadly, education historians have found that many common instructional practices—for example, using grammar worksheets or certain literary masterpieces in English—persist today for no other reason than habit—the way school has always been done (Applebee, 1974; Cuban, 1993; Krashen, 1993; Tyack & Cuban, 1995). In fact, studies have regularly demonstrated over the past century that grammar and language worksheets have little to no effect (and in some instances a negative effect) on students' learning to read (Krashen, 1993). Literacy scholars have documented the problem of irrelevance in traditional school literature (Allington, 2007). Similarly, modern overemphasis on reading drills or narrowed curriculum for test preparation can *lower* student achievement even though it is intended to do the opposite (Guthrie, 2002). We would prefer to think educators implement curriculum and instruction based on careful research and concern for best practices, but that's not always true (Cohen, 1988).

In order to address the problem of "struggling readers" today, many school districts still choose to pull children out of the regular classroom for one period a day to work on reading fluency, vocabulary, and comprehension with someone other than their regular teacher, using grade-level texts that are most likely too difficult for them to comprehend (Allington, 2007). Once this remedial period is completed, struggling readers are typically returned to regular classrooms where they've missed out on other important experiences and opportunities. Still, they are returned and expected to work even more on the same grade-level texts they couldn't read in the first place. These practices are not in place on the basis of any proven research that they help students learn but rather because state and national policies created by noneducators support them (Allington, 2007). They take less time, they are less expensive, and they seem efficient to outsiders. But, as Allington (2007) notes, "If struggling readers are provided with appropriate instruction only 10–20 percent of the school day [and in isolation from their disciplinary classrooms and peer groups], one doesn't need to hire a consultant to determine why these struggling readers...fail to meet goals for adequate yearly progress" (p. 8).

Scherff and Piazza's (2008) statistical studies of secondary students' opportunities to learn in secondary school classrooms echo Allington's critique. When policymakers, school administrators, and other stakeholders fail to acknowledge that students are lacking opportunities to access relevant curriculum, then educational opportunity becomes "something defined for students, and not *with* them" (Scherff & Piazza, 2008, p. 349). Excluding students from participation in their own learning is a direct violation of professional guidelines related to English language arts curriculum and instruction (NCTE, 2006) and international standards for reading assessment (International Reading Association, 2009). Middle grade English teachers must learn to use their knowledge of such guidelines, standards, and research to distinguish between practices based on pedagogical knowledge in students' best interest versus practices based on administrative expedience stemming from politics beyond the classroom.

For example, one entirely political reason why school administrators decide to pull students out of regular classrooms for remediation is the simple fact that schools (and the states that run them) must provide a clear and publicly obvious appearance of "doing something" to improve (Kroeger, 2008).They must give school boards, parents, community members, state governments, and federal bureaucrats the impression that students (and teachers) are working hard to do better. Nothing *looks* more like good schooling to the general public than a teacher standing at the front of the room and directing highly controlled children sitting in rows to read a textbook and recite answers to questions focused mostly on factual recall. Conversely, it does *not* look like good schooling to some traditionalists and public stakeholders when a teacher is circulating to coach small groups and pairs of students who are enthusiastically talking with one another (instead of the teacher) or using classroom time to "just" read something other than the textbook.

Beyond policy imperatives and administrative perceptions of efficiency that lead to unhealthy reading instruction, the limited time and resources teachers have to do their work makes it difficult to deviate from traditional practices and programmed curricula. Delivering content through direct instruction alone and then testing students' performance on worksheets is easier in some ways than designing reading experiences that blend disciplinary content and activities with students' funds of knowledge to position them as possible or primary knowers who actively engage with texts and schoolwork. As Kroeger (2008) points out, it can seem impossible to deliver individualized instruction when the teacher must address the needs of 150 different students every day.

Still, the conditions that force teachers to resort to practices we know are ineffective and even downright unhealthy are the direct results of school and educational policies. They are not accidental, incidental, or inevitable. Decisions about class size, the length of a class period, the number and kinds of texts purchased for classroom use, and the nature of instruction and assessment are all just that: decisions. Such decisions are made by individuals and groups, even though they may come about as matters of administrative expedience based on broad policies created by people who don't always know much about actual research on literacy and learning (Wise, 2007). Most reading policies and their resulting administrative implementation fail to consider the effects of the policy environ-

> Decisions about class size, the length of a class period, the number and kinds of texts purchased for classroom use, and the nature of instruction and assessment are all just that: decisions.

ment on teachers' abilities to teach and students' abilities to learn (Franzak, 2006). Therefore, when students or teachers appear to do poorly based on standardized test scores, there is a tendency to blame them individually for not helping themselves or trying hard enough. Policymakers generally assume that their policies are correct and they therefore are blameless. The typical response to perceived failure in schools is to take away even more autonomy from teachers and students and to remediate "struggling" readers by giving them an even more intense dose of the isolated drills, out-of-class interventions, and rigidly programmed curricula that did not work in the first place.

Given that the conditions described above are so common, Franzak (2006) argues that, rather than focusing on remediating children, teachers should instead focus on remediating the *curriculum*. Educators, after all, are the key players implementing any curriculum in a school bureaucracy (Cuban, 1993). Teachers work, figuratively speaking, "where the rubber hits the road." We have the most direct evidence available about whether a particular policy for reading instruction works or not. We are also public intellectuals capable of teaching noneducators what works best, based on sound research (Giroux, 1988; Kroeger, 2008). Given our unique insight into how teaching and learning really work, teachers need to become active in the policymaking processes at the local and state levels. We must learn to *make* policy rather than merely implement it (Burns, 2007; Franzak, 2006; Miller & Fox, 2006; Wise, 2007).

CURRICULUM AS POLICY

Perhaps the most effective way for teachers to inform and create policy at local levels is by focusing on the curriculum used to teach in their subject and/or grade level. Many view curriculum as an outcome of policy, but it is in fact policy in and of itself. In fact, curriculum is the keystone of the policy environment in any school (Weaver-Hightower, 2007). Based on standards set at the state and national levels, curriculum affects what can and cannot happen in a classroom. According to the National Middle School Association (NMSA, 2003a, 2003b), curriculum should be treated not only as the nuts and bolts of content for a subject area but as the entire school environment: the schedule, the resources, the facilities, the instructional styles, and more. Further, according to the NMSA, curriculum and instruction proceed from social constructivism in middle schools, "starting where students are," employing varying degrees of structure and pacing, a variety of teaching and learning strategies, and "significant opportunities for students to mature and be socialized" in collaborative groups that reflect the activities they will engage in later in life (Orb, 2001, pp. 16–17). It is telling that NMSA policies echo many research-based recommendations for supporting so-called struggling readers. It is also telling that state and national reading policies do not.

In obvious ways, the style of curriculum driven by standardized testing—in which all students are expected to work at the same pace and learn the same concepts all at the same time—violates most of what we know about quality reading instruction in middle school. This is not to say that "anything goes" or that there is no need for structure or high

standards when educating adolescents. Still, typical state-driven curricula simply are not responsive to the needs of middle grade students and
teachers. Given NMSA policies and research, such lack of responsiveness
is ironic. In a time and place where youth are being educated to assert
"a greater sense of control and autonomy through the development of
more complex identities," both teachers and students generally lack real
control and autonomy as a matter of policy (Reed, Schallert, Beth, &
Woodruff, 2004). Still, teachers have the capacity to change and adapt
curricula, and their political activity can make a difference.

But *how* can English teachers take political action? We are all busy
professionals. Our first priority (as it should be) is our students, and no
one should have to risk censure or loss of employment by doing what's
right. But political action does not have to take significant risk, time, or
energy for teachers to change policies and create conditions that support
quality reading instruction. With some planning and conscious decision
making, teachers can make their everyday interactions around school
serve political ends without being overtly "political" in the sense of radical activism. What follows are ways teachers can work in their communities every day to educate others about the work they do, thereby gaining
more control over how and why that work happens. By educating others,
especially parents, administrators, and policymakers, English teachers
can change conversations about literacy, teaching, testing, accountability,
and equity in ways that position all students to read without a struggle.

FINDING A VOICE IN POLICYMAKING

If teachers want to change curriculum policies so they can provide the
opportunities and instruction they know their students need, they must
first understand certain challenges they are likely to face. One reason
why educators are rarely listened to in conversations about educational
policy in the United States is that most members of the public—including
principals, school board members, parents, and politicians—believe they
understand how schools, teaching, and literacy work already. Unlike
doctors, lawyers, and other professionals whose work generally takes
place in more private settings, teachers do their jobs in an intensely public arena. By the time they graduate from high school, every U.S. citizen
spends over 13,000 hours in classrooms watching teachers work from
their point of view as students (Lortie, 1975). As a result, most people
believe they know what it takes to learn best, and they also think they
know best how teachers ought to do their jobs.

Commonly, noneducators believe teaching is a simple matter of telling children the information they need, drilling and training them, and
then testing them to determine which ones learned and which ones did

not. Most assume that all children learn in the same ways they learned themselves when they were in school (Lortie, 1975). These assumptions filter citizens' perceptions of education debates, and as a result they often see such traditions as using textbooks, worksheets, and standardized tests and remediating struggling readers as commonsense responses to educational problems. They honestly believe such practices are not only appropriate but important in providing quality education. It's not that they don't support public education but rather that they lack the information needed to understand and accept better alternatives.

Like the citizens they serve, most policymakers do not read educational research, let alone follow scholarly debates and new research findings about reading instruction, curriculum, teaching, and learning. Policymakers (and most other adults) simply have "neither the time nor any interest in figuring out what is nuance, much less who is right," in education theory and practice (Wise, 2007, p. 408). Most people, including policymakers, want to view policy in terms of black/white, either/or, and yes/no. Left to their own devices, they will predictably choose policies that seem simple and efficient.

While English teachers cannot and should not ignore the complexities of pedagogy and disciplinary knowledge when teaching in their classrooms, they can talk about that work and knowledge in ways that are clear, simple, straightforward, and concrete. When approaching administrators, parents, school boards, and politicians, teachers must present their expertise without using jargon or simply complaining based on ideology (Wise, 2007). If teachers cannot communicate their understanding of quality reading instruction clearly, potential allies will continue to ignore that input and support mandates that reflect their flawed beliefs about how education works. State legislators and school officials will continue to mandate methods for teaching reading that perpetuate labeling some students as "struggling readers." Parents will continue to applaud and vote for people who advocate so-called back-to-the-basics models and "rigorous" or "scientific" programs that lend themselves easily to standardized testing and instructional methods that do more harm than good (Goodman, 2008). But if teachers learn to share their knowledge in ways that enhance stakeholders' understanding of how reading instruction works, they can make a real difference.

BEYOND PROTEST:
REAL ACTIONS FOR REAL CHANGE

As professional educators, middle school English teachers can speak with greater authority, credibility, and knowledge than any other group of citizens in the area of reading policy. This is particularly true in local venues such as school site council meetings and district board meetings, but it is also true at the state and even national levels. The key is to be organized and strategic, and the most important activity for anyone seeking to reform curriculum and instruction is collecting and distributing accurate information about school practices in formats that are easily understood and used by others. Essentially, the kind of political action we advocate is really a matter of teaching other adults what we know about our professional work and establishing mutually supportive relationships that open up new policy conversations.

The political action we describe here is not the "bloody fist" mode of protest in which teachers hold up signs and chant slogans in bitter opposition and open conflict. Teachers are busy and don't normally have time to attend public demonstrations, protests, and the like. Beyond that, confrontational strategies are often limited in their success, and they are not productive in terms of genuinely persuading others to accept new perspectives. The political action we advocate, instead, involves teaching others how teaching and learning work from an insider's perspective. It is the kind of work teachers can do as part of their daily activities with minimal extra effort. It requires awareness, intentionality, cooperation, and a little organization. The strategies are basic and make use of the democratic process to generate dialogue about reform: identifying allies, gathering information, participating in public meetings, talking with parents and community members, contacting political representatives, and using media outlets.

The first step in taking political action is identifying allies—forming a group of like-minded people invested in improving reading instruction. Such a group doesn't have to be large, but it is important to form a group large enough to distribute the workload and carry out plans in a reasonable way. Again, teachers are busy, and so are the parents and community members who will support our efforts to improve schools. But with enough members no single individual will be overburdened, making it easier to act politically. Most teachers can identify at least five colleagues, parents, and community members who would support their work and who would help inform the community or act on relevant issues. These are the people we eat lunch with every day, the ones we talk shop with in the teachers' lounge, the ones who show up for parents' night and parent–teacher conferences. These are your friends and neighbors. By inviting these individuals to join, one English teacher can quickly establish a rich and efficient network without overwhelming investments of time and energy.

Once a sustainable group forms, it must meet as regularly as possible. Again, keep in mind that many allies are people you see every day in your community and school and that it shouldn't be impossible to meet once a month. Meetings should have clear agendas and take place in a local restaurant, a café, or a home if possible rather than a school site in order to avoid any conflict of interest in the eyes of school officials. Still, if necessary, groups can meet during a school lunch break or after school. The group should meet frequently at the beginning at a consistent time and location, and then settle into a monthly timeframe. As the group evolves, members should take on particular roles to guide action. Assigning roles allows the group to distribute time and effort evenly. Depending on how formal your group becomes, you may decide to choose a name, establish a website, and even offer press releases to raise community awareness. Regardless, members can share the workload to follow school board agendas, collect relevant research and information, write letters, make phone calls, and so on.

When the group has organized and set its priorities, the next step is to begin attending site-based council meetings (often called site-based decision-making meetings in some districts), school board meetings, legislative committee meetings, and other public forums where education is discussed. Such committees usually publish agendas in advance, and teacher-led groups can access these to determine and prioritize their actions. Obtaining agendas may require persistence because boards and committees are often not used to attracting true public interest in their activities. Thus, it's a good idea to put one group member in charge of obtaining agendas in order to plan around the activities of local policymakers. One or two members should be designated to collect news and research on relevant issues so the group can remain informed and up to date, and all these roles should be rotated periodically so that work is evenly shared by all members.

In addition to simply attending public meetings and speaking up in a calm, knowledgeable, well-reasoned manner, group members should establish regular contact with local, state, and federal politicians. Personal meetings are by far the best way to get a policymaker's attention.

As we have noted, politicians usually don't have the time or interest to read education research, and when they do they are easily frustrated by jargon and nuances. The key to effective communications with policymakers is planning and preparation. Because their time is at a premium, your group must come with a focused agenda composed of a single issue (for example, providing more textual variety in every classroom), and that agenda item should be clearly supported by citing at most, five to seven simply presented pieces of evidence or information that can be stated in a few minutes. When addressing an issue with a policymaker, it is often tempting to preach or rant out of passion for a strongly held viewpoint. Doing so, however, is almost always counterproductive. One angry outburst can guarantee that your group's first meeting with a policymaker will also be its last. Groups should communicate in a calm, straightforward manner with as much objectivity as possible. Stick to the facts, communicate your points clearly, and explain why supporting your position will benefit that policymaker's constituents.

As Wise (2007) advises, when educators present themselves as "serious-minded experts, and when they choose to focus on points of agreement, holding their professional debates in private ... they can indeed convince policymakers to listen and act" (p. 409). So, while teachers are often angered by what they view as unreasonable policies, and while they may even view some policy language as deliberately misleading (Goodman, 2008), attacking policymakers for ignorance, lack of ethics, or lack of care is obviously counterproductive to future partnership.

It is far more useful to state as experts that children *must* be taught to read. What policymaker, principal, school board member, or parent would disagree with a group of teachers who began a meeting with that statement? Once others have agreed on that point, your group can state its desire to work with them and offer expertise to help make decisions that ensure that teachers can do that work well. Teachers can then summarize concise research-based findings about the power of certain instructional strategies to improve students' learning and achievement—for example, reports by Marzano et al. (2001), Graham and Perin (2007), and Biancarosa and Snow (2006) report scientifically proven instructional methods, classroom conditions, curriculum, and school structures that increase academic learning and literacy achievement.

By offering these brief, easily understood recommendations, teachers seeking to support marginalized readers and reform reading education can demonstrate their use of the "scientific" claims that Goodman (2008) emphasizes are so valued by policymakers. By utilizing the rhetoric of science to talk about real research findings, teachers can ensure that policymakers—and especially the administrators and parents they work with locally—will not become what Goodman calls "easy prey to lies and disinformation" (p. 13). Most importantly, when teachers demonstrate their professional consideration of scientific research findings about reading and instruction, they position themselves to be seen as leaders and partners rather than adversaries and protesters who just don't want to be held accountable for their work. In a recent structured conversation at the National Council of Teachers of English 2009 annual convention (Burns, Scherff, & Botzakis, 2009), participants noted that when teachers actively work to explain their research-based rationales for using certain methods and texts rather than others to teach readers in the 21st century, they almost always find that concerned administrators and parents affirm their work and energetically support them as a result. We suggest that this will be true if teachers engage with local policymakers in similarly calm, professional, and evidence-based ways.

In many cases, it may not be feasible to meet personally with a policymaker, even at the local level. It is often the case that your group will have to meet instead with an assistant to the politician, a public relations person, or a staff aide. Still, such contacts can be highly advantageous, especially if your group is able to cultivate a friendly relationship with that individual. The individuals your group does meet with will always have greater access to policymakers than you do, and they can become powerful allies and persuaders if they support your cause.

Obviously, not everyone has easy access to policymakers, whether because of geography, professional work schedules, or other reasons. In such cases phone calls and letter writing can be extremely effective. However, it is important to avoid generic scripts for phone calls or form letters for writing campaigns. Officeholders and their staffs are adept at identifying form letters and scripted calls; so, if a group wants to get its message across, then each individual must speak in his or her own voice even when expressing much the same sentiment in supporting a position.

Email, while convenient, is rarely effective. Politicians receive hundreds of emails each day, and their staff members screen out all but the most significant ones (as viewed from their perspective). Handwritten letters, though, can be extremely powerful in generating responses from officeholders. A politician will generally perceive a single handwritten letter as representative of many voters; if one person felt strongly enough to *handwrite* a letter about some issue, then it was probably important to many others who did not take the time. Imagine how powerful it is when a politician's aides review *multiple* handwritten letters from citizens in their district. Some 10–15 letters can represent a significant block of voters, and they are more likely to get a serious response. When aides begin seeing a stream of similar yet individualized letters delivered to their inboxes, it becomes more and more likely they will bring the issue to their boss's attention. And, as the old adage goes, "When politicians feel the heat, they see the light."

Sometimes a group may not be able to get direct access to the appropriate policy contacts they need in order to instigate reform. Another way to cultivate relationships and spread your message is by working with journalists in local media outlets—whether newspapers, radio, or television. Members of a teacher-led political action group can become invaluable contacts for journalists. Typically radio and television stations or networks, as well as newspapers, assign one or two reporters to cover educational issues. Those reporters will almost always work with education insiders who can provide them with access to decision makers as well as accurate and expert information about the issues they must cover and report. Once such relationships have been established, teachers can amplify their voices by teaching journalists how to accurately represent issues from a professional's perspective. As Wise (2007) has observed, "Elected officials are more influenced by what appears in their local papers than by what's printed in *The New York Times*" (p. 411).

In addition to gaining the attention of reporters, writing editorials is a tried-and-true way to send your message to a broad audience in a forum where politicians will take notice. Letters to the editor in a local paper convey your group's messages to the public, and editorials are especially successful because they employ simple language in brief statements that are easily understood and remembered.

ALL TOGETHER NOW

Any discussion of political action is always in danger of becoming pie in the sky. See if you can't begin putting the ideas into more concrete terms right here. Can you list five colleagues who might be interested in making political action their work? Write their names down, and get these people together to talk. What would happen if lunchtime became the time to meet once a week and plan political local action? Parental involvement is useful, too. List five parents who might join you in working for changes in their neighborhood. Invite these people to join you.

Next, list three issues you would like to address in your school or school district related to reading instruction. For example, are standardized tests making it difficult for you to meet what you have judged to be the real needs of your students? Do you have to follow a rigid curriculum that keeps you from providing your students with texts they find truly interesting and relevant? Does your school's schedule or protocols prevent you from giving students sufficient time to practice their reading skills and apply them in useful ways? Do you have to follow a pacing guide that prevents you from pursuing "teachable moments"? Are you required to use textbooks that you know misrepresent or overlook important aspects of literacy? Write down these issues, and use your group network to find out what research has been done on these problems. Then find out what your political representatives and school board members know and believe about these issues, and begin working toward local partnerships and solutions.

In order to change the conversation about education in your community and school, it is necessary to become *a part* of that conversation. We may "just" be teachers, and we *are* busy working with students every day. But together in networks we can use our normal activities to develop a powerful voice and make a real difference in how education "happens."

In order to change the conversation about education in your community and school, it is necessary to become *a part* of that conversation. Together we can use our normal activities to develop a powerful voice and make a real difference in how education "happens."

Think in terms of the metaphor "A waterfall begins with a single drop." These opportunities for local action are what Kent Williamson, Executive Director of the National Council of Teachers of English, had in mind when he stated, "Our challenge today is to develop the grassroots organizational capacity to bring our expertise and carefully considered messages to policy makers." (Williamson, 2006, para. 7).

CONCLUSION: PERSISTENCE TO THE POINT OF SUCCESS

Using the strategies described in this chapter, English teachers *can* become politically active at the grassroots level. In addition to understanding the philosophy and research-based knowledge underpinning our work, we need to represent ourselves as the public intellectuals we are. We can teach our communities, and our communities in turn can make politicians, school board members, and administrators accountable to our conception of correctly structured reading instruction and curriculum. It is through (sometimes painstakingly slow) public intellectual action that teachers can eventually succeed in creating the conditions required for marginalized readers to learn and grow.

We likely will achieve our goals most expeditiously by operating as unabashed advocates in spaces where we already work—in faculty lounges, team and department meetings, school board meetings, site councils, steering committees, parent–teacher conferences, and through parent emails, phone calls, letters to the editor, and short conversations with political representatives. Any extra effort will pay off incrementally—20 phone calls from voters to a local representative about reading education will guarantee that representative's attention. What might 50 calls accomplish? A hundred? Would it really be so difficult to reach those levels of activity through concerted public discussion in your school's community?

Political activity doesn't need to be radical or angry, but rather professional and idealistic. The recommendations we make in this chapter for engaging in curriculum reform are not intended as an easy fix. Our calls for particular reforms and practices will be seen by some as controversial regardless of how calmly we offer them, and such work can be difficult and messy. It requires organization and planning. The key is to make sure that we don't act alone.

Some people will scoff at the idea that teachers can make a difference through reform of the system. Some critics may say "Just shut your door and teach" while others echo "Just *shut up* and teach!" But those who claim that working for change is *impossible* most often really mean that working for change is *difficult*. *Difficult* is not *impossible*. The teaching approaches and practices that we espouse in this book are not ready-made recipes for anything remotely "revolutionary." Rather, they represent a research-based perspective on incrementally improving education that helps middle school teachers think more profession-ally, act more decisively, and bring more real-life experience and contemporaneity into English classrooms (hopefully) forever.

> Looking beyond short-term "remedies," or palliatives, middle school teachers need to develop a comprehensive perspective on reading education that supports thinking more professionally, acting more decisively, and bringing more real-life experience and contemporaneity into English classrooms (hopefully) forever.

Positioning students for successful reading in middle schools today is far too important a mission to ignore, belittle, or abort prematurely, the history of reform in reading education having long been littered with examples of half-measures and quick fixes that didn't work. The plight of today's "struggling reader" is too fundamental and too critical an issue in today's schools to respond with a moderate's voice. Teaching reading capably in the 21st century is far too complex and onerous an undertaking for any quick fixes or "best practices" to work miracles. We have to communicate our best knowledge, however, to ensure "that vital information informs policy decisions" (Wise, 2007, p. 410). No one can communicate that knowledge better than English language arts teachers.

In the end, it seems important to remain idealistic in our work as professional teachers working in the public system to ensure that *all* of our students learn and succeed. It's a shame that a word like *idealism* now causes people to roll their eyes skyward and sigh at what they see as willful naïveté. Idealism, after all, is simply defined as the eternal pursuit of excellence. Shouldn't we expect *everyone* invested in the education of children to tirelessly support the pursuit of excellence? Isn't that what all teachers strive for? Isn't that why we work to position all our students to read without an undue struggle? If it is not, then why do we teach? And what should we think of anyone who would claim our idealism is foolish? We teach reading because we know there is nothing more important we can do for children in schools and society today. We teach English and the language arts because our students need us. We teach children to read, ultimately, because we know doing so will help make our society stronger. Helping our students move in from the periphery of our classrooms and positioning them for lifelong learning? Now, that's a struggle worth fighting for.

Questions for Reflection

1. What are the most pressing issues related to reading instruction in your classroom or school right now? What do you believe nonteachers involved with policymaking need to know most about how to help you meet all students' needs in learning to read?

2. Who are your local school board members and political representatives? What are their positions on education, especially literacy education?

3. Who reports news on education in your local community? What do their reports seem to reflect about current issues and concerns about literacy education and related topics?

4. Who do you know who could work with you to connect and communicate positively with policymakers and education advocates?

RECOMMENDED RESOURCES

Rethinking Schools Online
www.rethinkingschools.org

Susan Ohanian.Org
www.susanohanian.org
Winner of the George Orwell Award for Distinguished Contribution to Honesty and Clarity in Public Language.

SLATE, Support for the Learning and Teaching of English (National Council of Teachers of English)
www.ncte.org/action/slate

13

Conclusion
Promising Readers

David W. Moore

Empowering Struggling Readers, in its presentation of literacy learning as crucially situated within sociocultural contexts, is a highly timely volume. The sociocultural perspective is presented frequently in the research literature (Sperling & DiPardo, 2008); so, having it featured in a professional methods text now is quite sensible. The chances of sociocultural considerations informing the teaching and learning of middle-school struggling readers in ELA classrooms have increased substantially with the publication of this text.

To my mind, *Empowering Struggling Readers* presents two signature premises that deserve attention. One is that struggling readers' willingness to engage with academic literacy reflects how they wish to be identified as much as it does their attitudes, or strategic knowledge. Students' academic identities are a powerful dimension of classroom life, and teachers are well advised to take students' self-identification as readers seriously.

The other, related, premise is that middle school ELA teachers bear a great deal of responsibility in properly positioning students as readers and writers. Socially conscious assumptions that enhance struggling readers' opportunities to see themselves as capable learners are what is most needed. These two allied premises—taking students' self-identification seriously and positioning them accordingly—lead to productive ways of thinking about middle school ELA instruction.

David W. Moore, PhD, is Professor of Education in the College of Teacher Education and Leadership at Arizona State University.

CONTEXT

To gain perspective on *Empowering Struggling Readers,* consider some of the adolescent literacy reports published during the past decade by such organizations as the National Association of Secondary School Principals, National Association of State Boards of Education, and National Governors Association. Many such reports have been published. One review lists 22 reports, calling them "responses to the adolescent literacy crisis" (Jacobs, 2008, p. 10), and another lists 14, characterizing them as a "growing chorus" (Heller & Greenleaf, 2007, p. 3). In my opinion, *Empowering Struggling Readers* presents a needed counterargument in that its realistic appraisal of the sociocultural dimensions of literacy injects a significant dollop of dissonance into the excessively cognitive chorus of these reviews.

Reading Next (Biancarosa & Snow, 2006) famously presents 15 elements of effective adolescent literacy programs, including such ones as direct, explicit comprehension instruction, text-based collaborative learning, and a significant technology component. One of the 15 elements, motivation and self-directed learning, highlights the social-emotional aspect of literacy, and the report goes on to mention two time-honored ways to instill motivation, namely, providing choices and promoting relevance. This element "knocks on the same door" as literate identities and positions but does not go any further. Thus, *Reading Next* ultimately has nothing important to say about students' academic literacies being significantly shaped by their social and cultural worlds.

Improving Adolescent Literacy: Effective Classroom and Intervention Practices (Kamil et al., 2008) comes from the U.S. Institute of Education Sciences, which produces practice guides like this consistent with the What Works Clearinghouse standards. This guide offers five recommendations for advancing adolescents' reading:

1. Provide explicit vocabulary instruction.
2. Provide direct and explicit comprehension strategy instruction.
3. Provide opportunities for extended discussion of text meaning and interpretation.
4. Increase students' motivation and engagement in literacy learning.
5. Make available intensive and individualized interventions for struggling readers that can be provided by trained specialists.

Motivation and engagement are featured in this list as one element among five. Ways to increase motivation and engagement center on relevance (as is true with *Reading Next*) and go on to also include meaningful learning goals, a positive environment, self-directed learning, and collaboration with peers. The explicit call for developing a positive environment is a promising advance forward, but this report follows *Reading Next* in drawing attention only to teachers' providing sufficient choices as the key to such an environment.

The Alliance for Excellent Education surveyed people involved in running federally funded Striving Readers programs and compiled their recommendations in *Informing Adolescent Literacy Policy and Practice: Lessons Learned from the Striving Readers Program* (Ayers & Miller, 2009). Leaders who had at least 2 years of experience in running their adolescent literacy projects came up with the following five recommendations:

1. Allow sufficient time for planning and launching the program.
2. Choose the best program.
3. Build ownership and capacity.
4. Maintain fidelity and accountability.
5. Build the knowledge base while supporting students' learning.

The emphasis here is on implementing and sustaining programs, often commercial ones, with little attention directed at the internal elements. The Striving Readers program leaders offer little advice about determining the best program beyond encouraging planners to locate one that best fits their students' needs.

Finally, the well-funded and highly visible Carnegie Council on Advancing Adolescent Literacy recently issued its capstone report, *A Time to Act* (Carnegie Council on Advancing Adolescent Literacy, 2010). This report presents an agenda for reengineering middle and high schools to support adolescent literacy learners. In line with the response to intervention (RTI) model, it calls for targeted interventions in behalf of struggling readers and writers. Distinctive coursework is recommended to overcome youth's decoding, fluency, or comprehension difficulties. Additionally, *A Time to Act* appends a list of eight "essential elements of literacy for adolescent learners," specifically:

1. Phonemic awareness
2. Alphabetics
3. Fluency
4. Vocabulary
5. Comprehension
6. Writing
7. Speaking and listening
8. Critical thinking

This list adds three elements—writing, speaking and listening, and critical thinking—to the National Reading Panel (2000) report's five pillars that were emphasized in the federal Reading First primary grade program. While Reading First was found to focus instruction across the board on the first five elements, it did not produce a statistically significant impact on student reading comprehension test scores in grades 1, 2, or 3 (Gamse, Jacob, Horst, Boulay, & Unlu, 2008). In light of this record of underachievement, promoting these same literacy elements for older readers seems somewhat questionable.

Empowering Struggling Readers shows that a program of middle school ELA instruction necessarily involves more than what recently published reports have stipulated. Youth take up particular views of themselves as academic readers and writers in response to the norms and values presented in their classrooms. Being labeled as a "struggling reader" can severely threaten a student's self-view of him- or herself and undermine his or her academic performance. Middle school ELA teaching and learning inevitably involve a potent sociocultural dimension that cries out for attention. Reports that urge middle school educators to provide readers a positive environment and increase motivation and engagement are steps in the right direction, but they do not go anywhere nearly far enough.

In this chapter I present four major themes I discerned in *Empowering Struggling Readers* that the reports just reviewed tend to overlook. The themes are (1) embracing asset perspectives, (2) providing good teaching-"plus," (3) equipping readers for classroom norms, and (4) promoting critical responses to texts. I added a fifth theme, nearly intervening directly to bolster students' identities, to focus attention on some innovative practices with much potential that I have encountered in other writings. These five elements of middle school ELA teaching and learning, which are derived primarily from a sociocultural perspective, hold great promise for helping out struggling readers.

EMBRACING ASSET PERSPECTIVES

Empowering Struggling Readers characterizes struggling readers as tending to embrace highly-negative self-images of themselves. Several interviews scattered throughout this text present students as viewing their academic lives in intensely negative ways, leading them to marginalize themselves during potentially productive learning situations. For instance, some readers who see themselves as struggling with academic subjects choose to conceal their real or imagined shortcomings during reading discussions because these occasions for displaying knowledge entail huge social risks. To save face or preserve their dignity, these students often withdraw from or disrupt the discussions, preferring to appear disruptive or lazy rather than incompetent.

Middle school youth who enact negative self-images of themselves are in ironic situations. They might appear to be unmotivated when actually they are quite motivated. They might appreciate the choices of what to read, find school reading material sufficiently relevant, and want to participate in talk about the texts, but their words and actions indicate otherwise, and, so, in truth, they hold themselves back needlessly. This irony is deplorable.

What is more, substantial research indicates that educators who accept at face value these students' negative self-image of themselves tend to compound the problem by holding them back (Moll & Ruiz, 2002; Oakes, 1985). Such "deficit perspectives" in effect, lead teachers to distance themselves from struggling readers, and they thereby degrade the quality of day-to-day teaching. Whenever middle school ELA teachers (whether consciously or not) think in terms of perceived deficits, they end up reducing their curricula to rudimentary skills, having students answer questions about simple facts, and reproducing only basic written forms. Their verbal interactions with such students tend to decline, even if not intentionally. Such deficit perspectives align with the general consensus that struggling readers lack the necessary moral character, work ethic, or commitment to mainstream values and norms to succeed academically. As a consequence, instructional efforts are directed disproportionately to students considered more deserving (Anagnostopoulos & Rutledge, 2007)—when exactly the opposite should be occurring! (Who needs the teacher's time more, after all?)

Deficit perspectives tend to associate such students automatically with chronic negative attributes (e.g., distractedness, reluctance, ineptness) and thereby create self-fulfilling prophecies about what these students can actually accomplish (Valencia, 2009). And when students are repeatedly treated as substandard entities, or as basically "broken" inside, many gradually come to regard themselves in the same negative ways—as basically deficient—and act accordingly.

Both students and teachers would do well to start embracing asset— rather than deficit—perspectives. Asset perspectives begin by *presuming* competence and potential. All students are viewed as capable of engagement, motivation, and advanced literacies. Asset perspectives assume that all learners have cognitive and social strengths, even if these strengths might not be readily visible or greatly valued in academic situations. Rather than working to fix students' broken parts, educators embracing asset perspectives work to use what students bring to school as entry points to expanding their students' repertoires of academic thought and action.

A good first step for putting asset perspectives into action involves determining learners' strengths inside and outside of school. The interviews reported in earlier chapters admirably demonstrate the value of talking with and listening to students. Positioning students as key informants in their own teaching and learning sheds light on what is working, what is not working, and why (Cook-Sather, 2002). Soliciting and responding seriously to students' perspectives about teaching and learning in school is a way to begin capitalizing on learners' assets as avenues to academic learning and ways of acting.

Powerful teaching can occur when students' assets are recognized and utilized. Students and teachers do well to work on beliefs and practices that position all learners as having something to offer, as participants who come to school with assets that can be used for scaffolding advanced academic literacies. When middle school struggling readers see themselves and what they bring to school as respected, they make the most of whatever opportunities they are given to learn (Dillon, 1989).

PROVIDING GOOD TEACHING-PLUS

Empowering Struggling Readers presents many common ELA teaching approaches and practices. The table of contents presents familiar chapter titles relating to comprehension, vocabulary, discussion, and so on. The chapters describe key recommendations for all students, such as promoting metacognition, teaching independent word-learning strategies, and conducting peer-led discussions. An initial impression might be that this text just describes good teaching. But closer analysis reveals that it portrays good teaching-"plus." In other words, it presents ways to take good teaching to a whole new level.

This book's characteristic way of recommending good teaching-plus is exemplified well in Chapter 8, "Culturally Grounded Vocabulary Instruction." This chapter presents background on vocabulary development and details Graves's (2006) four-part program that calls for (1) providing frequent, varied, and extensive language experiences, (2) teaching individual words, (3) teaching independent word-learning strategies, and (4) fostering word consciousness.

Chapter 8 then takes vocabulary instruction to another level by describing how Graves's components can be grounded in sociocultural principles such as switching codes for various purposes and getting to know diverse cultures will in order to make more connections among students. For instance, it tells of a teacher reporting her use of different words and styles of language in different social situations and then having students tell how the words worked to her advantage. Rather than examining published authors' word choices, she focused on word choices within a much wider sociocultural realm. This practice involves fostering word consciousness-"plus" by helping to embed vocabulary instruction into participants' social and cultural worlds.

Culturally diverse youth generally do better academically when they are able to link what they know and do outside of school with the curriculum taught in school. Teachers can promote such links strategically by using learners' assets as scaffolds for academic learning, creating opportunities for learners to connect new academic knowledge with their funds of knowledge and specialized types of literacy acquired through their families, communities, peer groups, and various popular or mass media outlets (Lee, 2007). For instance, connecting literary elements (e.g., character, setting, point of view, theme) experienced through life and the media outside of school with literary texts inside of school can be a very productive teaching practice (Wilhelm & Smith, 2010). Showing youth how tracking the plot of a movie or television show compares with tracking the plot of imaginative fiction enlarges their literary capacities. Good teaching shows students how the knowledge of literary elements contributes usefully to their literary understanding; good teaching-plus shows students the links between their academic and non-academic worlds relative to literary elements.

Another way the curriculum inside school can be actively connected with what youth know and do outside of school involves teachers' linking academic language with English learners' primary languages (Goldenberg, 2008). To forge these links, teachers have students use their primary languages to clarify confusing ideas and information encountered in their new language. They have students compare related words (e.g., *pharmacy/farmacia*) and phrases (e.g., *cold water/agua fria*) across languages. They show how comprehension strategies that are used with a primary language apply to English. They use primary languages as assets, as scaffolds for learning a new language.

Sometimes cultures outside and inside school clash. Outside-of-school cultures that expect readers to obediently accept the written word hold different norms and values than academic ones that expect readers to question what they read. Outside-of-school cultures that endorse several individuals participating in story retellings differ from academic ones that expect one individual at a time to retell a story. To help students learn to question and retell texts, good teaching would explicitly demonstrate and explain these strategies and then hand them over to students through a gradual release of responsibility. Good teaching-plus would take this instruction to another level and link these strategies with what students do outside of school and encourage code-switching, adjustments as appropriate.

In short, good teaching-plus means teaching in accordance with sound general models while also enriching this instruction through accommodation with the specialized needs and unique backgrounds of one's students. It is grounded in and responsive to students' particular sociocultural circumstances. It is consistent with conceptions of the "third space," an idea originally introduced in Chapter 2 and occasionally referenced in succeeding chapters. Good teaching-plus and the third-space concept both spotlight the links between school and home, emphasizing the connections among what students know and can do outside and inside school. They point to creative ways of drawing on youth's natural assets as entry points to new subject matter knowledge. *Empowering Struggling Readers* goes far in showing how to incorporate the *plus* into *good teaching* for middle school struggling readers in ELA classes.

EQUIPPING READERS FOR CLASSROOM NORMS

Both thinking and acting productively in classrooms require that students observe the cultural norms of each classroom. Particular norms for accessing, producing, and communicating knowledge generally must be followed in order to achieve academic success. Equipping readers to participate well according to these norms is a crucial aspect of teaching.

The traditions of each academic discipline largely govern reading and writing practices within it (Lee & Spratley, 2010; Moje, 2008; Shanahan & Shanahan, 2008). For example, analyzing a poem in ELA differs radically from analyzing a frog in biology or a painting in art. In ELA, students make use of particular literary theories, language patterns, and participation structures to formalize and articulate their thoughts. These theories, patterns, and structures then become part of students' cultural tool kits, and students subsequently draw on them when entering into and participating in ELA classes in the future.

Some variations may occur within the disciplines as teachers shape and sustain what is considered most appropriate within their particular classes (Moje & Dillon, 2006). For instance, students in a seventh-grade ELA class might be expected to act as precise problem solvers who scrutinize authors' uses of literary elements. When these students progress the next year to an eighth-grade ELA class, they might be expected to act as creative problem solvers who discuss more speculative adventurous interpretations of deliberately ambiguous texts. To do well, these students need to embrace the role of precise problem solvers in one ELA class and creative problem solvers at the next level.

Empowering Struggling Readers addresses the need to help youth grasp the values and norms of the ELA traditions they inherit as well as the particular forms of literacy that are appropriate and often necessary in particular classrooms. Chapter 2 is noteworthy in this regard by tracing the development of English as an academic discipline and revealing the historical forces that helped to shape through evolution ELA's curricular attributes in modern-day classrooms. It explains how too rigid an adherence to the traditional values and norms of ELA might well shortchange students who still are developing general literacy competencies.

Chapter 7 presents ELA-specific theories that can serve as scaffolds, or frameworks, for students to embrace when faced with the challenges of analyzing literature. Chapter 9 puts forward socially based principles of teaching and learning that contribute to students' participating actively in discussing texts. Such practices better enable struggling students to read and write in line with disciplinary and classroom expectations and in some sense to respond to texts according to particular traditions and conventions.

PROMOTING CRITICAL RESPONSES TO TEXTS

Proficient readers readily appreciate the great influence that authors can have on their thoughts and beliefs. Such readers discern the ways that authors (both knowingly and unknowingly) can literally shake their worlds, being especially sensitive to how written messages significantly shape their views of themselves and their places in society. Proficient readers realize, for instance, how advertisements inevitably depict commercial products favorably, how news sources may slant their coverage of events, and how fictional characters can represent imaginative possibilities for real life.

Promoting critical responses to texts means putting readers in the driver's seat, enabling them to take charge of their own thinking and beliefs—which is especially important in today's media-saturated society. It calls for readers to pause and reflect on texts' stated but also implicit values, to step back and strive to apply a more distanced and nuanced perspective on texts' various meanings. Promoting critical responses entails embracing mindsets and strategies that readers can use to better cope with authors' own hidden agendas.

Critical responses to texts largely consist of evaluations and judgments of authors' messages. One form of critical response assesses how well authors present their messages. Students may effectively interrogate the author (Beck & McKeown, 2006) and clarify passages (Palincsar, 2002) by answering to themselves such questions as the following:

"What did the author do to help *me* understand the passage? How can I use this help?"

"Did the author put the ideas in logical order?"

"What did the author not explain clearly?"

"What concepts, words, or phrases are left unclear?"

Another form of critical response urges readers to evaluate evidence systematically before expressing their own conclusions (Copeland, 2005), which in turn traditionally requires that they judge the credibility of sources, the validity of assertions, and the quality of arguments. Responding critically to texts in this way begins with a skeptical frame of mind that leads to constantly questioning, cross checking, and reflecting on the logic of the received knowledge. Socratic teaching methods exemplify instruction along these lines by subjecting all texts to critique, continually doubting and testing authors' ideas. Under this approach, readers come to conclusions only after checking ideas rigorously against the relevant criteria.

Insights from critical inquiry theorists have expanded traditional notions of critical response by concentrating on the links between texts and power (Rogers, Kramer, & Mosely, 2009). Much of the work in critical literacy suggests that contemporary academic reading and writing practices may well reflect and replicate the gender, racial, and class biases of the broader society or culture. Like most everything else, ELA clearly is situated within the broader school and nonschool relations of power and thus subject to society's dictates.

Critical inquiry educators have readers evaluate the ways in which print maintains or transforms privilege, investigating whose interests various texts serve. They guide students in ascertaining how textual representations support or impede marginalized groups' access to full participation in society. For instance, they call attention to materials that predominantly portray scientists as male. They examine the adjectives that ascribe positive or negative attributes to members of different racial and ethnic groups. They analyze the settings in which teenagers typically are presented. In general, they examine the ways in which texts help position various groups in society.

Empowering Struggling Readers touches on critical responses in practically every chapter if such responses are thought to comprise reflective, self-regulated control of the ideas one encounters in texts. This volume most emphatically deals with critical responses to texts in Chapter 11. Viewing critical literacy as an ongoing discussion with the world as a whole, this chapter explores and in fact champions diverse notions of text (literature, film, graphic novels, and media) and corresponding methods of analysis (making inferences, learning vocabulary, synthesizing), as this view is key to promoting dynamic and active conceptions of readers.

Chapter 11 offers up opportunities to think beyond the hype surrounding the new digital technologies as textual tools move from pencils, paper, and books to keyboards, websites, and podcasts. It invites reflection on youth's engagement with multimodal representations and how all forms of critical response fit them.

INTERVENING DIRECTLY
TO BOLSTER STUDENTS' IDENTITIES

The middle school ELA teaching and learning themes I found in *Empowering Struggling Readers* are based on solid scholarship. This final section describes practices that are promising yet lack the bedrock support of education that the practices presented so far can boast. This section also differs from the previous ones because it describes interventions that directly address youth's identities. Finally, the practices presented here have been developed in situations that are related to but definitely different from middle school ELA classes with struggling readers. They suggest possible *future* directions.

Writing Self-Affirmations

Writing self-affirmations tends to bolster feelings of self-worth and diminish stress (Cohen, Garcia, Purdie-Vaughns, Apfel, & Brzustoski, 2009). Self-affirmations are statements about personal values that focus on a wide variety of core values to which individuals may subscribe. Self-affirmations may relate to such attributional areas as the following:

1. Abilities in athletic, artistic, or writing pursuits
2. Activities in school or outside-of-school clubs
3. Affiliations with one's race, ethnicity, or nationality
4. Interests in such diverse pursuits as politics, popular culture, or even automobiles
5. Personality traits—for example, being creative, faithful, or independent
6. Relationships with one's friends or family
7. Religion
8. Sense of adventure, humor, or loyalty

Writing self-affirmations begins with a list of attributes like the ones just suggested. Teachers ask students to identify particular attributes that they value highly, one that is most important to them personally, and then indicate their level of agreement about the value on a 4-point scale that measures the following statements:

"This value has influenced my life."
"In general, I try to live up to this value."
"This value is an important part of who I am."
"I care about this value."

Finally, students write about the one or more times in their lives when the value was especially important to them. Students are told there are no right or wrong answers, and they are to focus on their thoughts and feelings rather than spelling, grammar, or other conventions. Students might share their affirmations with a classroom partner or keep them private in a journal. Setting aside about 15 minutes several times a year to give students a specific opportunity to reflect further on the written affirmations is recommended.

Informed Internal Dialogues

Internal dialogues consist of what people say to themselves (Purkey, 2000). They are a form of self-talk that contributes to people positioning themselves, that is, talking themselves into particular identities. Struggling readers' internal dialogues can be directed toward shaping their literate academic identities.

To inform youth's internal dialogues, ask youth to brainstorm the thoughts they have or questions they ask themselves when they are avoiding reading and writing (Ortiz, 1996). These thoughts, called *shut-downs* or *avoidance talk*, consist of items such as the following:

"I'm not a very good reader."
"Reading isn't for me."
"I should be doing something else."
"What else could I be doing?"
"I'm going to look bad."

Next, have students brainstorm statements they can use when they want to convince themselves to read and write. These thoughts, called *open-ups* or *approach talk*, consist of statements such as the following:

"I can do this."
"If not me, who? If not now, when?"
"No one is perfect."

"Reading is for everyone."
"Just do it!"

The role of internal dialogues can be introduced early in the school year, and all students, including struggling readers, can be encouraged to use this self-talk to their advantage throughout the year. Displaying possible shut-downs and open-ups on a bulletin board or wall reminds youth to use them.

Personal Literacy Narratives

Personal literacy narratives are stories youth tell about their development as readers and writers. Theses narratives promote youth's awareness of how they came to embrace their current literate academic identities. They are designed to help struggling readers to (re)claim and (re)name themselves as fully functioning readers and writers.

Personal literacy narratives involve students in writing portions of their literate lives throughout the school year. Students describe the major experiences they had at certain ages that contributed to their being the readers they have become. The narratives can center about home or community experiences one time and school experiences another. Students' ages can be group into such segments as 1–5, 6–8, 9–11, 12–13, and possibly 14–present. These segments can then be compiled or synthesized into complete narratives covering youth's lifetimes.

Putting a critical edge on such narratives helps to place students in control of their past literacy learning (Lesley, 2004). Teachers create such an edge by having students assess the power others exerted over them while shaping their identities as readers. Students are shown how to actively question the ways in which they were previously positioned as readers and writers in the past. Then they can explicitly appreciate and celebrate the subsequent positive experiences, and they can work to reconcile and rehabilitate what resulted in any negative experiences.

Written affirmations, informed internal dialogues, and personal literacy narratives are deliberate interventions that directly address youth's identities. While teachers play a powerful role in promoting students' identities through day-to-day interactions, some targeted mediations seem appropriate, too. The three presented here seem worth considering for struggling readers in middle school.

CLOSING WORDS

ELA teachers today, as never before, teach amid conditions shaped by state and federal educational policies. All students, including those most socially and economically underserved, now are expected to become literate at sophisticated, advanced levels. Requirements for standards-based accountability, high-stakes tests, evidence-based instruction, and fidelity to program protocols now play significant roles in school administration. The main rationale underlying such curriculum changes seems to be that standardization is best and that first-rate learning results are the product of an established sequence of actions aimed toward agreed-upon goals. Teachers' responses to these new conditions directly affect their interactions with their students (Dooley & Assaf, 2009).

Empowering Struggling Readers shows how undue emphasis on standardization misses the point. Excessive attention to running middle school youth through an ELA program's instructional path can interfere with the relationships needed to uphold high-quality instruction. Efforts at promoting the literacies of middle school readers, especially those who struggle in school, do well to acknowledge the role of youth's socially embedded identities as readers.

This book presents a generous view of middle school youth who struggle with academic reading. It portrays these youth individually as uniquely endowed, culturally informed, and socially embedded learners. It assumes that ultimately all youth are capable of accomplishing rigorous ELA work—so long as they are provided suitable social and academic opportunities, ones that fully take into account their own funds of knowledge.

References

ACT. (2008). The forgotten middle: Ensuring that all students are on target for college and career readiness before high school. Retrieved January 12, 2009, from *www.act.org/research/policymakers/pdf/ForgottenMiddle.pdf*.

Afflerbach, P., Pearson, P. D., & Paris, S. G. (2008). Clarifying differences between reading skills and reading strategies. *Reading Teacher, 61,* 364–373.

Alexie, S. (2007). *The absolutely true diary of a part-time Indian.* New York: Little, Brown.

Allington, R. L. (2005). Ideology is still trumping evidence. *Phi Delta Kappan, 86,* 462–468.

Allington, R. L. (2007). Intervention all day long: New hope for struggling readers. *Voices from the Middle, 14*(4), 7–14.

Almasi, J. F. (1995). The nature of fourth graders' sociocognitive conflicts in peer-led and teacher-led discussions of literature. *Reading Research Quarterly, 30,* 314–351.

Alvermann, D. E. (2001a). Reading adolescents' reading identities: Looking back to see ahead. *Journal of Adolescent and Adult Literacy, 44,* 676–690.

Alvermann, D. E. (2001b). Effective literacy instruction for adolescents. Executive summary and paper commissioned by the National Reading Conference. Chicago, IL: National Reading Conference. Retrieved August 17, 2009, from *www.nrconline.org/publications/alverwhite2.pdf*.

Alvermann, D. E., Hinchman, K. A., Moore, D. W., Phelps, S. F., & Waff, D. R. (2006). *Reconceptualizing the literacies in adolescents' lives* (2nd ed.). Mahwah: NJ: Erlbaum.

Alvermann, D. E., & McLean, C. A. (2007). The nature of literacies. In L. S. Rush, A. J. Eakle, & A. Berger (Eds.), *Secondary school literacy: What research reveals for classroom practice* (pp. 1–20). Urbana, IL: National Council of Teachers of English.

Anaya, R. (1999). *Bless me, Ultima* (7th ed.). New York: Grand Central.

Anagnostopoulos, D., & Rutledge, S. A. (2007). Making sense of school sanctioning policies in urban high schools. *Teachers College Record, 109,* 1261–1302.

Anzaldua, G. (1987). *Borderlands/La frontera: The new mestiza.* San Francisco: Aunt Lute.

Applebee, A. (1974). *Tradition and reform in the teaching of English: A history.* Urbana, IL: National Council of Teachers of English.

Applebee, A. N., Langer, J. A., Nystand, M., & Gamoran, A. (2003). Decision-based approaches to developing understanding: Classroom instruction and student performance in middle and high school English. *American Educational Research Journal, 40,* 685–730.

Appleman, D. (2000). *Critical encounters in high school English: Teaching literary theory to adolescents.* New York and Urbana, IL: Teachers College Press and National Council of Teachers of English.

Athanases, S. Z. (1998). Diverse learners, diverse texts: Exploring identity and difference through literary encounters. *Journal of Literacy Research, 30,* 273–296.

Aukerman, M. S. (2007). When reading it wrong is getting it right: Shared evaluation pedagogy among struggling fifth grade readers. *Research in the Teaching of English, 42,* 56–103.

Ayers, J., & Miller, M. (2009). *Informing adolescent literacy policy and practice: Lessons learned from the Striving Readers program.* Washington, DC: Alliance for Excellent Education. Retrieved August 17, 2009, from *www.all4ed. org/publication_material/adlit.*

Baker, S. K., Simmons, D. C., & Kame'enui, E. J. (1995). *Vocabulary acquisition: Synthesis of the research* (Technical report no. 13). Eugene: National Center to Improve the Tools of Educators, University of Oregon.

Balfanz, R., McPartland, J., & Shaw, A. (2002, April). *Re-conceptualizing extra help for high school students in a high standards era.* Paper commissioned for "Preparing America's Future: The High School Symposium," Washington, DC.

Bartlett, L. (2005). Identity work and cultural artifacts in literacy learning and use: A sociocultural analysis. *Language and Education, 19,* 1–9.

Bartlett, L. (2007). To seem and to feel: Situated identities and literary practices. *Teachers College Record, 109,* 51–69.

Basmadjian, K. G. (2008). Watching what we say: Using video to learn about discussions. *English Education, 14,* 13–38.

Bass, J. F., Dasinger, S., Elish-Piper, L., Matthews, M. W., & Risko, V. J. (2008). *A declaration of readers' rights.* Boston: Pearson Education.

Baumann, J. F., Ware, D., & Edwards, E. C. (2007). "Bumping into spicy, tasty words that catch your tongue": A formative experiment on vocabulary instruction. *The Reading Teacher, 61,* 108–122.

Baumann, J. F., Edwards, E. C., Boland, E. M., Olejnik, S., & Kame'enui, E. J. (2003). Vocabulary tricks: Effects of instruction in morphology and context on fifth-grade students' ability to derive and infer word meanings. *American Educational Research Journal, 40,* 447–494.

Beach, R., & O'Brien, D. G. (2007). Adopting reader and writer stances in understanding and producing texts. In L. S. Rush, A. J. Eakle, & A. Berger (Eds.),

Secondary school literacy: What research reveals for classroom practice (pp. 217–242). Urbana, IL: National Council of Teachers of English.

Beck, I. L., & McKeown, M. G. (2006). *Improving comprehension with Questioning the Author: A fresh and expanded view of a powerful approach.* New York: Scholastic.

Berne, J. I., & Clark, K. F. (2005). Making meaning in ninth grade: An exploratory study of peer-led literature discussions. *Illinois Reading Council Journal, 33,* 31–38.

Berne, J. I., & Clark, K. F. (2006). Comprehension strategy use during peer-led discussions of text: Ninth-graders tackle "The Lottery." *Journal of Adolescent and Adult Literacy, 49,* 674–686.

Berry, M. (1981). Systemic linguistics and discourse analysis: A multi-layered approach to exchange structure. In M. Coulthard & M. Montgomery (Eds.), *Studies in discourse analysis.* London: Routledge & Kegan Paul.

Biancarosa, C., & Snow, C. (2006). *Reading next—a vision for action and research in middle and high school literacy: A report to Carnegie Corporation of New York* (2nd ed.). Washington, DC: Alliance for Excellent Education.

Biggers, D. (2001). The argument against Accelerated Reader. *Journal of Adolescent and Adult Literacy, 45*(1), 72–75.

Black, A. (2005). The use of asynchronous discussion: Creating a text of talk. *Contemporary Issues in Technology and Teacher Education, 5,* 5–24.

Bloome, D., & Egan-Roberston, A. (1993). The social construction of intertextuality in classroom reading and writing lessons. *Reading Research Quarterly, 28,* 304–333.

Blum, T., Lipsett, L. R., & Yocom, D. J. (2002). Literature circles: A tool for self-determination in one middle school inclusive classroom. *Remedial and Special Education, 23,* 99–108.

Botzakis, S. (2007). *Pretty in print: Questioning magazines.* Mankato, MN: Capstone Press.

Botzakis, S. (2009). *What's your source?: Questioning the news.* Mankato, MN: Capstone Press.

Brabham, E. G., & Villaume, S. K. (2002). Leveled text: The good news and the bad news. *The Reading Teacher, 55,* 438–441.

Brass, J. (2009, August). *The emergence of 'English' in the U.S.: Reconstructing 'the cure of souls' as popular education.* Paper presented at the International Standing Conference for the History of Education, Uttrecht, Netherlands.

Brookfield, S. D., & Preskill, S. (2005). *Discussion as a way of teaching: Tools and techniques for democratic classrooms* (2nd ed.). San Francisco: Jossey-Bass.

Brooks, L. (2008). *Selkie Girl.* New York: Knopf.

Brooks, W., Browne, S., & Hampton, G. (2008). "There ain't no accounting for what folks see in their own mirrors": Considering colorism within a Sharon Flake narrative. *Journal of Adolescent and Adult Literacy, 51,* 660–669.

Brown, J. E., & Stephens, E. C. (1995). *Teaching young adult literature: Sharing the connection.* Belmont, CA: Wadsworth.

Brown, K. J., Morris, D., & Fields, M. (2005). Intervention after grade 1: Serving increased numbers of struggling readers effectively. *Journal of Literacy Research, 37,* 61–94.

Bruner, J. (1977). *The process of education.* Cambridge, MA: Harvard University Press. (Original work published 1960)

Burns, L. (2007). A practical guide to political action: Grassroots and English teaching. *English Journal, 96*(4), 56–61.

Burns, L. D. (2008). Relevance, new literacies, and pragmatic research for middle grades education. *Middle Grades Research Journal, 3,* 1–28.

Burns, L., Scherff, L., & Botzakis, S. (2009, November). *The kids are alright: Making English relevant for 21st century youth.* Paper presented at the annual convention of the National Council for Teachers of English, Philadelphia, PA.

Caldwell, J., & Leslie, L. (2004). Does proficiency in middle school reading assure proficiency in high school reading?: The possible role of think-alouds. *Journal of Adolescent and Adult Literacy, 47,* 324–335.

Cambourne, B. (1995). Toward an educationally relevant theory of literacy learning: Twenty years of inquiry. *The Reading Teacher, 49*(3), 182–190.

Carico, K. M. (2001). Negotiating meaning in classroom literature discussions. *Journal of Adolescent and Adult Literacy, 44,* 510–518.

Carnegie Council on Advancing Adolescent Literacy (2010). *Time to act: An agenda for advancing adolescent literacy for college and career success.* New York: Carnegie Corporation of New York. Retrieved November 3, 2009, from *www.carnegie.org/literacy/tta/index.html.*

Center for Media Literacy. (2004). CML MediaLit Kit: A framework for learning and teaching in a media age. Retrieved July 3, 2009, from *www.medialit. org.*

Clark, K. F. (2009). The nature and influence of comprehension strategy use during peer-led literature discussions: An analysis of intermediate grade students' practice. *Literacy Research and Instruction, 48,* 95–119.

Clark, K. F., & Graves, M. F. (2005). Scaffolding students' comprehension of text. *The Reading Teacher, 58,* 570–580.

Cohen, D. (1988). Teaching practice: Plus ça change. In P. W. Jackson (Ed.), *Contributing to educational change: Perspectives on research and practice* (pp. 27–84). Berkeley, CA: McCutchan.

Cohen, G. L., Garcia, J., Purdie-Vaughns, V., Apfel, N., & Brzustoski, P. (2009). Recursive processes in self-affirmation: Intervening to close the minority achievement gap. *Science, 324,* 400–403.

Coiro, J. (2003). Reading comprehension on the Internet: Expanding our understanding of reading comprehension to encompass new literacies. *The Reading Teacher, 56,* 458–464.

Coiro, J. (2009). A beginning understanding of the interplay between offline and online reading comprehension ability when adolescents read on the Internet. Presentation given at the 29th annual University of Wisconsin Research Symposium, Appleton.

Coiro, J., & Dobler, E. (2007). Exploring the online reading comprehension strategies used by sixth-grade skilled readers to search for and locate information on the Internet. *Reading Research Quarterly, 42,* 214–257.

Cole, P. (2008). *Young adult literature in the 21st century.* New York: McGraw-Hill.

Collins, P. H. (1990). Black feminist thought in the matrix of domination. Retrieved April 26, 2009, from *www.hartford-hwp.com/archives/45a/252.html.*

Compton-Lilly, C. (2008). Teaching struggling readers: Capitalizing on diversity for effective learning. *The Reading Teacher, 61,* 668–672.

Conley, M. (2008). Cognitive strategy instruction for adolescents: What we know about the promise, what we don't know about the potential. *Harvard Educational Review, 78,* 84–106.

Cook-Sather, A. (2002). Authorizing students' perspectives: Toward trust, dialogue, and change in education. *Educational Researcher, 31,* 3–14.

Cormier, R. (2007). *I am the cheese.* New York: Knopf.

Cromley, J. G., & Azevedo, R. (2009). Locating information within extended hypermedia. *Educational Technology Research and Development, 57,* 287–313.

Cuban, L. (1993). *How teachers taught: Constancy and change in American classrooms, 1890–1990.* New York: Teachers College Press.

Curtis, C. P. (2000). *The Waltons go to Birmingham—1963.* New York: Laurel-Leaf Books.

Cushman, K. (1995). *Catherine called Birdy.* New York: HarperCollins.

Damico, J. S. (2005). Multiple dimensions of literacy and conceptions of readers: Toward a more expansive view of accountability. *The Reading Teacher, 58,* 644–652.

Daneman, M. (1991). Individual differences in reading skills. In R. Barr, M. L. Kamil, P. Mosental, & P. D. Pearson (Eds.), *Handbook of reading research* (Vol. 2, pp. 512–538). White Plains, NY: Longman.

Deci, E. L., & Ryan, R. M. (2000). The "what" and "why" of goal pursuits: Human needs and the self-determination of behavior. *Psychological Inquiry, 11*(4), 227"268.

Dennis, D. V. (2008). Are assessment data really driving middle school reading instruction?: What we can learn from one student's experience. *Journal of Adolescent and Adult Literacy, 51,* 578–587.

Delpit, D., & Dowdy, J. K. (Eds.). (2008). *The skin that we speak: Thoughts on language and culture in the classroom.* New York: New Press.

Dewitz, P., Jones, J., & Leahy, S. (2009). Comprehension strategy instruction in core reading programs. *Reading Research Quarterly, 44,* 102–126.

Diamandis, P. (1989). *Peter's laws: The creed of the sociopathic obsessive–compulsive.* Cincinnati, OH: Author.

Dillon, D. R. (1989). Showing them that I want them to learn and that I care about who they are: A microethnography of the social organization of a secondary low track English Reading classroom. *American Educational Research Journal, 26,* 227–259.

Doering, A., Beach, R., & O'Brien, D. (2007). Infusing multimodal tools and digital literacies into an English education program. *English Education, 40,* 41–60.

Dooley, C. M., & Assaf, L. C. (2009). Contexts matter: Two teachers' language arts instruction in this high-stakes era. *Journal of Literacy Research, 41,* 354–391.

Draper, S. (2008). *Copper sun.* New York: Antheum.

Duke, N. K., & Pearson, P. D. (2002). Effective practices for developing reading comprehension. In A. E. Farstrup & S. J. Samuels (Eds.), *What research has to say about reading instruction* (pp. 205–242). Newark, DE: International Reading Association.

Dunston, P. J. (2007). Instructional practices, struggling readers, and a university-based reading club. *Journal of Adolescent and Adult Literacy, 50,* 328–336.

Dymock, S. (2007). Comprehension strategy instruction: Teaching narrative text structure awareness. *The Reading Teacher, 61,* 161–167.

Dzaldov, B. S., & Peterson, S. (2005). Book leveling and readers. *The Reading Teacher, 59,* 222–229.

Eagleton, M., Guinee, K., & Langlais, K. (2003). Teaching the Internet literacy strategies: The hero inquiry project. *Voices from the Middle, 10,* 28–35.

Eeds, M., & Wells, D. (1989). Grand conversations: An exploration of meaning construction in literature study groups. *Research in the Teaching of English, 23,* 4–29.

Egan-Robertson, A. (1998). Learning about culture, language, and power: Understanding relationships among personhood, literacy practices, and intertextuality. *Journal of Literacy Research, 30,* 449–487.

Eisner, W. (2006). *Will Eisner's New York: Life in the big city.* New York: Norton.

Eliopoulos, D., & Gotlieb, C. (2003). Evaluating web search results rankings. *Online, 27,* 42–48.

Evans, K. S. (2002). Fifth-grade students' perceptions of how they experience literature discussion groups. *Reading Research Quarterly, 37,* 46–69.

Fang, Z. (2008). Going beyond the Fab Five: Helping students cope with the unique linguistic challenges of expository reading in intermediate grades. *Journal of Adolescent and Adult Literacy, 51*(6), 476–487.

Farmer, M., & Soden, J. A. (2005). The seven Cs of comprehension. *Voices from the Middle, 13*(2), 20–23.

Fecho, B. (2004). *"Is this English?": Race, language, and culture in the classroom.* New York: Teachers College Press.

Fecho, B., & Botzakis, S. (2007). Feasts of becoming: Imagining a literacy classroom based on dialogic beliefs. *Journal of Adolescent and Adult Literacy, 50,* 548–558.

Fisher, A. (2008). Teaching comprehension and critical literacy: Investigating guided reading in three primary classrooms. *Literacy, 42*(1), 19–28.

Fisher, D., & Frey, N. (2008). What does it take to create skilled readers?: Facilitating the transfer and application of literacy strategies. *Voices from the Middle, 15*(4), 16–22.

FitzPatrick, D. (2008). Constructing complexity: Using reading levels to differentiate reading comprehension activities. *English Journal, 98*(2), 57–63.

Frank, A. (1953). *The diary of Anne Frank.* New York: Bantam.

Franzak, J. (2006). Zoom: A review of the literature on marginalized adolescent readers, literacy theory, and policy implications. *Reviews of Research in Education, 76*(2), 209–248.

Frey, N., & Fisher, D. (2004). Using graphic novels, anime, and the Internet in an urban high school. *English Journal, 93*(3), 19–25.

Frey, N., & Fisher, D. (2008). Doing the right thing with technology. *English Journal, 97*(6), 38–42.

Friese, E., Alvermann, D., Parkes, A., & Rezak, A. (2008). Selecting texts for English language arts classrooms: When assessment is not enough. *English Teaching: Practice and Critique 7*(3), 74–99.

Frye, N. (2001). The archetypes of literature. In V. B. Leitch (Ed.), *The Norton anthology of theory and criticism* (pp. 1445–1456). New York: Norton.

Galda, L., & Beach, R. (2004). Response to literature as a cultural activity. In R. B. Ruddell & N. J. Unrau (Eds.) *Theoretical models and processes of reading* (5th ed., pp. 852–869). Newark, DE: International Reading Association.

Gamoran, A. (1993). Alternative uses of ability grouping in secondary schools: Can we bring high-quality instruction to low-ability classes? *American Journal of Education, 101*, 1–22.

Gee, J. P. (1996). *Social linguistics and literacies: Ideology in discourse.* Bristol, PA: Taylor & Francis.

Giroux, H. (1988). *Teachers as intellectuals: Toward a critical pedagogy of learning.* New York: Bergin & Garvey.

Glenn, W. (2008). Gossiping girls, Insider boys, A-list achievement: Examining and exposing young adult novels consumed by conspicuous consumption. *Journal of Adolescent and Adult Literacy, 52*(1), 34–42.

Golden, J. (2001). *Reading in the dark: Using film as a tool in the English classroom.* Urbana, IL: National Council of Teachers of English.

Goldenberg, C. (2008, Summer). Teaching English language learners: What the research does—and does not—say. *American Educator.* Retrieved August 13, 2008, from *www.aft.org/pubs-reports/american_educator/issues/summer08/index.htm.*

Gonzalez, N. E. (2005). *Funds of knowledge: Theorizing practices in households and classrooms.* Mahwah, NJ: Erlbaum.

Goodman, K. (2008). Making reading curriculum by professional consensus and by legislative mandate. *Journal of Reading Education, 34*(1), 5–15.

Grabill, J. T., & Hicks, T. (2005). Multiliteracies meet methods: The case for digital writing in English education. *English Education, 37*, 301–311.

Graham, S., & Perin, D. (2007). *Writing next: Effective strategies to improve writing of adolescents in middle and high schools—a report to Carnegie Corporation of New York.* Washington, DC: Alliance for Excellent Education.

Graves, M. F. (2006). *The vocabulary book: Learning and instruction.* New York: Teachers College Press.

Graves, M. F., & Philippot, R. A. (2002). High-interest, easy reading: An important resource for struggling readers. *Preventing School Failure 46*(4), 179–181.

Greenfield, E. (1972). *Honey, I love and other love poems.* New York: HarperCollins.

Greenleaf, C., Schoenbach, R., Cziko, C., & Mueller, F. (2001). Apprenticing adolescent readers to academic literacy. *Harvard Educational Review*, 71(1), 79–130.

Groenke, S. & Scherff. L. (in press). *Teaching young adult literature through differentiated instruction*. Urbana, IL: National Council of Teachers of English.

Grolnick, W. S., & Ryan, R. M. (1987). Autonomy in children's learning: An experimental and individual difference investigation. *Journal of Personality and Social Psychology*, 52, 890–898.

Grossman, P. (1990). *The making of a teacher: Teacher knowledge and teacher education*. New York: Teachers College Press.

Guitiérrez, K. D. (2008). Developing a sociocritical literacy in the Third Space. *Reading Research Quarterly*, 43(2), 148–164.

Guthrie, J. (2002). Preparing students for high-stakes test taking in reading. In A. Farstrup & S. J. Samuels (Eds.), *What research has to say about reading instruction* (pp. 370–391). Newark, DE: International Reading Association.

Guthrie, J., & Alao, S. (1997). Designing contexts to increase motivation for reading. *Educational Psychologist*, 32, 95–107.

Guthrie, J. T., Alao, S., & Rinehart, J. (1997). Engagement for young adolescents. *Journal of Adolescent and Adult Literacy*, 40(6), 438–446.

Guthrie, J., Coddington, C., & Wigfield, A. (2009). Profiles of reading motivation among African American and Caucasian students. *Journal of Literacy Research*, 41(3), 317–353.

Guthrie, J. T., & Davis, M. H. (2003). Motivating struggling readers in middle school through an engagement model of classroom practice. *Reading and Writing Quarterly: Overcoming Learning Difficulties*, 19, 59–85.

Guthrie, J., Perencevich, K., Wigfield, A., Taboada, A., Humenick, N., & Barbosa, P. (2006). Influences of stimulating tasks on reading motivation and comprehension. *Journal of Educational Research*, 99(4), 232–245.

Guthrie, J. T., & Wigfield, A. (2001). Engagement and motivation in reading. In M. L. Kamil, P. B. Mosenthal, P. D. Pearson, & R. Barr (Eds.), *Handbook of reading research* (Vol. 3, pp. 403–422). Mahwah, NJ: Erlbaum.

Hagood, M. (2000). New times, new millennium, new literacies. *Reading Research and Instruction*, 39, 311–328.

Hall, L. A. (2005a). Comprehending expository texts: Promising strategies for struggling readers and students with reading disabilities? *Reading Research and Instruction*, 44, 75–95.

Hall, L. A. (2005b). Struggling readers and content area text: Interactions with and perceptions of comprehension, self, and success. *Research in Middle-Level Education*, 39(4), 1–19.

Hall, L. A. (2007). Understanding the silence: Struggling readers discuss decisions about reading expository text. *Journal of Educational Research*, 100, 132–141.

Hall, L. A. (2009). Struggling reader, struggling teacher: An examination of student–teacher transactions with reading instruction and text in social studies. *Research in the Teaching of English*, 43, 286–309.

Hall, L. A. (2010). The negative consequences of becoming a good reader: Identity theory as a lens for understanding struggling readers, teachers, and reading instruction. *Teachers College Record, 117,* 1792–1829.

Hall, L. A., Johnson, A., Juzwik, M. M., Wortham, S., & Mosley, M. (2010). Teacher identity in the context of literacy teaching: Three explorations of classroom positioning and interaction in secondary schools. *Teaching and Teacher Education, 26,* 234–243.

Hall, L. A., & Nellenbach, K. (2009). *The role of reading identities and reading abilities in students' discussions about texts and comprehension strategies.* Paper presented at the National Reading Conference, Albuquerque, NM.

Hall, L. A., & Piazza, S. V. (2008, December). Critically reading texts: What students do and how teachers can help. *The Reading Teacher, 62,* 32–41.

Halladay, J. L. (2008). Reconsidering frustration-level texts: Second-graders' experiences with difficult texts. Retrieved December 12, 2009, from *conflibs.nrconline.org/58th_Annual_Mtg/Halladay_NRC_2008.pdf.*

Heller, R., & Greenleaf, C. L. (2007). *Literacy instruction in the content areas: Getting to the core of middle and high school improvement.* Washington, DC: Alliance for Excellent Education. Retrieved August 25, 2007, from the Alliance for Excellent Education site, *www.all4ed.org/adolescent_literacy/index.html.*

Henk, W. A., & Melnick, S. A. (1995). The reader self-perception scale (RSPS): A new tool for measuring how children feel about themselves as readers. *The Reading Teacher, 48,* 470–482.

Henry, L. A. (2006). SEARCHing for an answer: The critical role of new literacies while reading on the Internet. *The Reading Teacher, 59,* 614–627.

Heron-Hruby, A., Hagood, M. C., & Alvermann, D. E. (2008). Switching places and looking to adolescents for the practices that shape school literacies. *Reading and Writing Quarterly, 24,* 311–334.

Hiebert, E. H., & Kamil, M. L. (2005). *Teaching and learning vocabulary: Bringing research to practice.* Mahwah, NJ: Erlbaum.

Hill, D. K. (2008). Conflict in a sixth-grade book club: The impact of a rule driven discourse. *Voices from the Middle, 16,* 16–24.

Hillocks, G. (1980). Toward a hierarchy of skills in the comprehension of literature. *English Journal, 69*(3), 54–59.

Hinton, K. (2004). "Sturdy black bridges": Discussing race, class, and gender. *English Journal, 94*(2), 60–64.

Hinton-Johnson, K. (2003). *Expanding the power of literature: African American literary theory and young adult literature.* Unpublished doctoral dissertation, The Ohio State University, Columbus.

Hipple, T. (2000). With themes for all: The universality of the young adult novel. In V. R. Monseau & G. M. Salvner (Eds.), *Reading their world: The young adult novel in the classroom* (pp. 1–14). Portsmouth, NH: Heinemann.

Hirsch, E. D. (1988). *Cultural literacy: What every American needs to know.* New York: Vintage.

Hirsch, E. D. (2006). *The knowledge deficit: Closing the shocking education gap for American children.* Boston: Houghton Mifflin.

Hobbs, R. (2007). *Reading the media: Media literacy in high school English.* New York: Teachers College Press.

Holland, D., & Lave, J. (2001). *History in person: Enduring struggles, contentious practice, intimate identities.* Sante Fe, NM: School of American Research Press.

Hook, J. N. (1979). *A long way together: A personal view of National Council of Teachers of English's first sixty-seven years.* Urbana, IL: National Council of Teachers of English.

Howley, K. (2007). Reading reality television: Cultivating critical media literacy. In M. T. Christel & S. Sullivan (Eds.), *Lesson plans for creating media-rich classrooms* (pp. 148–155). Urbana, IL: National Council of Teachers of English.

International Reading Association. (2009). Standards for the assessment of reading and writing (rev. ed.). Retrieved December 10, 2009, from *www.reading.org/General/CurrentResearc/Stnadards/AssessmentStandards.aspx.*

Ivey, G., & Broaddus, K. (2000). Tailoring the fit: Reading instruction and middle school readers. *The Reading Teacher, 54,* 68–78.

Ivey, G., & Broaddus, K. (2001). "Just plain reading": A survey of what makes students want to read in middle school classrooms. *Reading Research Quarterly, 36*(4), 350–377.

Ivey, G., & Fisher, D. (2005). Learning from what doesn't work. *Educational Leadership. 63*(2), 8–14.

Jacobs, D. (2007). More than words: Comics as a means of teaching multiple literacies. *English Journal, 96*(3), 19–25.

Jacobs, V. A. (2008). Adolescent literacy: Putting the crisis in context. *Harvard Educational Review, 78,* 7–39.

Jago, C. (2003). *The call of the wild:* Using the elements of literature for comprehension. *Voices from the Middle, 11*(1), 64–65.

Jewitt, C. (2008). Miltimodality and literacy in school classrooms. *Review of Research in Education, 32,* 241–267.

Johannessen, L. R. (2004). Helping "struggling" students achieve success. *Journal of Adolescent and Adult Literacy, 47,* 638–647.

Johannessen, L. R., & McCann, T. M. (2009). Adolescents who struggle with literacy. In L. Christenbury, R. Bomer, & P. Smagorinsky (Eds.), *Handbook of adolescent literacy research* (pp. 65–79). New York: Guilford Press.

Johnson, H., & Freedman, L. (2005). *Developing critical awareness at the middle level: Using texts as tools for critique and pleasure.* Newark, DE: International Reading Association.

Johnson, S. (2005). *Everything bad is good for you: How today's popular culture is actually making us smarter.* New York: Riverhead Books.

Johnston, P. (2004). *Choice words: How our language affects children's learning.* Portland, ME: Stenhouse.

Johnston, P., & Costello, P. (2005). Principles for literacy assessment. *Reading Research Quarterly, 4*(2), 256–267.

Jung, M. (2009). Selkie girl [Review]. *Journal of Adolescent and Adult Literacy, 52,* 725.

Kamil, M. (2008). How to get recreational reading to increase reading achievement. *Fifty-seventh Yearbook of the National Reading Conference* (pp. 31–40). Oak Creek, WI: National Reading Conference.

Kamil, M. L., Borman, G. D., Dole, J., Kral, C. C., Salinger, T., & Torgesen, J. (2008). *Improving adolescent literacy: Effective classroom and intervention practices: A practice guide* (NCEE #2008–4027). Washington, DC: Institute of Education Sciences, U.S. Department of Education. Retrieved September 4, 2008, from *ies.ed.gov/ncee/wwc*.

Karchmer, R. A. (2004). Creating connections: Using the Internet to support struggling readers' background knowledge. *Reading and Writing Quarterly, 20,* 331–335.

Keene, E. O. (2007). The essence of understanding. In K. Beers, R. E. Probst, & L. Rief (Eds.). *Adolescent literacy: Turning promise into practice* (pp. 27–38). Portsmouth, NH: Heinemann.

Keene, E. O., & Zimmerman, S. (2007). *Mosaic of thought: The power of comprehension strategy instruction* (2nd ed.). Portsmouth, NH: Heinemann.

Kelley, M., & Clausen-Grace, N. (2008). Ensuring transfer of strategies by using a metacognitive teaching framework. *Voices from the Middle, 15,* 23–31.

King, A., & Brownell, J. (1966). *The curriculum and the disciplines of knowledge: A theory of curriculum practice.* New York: Wiley.

Kintsch, W., & Kintsch, E. (2005). Comprehension. In S. G. Paris & S. A. Stahl (Eds.), *Current issues in reading comprehension and assessment* (pp. 71–92). Mahwah, NJ: Erlbaum.

Kist, W. (2005). *New literacies in action: Teaching and learning in multiple media.* New York: Teachers College Press.

Klem, A., & Connell, P. (2004, March 11–14). *Relationships matter: Linking teacher support to student engagement and achievement.* Paper presented at the 10th biennial meeting of the Society for Research on Adolescence, Baltimore, MD.

Knickerbocker, J. L., & Rycik, J. A. (2006). Reexamining literature study in the middle grades: A critical response framework. *American Secondary Education, 34,* 43–56.

Knowles, J. (1960). *A separate peace.* Austin, TX: Holt, Rinehart & Winston.

Kottke, S. (2008). *RSVPs to reading: Gendered responses to the permeable curriculum.* Paper presented at the National Reading Conference, Orlando, FL.

Krashen, S. (1993). *The power of reading: Insights from the research.* Englewood, CA: Libraries Unlimited.

Krashen, S. (2001). More smoke and mirrors: A critique of the National Reading Panel Report on Fluency. *Phi Delta Kappan, 83*(2), 119–123.

Kraver, J. R. (2007). Engendering gender equity: Using literature to teach and learn democracy. *English Journal, 96*(6), 67–73.

Kroeger, D. (2008). Thoughts on narrowing the policy–practice gap: Literacy teachers as critical bureaucrats. *Journal of Reading Education, 34*(1), 46–50.

Lacquer, T. (1976). *Religion and respectability: Sunday schools and working class culture, 1780–1850.* New Haven, CT, and London: Yale University Press.

Ladson-Billings, G. (1992). Reading between the lines and beyond the pages: A culturally relevant approach to teaching literacy. *Theory into Practice, 31,* 312–320.

Ladson-Billings, G. (1994). *The dreamkeepers: Successful teachers of African American children.* San Francisco, CA: Jossey-Bass.

Lain, S. (2003). The dimensions of reading. *Voices from the Middle, 11*(1), 24–28.

Landt, S. M. (2006). Multicultural literature and young adolescents: A kaleidoscope of opportunity. *Journal of Adolescent and Adult Literacy, 49*(8), 690–697.

Lanham, R. A. (2001). What's next for text? *Education, Communication and Information, 1*(1), 15–36.

Lankshear, C., & Knobel, M. (2003). *New literacies: Changing knowledge and classroom learning.* Philadelphia: Open University Press.

Larrotta, C., & Gainer, J. (2008). Text matters: Mexican immigrant parents reading their world. *Multicultural Education, 16,* 45–51.

Lawless, K. A., Schrader, P. G., & Mayall, H. J. (2007). Acquisition of information online: Knowledge, navigation, and learning outcomes. *Journal of Literacy Research, 39,* 289–306.

Lee, C. (1998). Culturally responsive teaching and performance-based assessment. *Journal of Negro Education, 67*(3), 268–279.

Lee, C. (2007). *Culture, literacy, and learning: Taking bloom in the midst of the whirlwind.* New York: Teachers College Press.

Lee, C. D., & Spratley, A. (2010). *Reading in the disciplines: The challenges of adolescent literacy.* New York: Carnegie Corporation of New York.

Lee, H. (2002). *To kill a mockingbird.* New York: Harper Perennial Modern Classics.

Lei, J. (2009). Digital natives as preservice teachers: What technology preparation is needed? *Journal of Computing in Teacher Education, 25,* 87–97.

Lenters, K. (2006). Resistance, struggle, and the adolescent reader. *Journal of Adolescent and Adult Literacy, 50,* 136–146.

Lesley, M. (2004). Refugees from reading: Students' perceptions of "remedial" literacy pedagogy. *Reading Research and Instruction, 44,* 62–85.

Leu, D. J., Kinzer, C. K., Coiro, J. L., & Cammack, D. W. (2004). Toward a theory of new literacies emerging from the Internet and other information and communication technologies. In R. B. Ruddell & N. J. Unrau (Eds.), *Theoretical models and processes of reading* (5th ed., pp. 1570–1613). Wilmington, DE: International Reading Association.

Levine, E., & Bjorkman, S. (1995). *I hate English.* New York: Scholastic.

Lewis, J. (Ed.). (2009). *Essential questions in adolescent literacy: Teachers and researchers describe what works in classrooms.* New York: Guilford Press.

Lincoln, A. (1848). To Thomas Lincoln and John D. Johnston, December 24, 1898. In D. Fehrenbacher (Ed.), *Lincoln: Speeches and writings* (p. 224). New York: Library of America.

Linn, R., Baker, E., & Dunbar, S. (1991). Complex, performance-based assessment: Expectations and validation criteria. *Educational Researcher, 20,* 15–21.

London, J. (2008). *The call of the wild.* [The Project Gutenberg EBook of *The call of the wild*]. Retrieved April 26, 2009, from *www.gutenberg.org/etext/215*. (Original work published 1903)

Lortie, D. (1975). *Schoolteacher: A sociological study*. Chicago: University of Chicago Press.

Lowry, L. (1993). *The giver*. New York: Delacorte Books for Young Readers.

Luke, A. (2004). The trouble with English. *Research in the Teaching of English, 39*(1), 85–95.

Mallette, M. H., Henk, W. A., Waggoner, J. E., & DeLaney, C. J. (2005). What matters most?: A survey of accomplished middle-level educators' beliefs and values about literacy. *Action in Teacher Education, 27*, 33–42.

Manguel, A. (1997). *The history of reading*. New York: Penguin.

Margolis, H., & McCabe, P. H. (2006). Motivation struggling readers in an era of mandated instructional practices. *Reading Psychology, 27*, 435–455.

Marsh, J. (2006). Popular culture in the literacy curriculum: A Bourdieuan analysis. *Reading Research Quarterly, 41*(2), 160–174.

Marshall, J., Smith, J., & Schaafsma, D. (1997). Teaching as we're taught: The university's role in the education of English teachers. *English Education, 29*(4), 246–268.

Marzano, R., Pickering, D., & Pollock, J. (2001). *Classroom instruction that works: Research-based strategies for increasing student achievement*. Upper Saddle River, NJ: Pearson Education.

Mathieson, M. (1975). *The preachers of culture: A study of English and its teachers*. Totowa, NJ: Rowman & Littlefield.

McCarthey. S. J. (1998). Constructing multiple subjectivities in classroom literacy contexts. *Research in the Teaching of English, 32*, 126–160.

McCarthey, S. (2001). Identity construction in elementary readers and writers. *Reading Research Quarterly, 36*, 122–151.

McCloud, S. (1993). *Understanding comics: The invisible art*. Northampton, MA: Tundra.

McCormick, K. (1994). *The culture of reading and the teaching of English*. Manchester, UK: Manchester University Press.

McCormick, P. (2006). *Sold*. New York: Hyperion.

McDermott, R., & Varenne, H. (1995). Culture as disability. *Anthropology and Education Quarterly, 26*, 324–348.

McGill-Franzen, A., & Allington, D. (2001, June/July). Summer reading: Improving access to books and opportunities to read. *Reading Today*, p. 10.

McRae, A., & Guthrie, J. T. (2009). Promoting reasons for reading teacher practices that impact motivation. In E. H. Hiebert (Ed.) *Reading more, reading better* (pp. 55–78). New York: Guilford Press.

McVee, M. B., Bailey, N. M., & Shanahan, L. E. (2008). Teachers and teacher educators learning from new literacies and new technologies. *Teaching Education, 19*, 197–210.

Meier, D., & Wood, G. (2004). *Many children left behind: How the No Child Left Behind Act is damaging our children and our schools*. Boston: Beacon Press.

Mesmer, H. A. E. (2006). Beginning reading materials: A national survey of primary teachers' reported use and beliefs. *Journal of Literacy Research, 38*, 389–425.

Meyer, S. (2006). *Twilight*. New York: Little, Brown.

Miller, S. (1991). *Textual carnivals: The politics of composition*. Carbondale, IL: Southern Illinois University Press.

Miller, S., & Fox, D. (2006). *Reconstructing English education for the 21st century: A report on the CEE leadership and policy summit*. Conference on English Education. Retrieved May 15, 2006, from *www.ncte.org/groups/cee/featuredinfo/122846.htm*.

Minnick, J. B., & Mergil, F. (2008). The doubling moment: Resurrecting Edgar Allan Poe. *Voices from the Middle, 16*, 37–46.

Moje, E. (2008). Foregrounding the disciplines in secondary literacy teaching and learning: A call for change. *Journal of Adolescent and Adult Literacy, 52*, 96–107.

Moje, E., Ciechanowski, K., Kramer, K., Ellis, L., Carrillo, R., & Collazo, T. (2004). Working toward third space in content area literacy: An examination of everyday funds of knowledge and discourse. *Reading Research Quarterly, 39*, 38–70.

Moje, E. B., & Dillon, D. R. (2006). Adolescent identities as mediated by science classroom discourse communities. In D. E. Alvermann, K. A. Hinchman, D. W. Moore, S. F. Phelps, & D. R. Waff (Eds.), *Reconceptualizing the literacies in adolescents' lives* (2nd ed., pp. 85–106). Mahwah, NJ: Erlbaum.

Moje, E., Overby, M., Tysvaer, N., & Morris, K. (2008). The complex world of adolescent literacy: Myths, motivations, and mysteries. *Harvard Educational Review, 78*, 1–35.

Moje, E., Young, J., Readence, J. E., & Moore, D. W. (2000). Reinventing adolescent literacy for new times: Perennial and millennial issues. *Journal of Adolescent and Adult Literacy, 43*, 400–410.

Moll, L., Amanti, C., Neff, D., & Gonzalez, N. (1992). Funds of knowledge for teaching: A qualitative approach to connect homes and classrooms. *Theory into Practice, 31*(2), 132–141.

Moll, L., & Gonzalez, N. (2001). Lessons from research with language-minority children. In E. Cushman, E. Kintgen, B. Kroll, & M. Rose (Eds.), *Literacy: A critical sourcebook* (pp. 156–172). New York: Bedford/St. Martins.

Moll, L., & Ruiz, R. (2002). The schooling of Latino students. In M. Suarez-Orozco & M. Paez (Eds.), *Contexts for learning: Sociocultural dynamics in children's development* (pp. 19–42). New York: Oxford University Press.

Moller, K. J. (2004–2005). Creating zones of possibility for struggling readers: A study of one fourth grader's shifting roles in literature discussions. *Journal of Literacy Research, 36*, 419–460.

Monnin, K. (2009). Finding literacy in Neverland. *Voices from the Middle, 16*(3), 54–56.

Montgomery, W. (2000). Literature discussion in the elementary school classroom: Developing cultural understanding. *Multicultural Education, 8*, 33–36.

Moore, D. W., & Cunningham, J. W. (2006). Adolescent agency and literacy. In D. E. Alvermann, K. A. Hinchman, D. W. Moore, S. F. Phelps, & D. R. Waff (Eds.), *Reconceptualizing the literacies in adolescents' lives* (2nd ed., pp. 129–146). Mahwah, NJ: Erlbaum.

Moore, J. N. (1997). *Interpreting young adult literature: Literary theory in the secondary classroom*. Portsmouth, NH: Boynton/Cook.

Morrell, E. (2004). *Linking literacy and popular culture: Finding connections for lifelong learning*. Norwood, MA: Christopher-Gordon.

Mraz, M., Rickleman, R. J., & Vacca, R. T. (2009). Content-area reading: Past, present, and future. In K. D. Wood & W. E. Blanton (Eds.), *Literacy instruction for adolescents: Research-based practices* (pp. 77–91). New York: Guilford Press.

Myers, D. W. (1995). *Slam!* New York: Scholastic.

Nagy, W. E. (2005). Why vocabulary instruction needs to be long-term and comprehensive. In E. H. Hiebert & M. L. Kamil (Eds.), *Teaching and learning vocabulary: Bringing research to practice*. Mahwah, NJ: Erlbaum.

Nagy, W. E., & Scott, A. (2000). Vocabulary processes. In M. L. Kamil, P. Mosenthal, P. D. Pearson, & R. Barr (Eds.), *Handbook of reading research* (Vol. 3, pp. 269–284). Mahwah, NJ: Erlbaum.

National Assessment of Educational Progress. (2005). *2005 reading assessment results*. Retrieved May 5, 2009, from *nationsreportcard.gov/reading_math_grade12_2005/s0201.asp*.

National Assessment of Educational Progress. (2007). *2007 reading assessment results*. Retrieved May 5, 2009, from *nationsreportcard.gov/reading_2007*.

National Assessment of Educational Progress. (2008). *2008 long-term trend assessment in reading*. Retrieved May 5, 2009, from *nationsreportcard.gov/ltt_2008*.

National Council of Teachers of English. (1996a). *Guidelines for the preparation of teachers of English language arts*. Urbana, IL: Author.

National Council of Teachers of English. (1996b). *Standards for the English language arts*. Urbana, IL: Author.

National Council of Teachers of English. (2004a). A call to action: What we know about adolescent literacy and ways to support teachers in meeting students' needs. Retrieved July 29, 2009, from *www.ncte.org/positions/statements/adolescentliteracy*.

National Council of Teachers of English. (2004b). On reading, learning to read, and effective reading instruction: An overview of what we know and how we know it. Retrieved March 11, 2010, from *www.ncte.org/positions/statements/onreading*.

National Council of Teachers of English. (2006). *Guidelines for the preparation of teachers of English language arts*. Urbana, IL: Author.

National Institute for Literacy. (2007). *What content-area teachers should know about adolescent literacy*. Washington, DC: U.S. Government Printing Office.

National Middle School Association. (2003a). *This we believe: Successful schools for young adolescents*. Westerville, OH: Author.

National Middle School Association. (2003b). *Research and resources in support of this we believe*. Westerville, Author.

National Reading Panel. (2000). *Teaching children to read: An evidence-based assessment of the scientific research literature on reading and its implications for reading instruction: Reports of the subgroups*. Bethesda, MD: National Institute of Child Health and Human Development, National Institutes of Health.

New London Group. (1996). A pedagogy of multiliteracies: Designing social futures. *Harvard Educational Review, 66*(1), 60–92.

New London Group. (1999). A pedagogy of multiliteracies designing social futures. In B. Cope & M. Kalantzis (Eds.), *Multiliteracies: Literacy learning and the design of social futures* (pp. 9–38). New York: Routledge.

Niday, D., & Allender, D. (2000). Standing on the border: Issues of identity and border crossings in young adult literature. *The ALAN Review, 27*(2), 60–63.

Oakes, J. (1985). *Keeping track: How schools structure inequality.* New Haven, CT: Yale University Press.

O'Brien, D. (2006). "Struggling" adolescents' engagement in multimediating: Countering the institutional construction of incompetence. In D. E. Alvermann, K. A. Hinchman, D. W. Moore, S. F. Phelps, & D. R. Waff (Eds.), *Reconceptualizing the literacies in adolescents' lives* (2nd ed., pp. 29–46). Mahwah, NJ: Erlbaum.

O'Brien, D., Beach, R., & Scharber, C. (2007). "Struggling" middle schoolers: Engagement and literate competence in a reading–writing intervention class. *Reading Psychology, 28,* 51–73.

O'Brien, D., Stewart, R., & Beach, R. (2009). Proficient reading in school: Traditional paradigms and new textual landscapes. In L. Christenbury, R. Bomer, & P. Smagorinsky (Eds.), *Handbook of adolescent literacy research* (pp. 80–97). New York: Guilford Press.

O'Dell, S. (1960). *Island of the blue dolphins.* New York: Sandpiper.

O'Flahavan, J., & Wallis, J. (2005). Rosenblatt in the classroom: Her texts, our reading, our classrooms. *Voices from the Middle, 12,* 32–33.

Ogle, D. M. (1986). K–W–L: A teaching model that develops active reading of expository text. *The Reading Teacher, 39,* 564–570.

Ohanian, S. (2009). On assessment, accountability, and other things that go bump in the night. *Language Arts, 86*(5), 371–381.

Oldfather, P., & Dahl, K. (1994). Toward a social constructivist reconceptualization of intrinsic motivation for literacy learning. *Journal of Reading Behavior, 26*(2), 139–158.

Oldfather, P., & McLaughlin, H. J. (1993). Gaining and losing voice: A longitudinal study of students' continuing impulse to learn across elementary and middle level contexts. *Research in Middle Level Education, 3,* 1–25.

Olson, M. R., & Truxaw, M. P. (2009). Preservice science and mathematics teachers and discursive metaknowledge of text. *Journal of Adolescent and Adult Literacy, 52,* 422–431.

Orb, T. (Ed.). (2001). *This we believe.* Westerville, OH: National Middle School Association.

Ornstein, A., Lasley, T., & Mindes, G. (2005). *Secondary and middle school methods.* Boston: Pearson Education.

Ortiz, R. K. (1996). Awareness of inner dialogues can alter reading behaviors. *Journal of Adolescent and Adult Literacy, 39*(6), 494–495.

Otis, N., Grouzet, F., & Pelletier, L. (2005). Latent motivational change in an academic setting: A 3-year longitudinal study. *Journal of Educational Psychology, 97*(2), 170–183.

Palincsar, A. S. (2002). Reciprocal teaching. In B. J. Guzzetti (Ed.), *Literacy in America: An encyclopedia of history, theory, and practice* (Vol. 2, pp. 535–538). Santa Barbara, CA: ABC-CLIO.

Peire, M., Grigg, W., & Donahue, P. (2005). *The nation's report card: Reading 2005* (NCES 2006–451). Washington, DC: U.S. Department of Education.

Poe, E. A. (2000). *The pit and the pendulum.* London: Travelman.

Prensky, M. (2001). Digital natives, digital immigrants. *On the Horizon, 9,* 1–6.

Pressley, M. (2004). The need for research on secondary literacy education. In T. L. Jetton & J. A. Dole (Eds). *Adolescent literacy research and practice* (pp. 415–432). New York: Guilford Press.

Pressley, M., & Hilden, K. (2006). Cognitive strategies: Production deficiencies and successful strategy instruction everywhere. In D. Kuhn & R. Siegler (Eds.) (W. Damon & R. Lerner, Series Editors), *Handbook of Child Psychology:* Vol. 2. *Cognition, perception, and language* (6th ed., pp. 511–556). Hoboken NJ: Wiley.

Probst, R. E. (2004). *Response and analysis: Teaching literature in secondary school* (2nd ed.). Portsmouth, NH: Heinemann.

Protherough, R., & Atkinson, J. (1991). *The making of English teachers.* Philadelphia: Open University Press.

Purcell-Gates, V. (2008). " ... As soon as she opened her mouth!": Issues of language, literacy, and power. In L. Delpit & J. K. Dowdy (Eds.), *The skin that we speak: Thoughts on language and culture in the classroom* (pp. 121–141). New York: New York Press.

Purkey, W. W. (2000). *What students say to themselves: Internal dialogue and school success.* Thousand Oaks, CA: Corwin Press.

Rasinski, T., & Padak, N. D. (2005). Fluency beyond the primary grades: Helping adolescent struggling readers. *Voices from the Middle, 13,* 34–41.

Reed, J., Shallert, D., Beth, A., & Woodruff, A. (2004). Motivated reader, engaged writer: The role of motivation in the literate acts of adolescents. In T. Jetton & J. Dole (Eds.), *Adolescent literacy research and practice* (pp. 251–282). New York: Guilford Press.

Reeve, J., & Jang, H. (2006). What teachers say and do to support students' autonomy during a learning activity. *Journal of Educational Psychology, 98*(1), 209–218.

Rice, P. S. (2005). It "ain't" always so: Sixth graders' interpretations of Hispanic-American stories with universal themes. *Children's Literature in Education, 36,* 343–362.

Risko, V., & Walker-Dalhouse, D. (2007). Tapping students' cultural funds of knowledge to address the achievement gap. *The Reading Teacher, 61*(1), 98–100.

Roe, B. D., & Smith, S. H. (2005). *Teaching reading in today's middle schools.* New York: Houghton Mifflin.

Rogers, R., Kramer, M. A., & Mosely, M. (Eds.). (2009). *Designing socially just learning communities: Critical literacy education across the lifespan.* New York: Routledge.

Root, M. P. P. (1996). *Multiracial experience: Racial borders as a new frontier.* Thousand Oaks, CA: Sage.

Rosenblatt, L. M. (1978). *The reader, the text, the poem: The transactional theory of the literary work.* Carbondale: Southern Illinois University Press.

Rosenblatt, L. M. (2004). The transactional theory of reading and writing. In R. B. Ruddell & N. J. Unrau (Eds.), *Theoretical models and processes of reading* (5th ed., pp. 1363–1398). Newark, DE: International Reading Association.

Sarroub, L., & Pearson, P. D. (1998). Two steps forward, three steps back: The stormy history of reading comprehension assessment. *The Clearing House, 72*(2), 97–105.

Sarup, M. (1996). *Identity, culture, and the postmodern world.* Athens: University of Georgia Press.

Scherff, L., & Piazza, L. (2008). Why now, more than ever, we need to talk about opportunity to learn. *Journal of Adolescent and Adult Literacy, 52*(4), 343–352.

Scherff, L., & Wright, C. L. (2007). Getting beyond the cuss words: Using Marxism and binary opposition to teach *Ironman* and *The catcher in the rye. The ALAN Review, 35*(1), 51–61.

Schiefele, U. (1996). Topic interest, text representation, and quality of experience. *Contemporary Educational Psychology, 21,* 3–18.

Schnur, S. (1994). *The shadow children.* New York: Morrow.

Scholes, R. (1985). *Textual power.* New Haven, CT: Yale University Press.

Schraw, G. (1997). Situational interest in literary text. *Contemporary Educational Psychology, 22*(4), 436–456.

Schraw, G., Flowerday, T., & Reisetter, M. F. (1998). The role of choice in reader engagement. *Journal of Educational Psychology, 90*(4), 705–714.

Schunk, D. H., & Rice, J. M. (1993). Strategy fading and progress feedback: Effects on self-efficacy and comprehension among students receiving remedial reading services. *Journal of Special Education, 27*(3), 257–276.

Scieszka, J. (1996). *The true story of the three little pigs.* New York: Puffin. (Original work published 1989)

Scieszka, J., & Smith, L. (1996). *The true story of the three little pigs.* New York: Puffin.

Scott, J. A., & Nagy, W. E. (2004). Developing word consciousness. In J. F. Baumann & E. J. Kame'enui (Eds.), *Vocabulary instruction: Research to practice* (pp. 201–217). New York: Guilford Press.

Shan, D. (2005). *Cirque Du Freak: The lake of the souls.* Boston: Little, Brown.

Shanahan, T., & Shanahan, C. (2008). Teaching disciplinary literacy to adolescents: Rethinking content-area literacy. *Harvard Education Review, 78*(1), 40–59.

Shumway, D., & Dionne, C. (Eds.). (2002). *Disciplining English: Alternative histories, critical perspectives.* New York: State University of New York Press.

Skinner, E. A., & Belmont, M. J. (1993). Motivation in the classroom: Reciprocal effects of teacher behavior and student engagement across the school year. *Journal of Educational Psychology, 85*(4), 571–581.

Slavin, R., Cheung, A., Groff, C., & Lake, C. (2008). Effective reading programs for middle and high schools: A best-evidence synthesis. *Reading Research Quarterly, 43*(3), 290–322.

Smiles, T. (2008). Connecting literacy and learning through collaborative action research. *Voices from the Middle, 15,* 32–39.

Smith, M., & Wilhelm, J. D. (2004). "I just like being good at it": The importance of competence in the literate lives of young men. *Journal of Adolescent and Adult Literacy, 47,* 454–461.

Spear-Swerling, L. (2004). Fourth graders' performance on a state-mandated assessment involving two different measures of reading comprehension. *Reading Psychology, 25,* 121–148.

Sperling, M., & DiPardo, A. (2008). English education research and classroom practice: New directions for new times. *Reviews of Research in Education, 32,* 62–108.

Spiegel, D. L. (2005). *Classroom discussion: Strategies for engaging all student, building higher-level thinking skills, and strengthening reading and writing across the curriculum.* New York: Scholastic.

Spires, H. A., & Donley, J. (1998). Prior knowledge activation: Inducing engagement with informational texts. *Journal of Educational Psychology, 90*(2), 249–260.

Stahl, S. (1999). *Vocabulary development.* Cambridge, MA: Brookline.

Stahl, S. A., & Nagy, W. E. (2006). *Teaching word meanings.* Mahwah, NJ: Erlbaum.

Stevens, L. P., & Bean, T. W. (2007). *Critical literacy: Context, research, and practice in the K–12 classroom.* Thousand Oaks, CA: Sage.

Street, B. V. (1985). *Literacy in theory and practice.* Cambridge, UK: Cambridge University Press.

Street, B. V. (1995). *Social literacies: Critical approaches to literacy development, ethnography, and education.* Reading, MA: Addison–Wesley.

Swenson, J., Young, C. A., McGrail, E., Rozema, R., & Whitin, P. (2006). Extending the conversation: New technologies, new literacies, and English education. *English Education, 38,* 351–369.

Tatum, A. W. (2006). Adolescents' multiple identities and teacher professional development. In D. E. Alvermann, K. A. Hinchman, D. W. Moore, S. F. Phelps, & D. R. Waff (Eds.), *Reconceptualizing the literacies in adolescents' lives* (2nd ed., pp. 65–82). Mahwah, NJ: Erlbaum.

Tatum, A. (2008a). Toward a more anatomically complete model of literacy instruction: A focus on African American male adolescents and texts. *Harvard Educational Review, 78*(1), 155–180.

Tatum, A. (2008b). Discussing texts with adolescents in culturally responsive ways. In K. Hinchman & H. Sheridan-Thomas (Eds.), *Best practices in adolescent literacy* (pp. 3–19). New York: Guilford Press.

Tennessee Department of Education. (2009). English/language arts—sixth grade: Standards, learning expectations, accomplishments, and indicators. Retrieved August 25, 2009, from *www.state.tn.us/education/ci/english/grade_6_pf.shtml.*

Thoman, E., & Jolls, T. (2004). Media literacy—a national priority for a changing world. *American Behavioral Scientist, 48*(1), 18–29.

Thomas, P. L. (2008). Challenging texts. *English Journal, 98,* 81–84.

Thomas, S., & Oldfather, P. (1997). Intrinsic motivations, literacy, and assessment practices: "That's my grade. That's me." *Educational Psychologist,* 32(2), 107–123.

Thompson, G., Madhuri, M., & Taylor, D. (2008). How the Accelerated Reader program can become counterproductive for high school students. *Journal of Adolescent and Adult Literacy,* 51(7), 550–560.

Tierney, R. (2007). New literacies learning strategies for new times. In L. S. Rush, A. J. Eakle, & A. Berger (Eds.), *Secondary school literacy: What research reveals for classroom practice* (pp. 21–36). Urbana, IL: National Council of Teachers of English.

Tolstoy, L. (1903). *Padagogicheskie statli [Pedagogical writings].* Moscow: Kushnerev.

Triplett, C. F. (2007). The social construction of "struggle": Influences of school literacy contexts, curriculum, and relationships. *Journal of Literacy Research,* 39, 95–126.

Underwood, T., & Pearson, P. D. (2004). Teaching struggling adolescent readers to comprehend what they read. In T. L. Jetton & J. A. Dole (Eds.), *Adolescent literacy research and practice* (pp. 135–161). New York: Guilford Press.

Valencia, R. R. (2009). A response to Ruby Payne's claim that the deficit thinking model has no scholarly utility. *Teachers College Record.* Retrieved July 24, 2009, from *www.tcrecord.org/Content.asp?ContentID=15691.*

Voight, C. (2003). *Homecoming.* New York: Aladdin.

Vygotsky, L. S. (1978). *Mind in society: The development of higher psychological processes.* Cambridge, MA: Harvard University Press.

Walsh, M. (2008). Worlds have collided and modes have merged: Classroom evidence of changed literacy practices. *Literacy,* 42, 101–108.

Weaver-Hightower, M. B. (2007). An ecology metaphor for educational policy analysis: A call to complexity. *Educational Researcher,* 37(3), 153–167.

Weih, T. G. (2008). A book club sheds light on boys and reading. *Middle School Journal,* 40, 19–25.

Wentzel, K. (1997). Student motivation in middle school: The role of perceived pedagogical caring. *Journal of Educational Psychology,* 89(3), 411–419.

Wigfield, A. (1997). Reading motivation: A domain-specific approach to motivation. *Educational Psychologist,* 32(2), 59–68.

Wilder, P., & Dressman, M. (2006). New literacies, enduring challenges?: The influence of capital on adolescent readers' Internet practices. In D. E. Alvermann, K. A. Hinchman, D. W. Moore, S. F. Phelps, & D. R. Waff (Eds.). *Reconceptualizing the literacies in adolescents' lives* (2nd ed., pp. 205–230). Mahwah, NJ: Erlbaum.

Wilhelm. J. D., & Smith, M. W. (2010). *Fresh takes on teaching literary elements: How to teach what really matters about character, setting, point of view, and theme: Grades 6–12.* New York: Scholastic Teaching Resources.

Wilhelm, J. (1997). *You gotta be the book.* Urbana, IL: National Council of Teachers of English.

Williamson, K. (2006). The National Council of Teachers of English Legislative Platform. *Council Connection: News From National Council of Teachers of*

English. Retrieved August 14, 2009, from *www.ncte.org/about/gov/cgrams/ news/124241.htm*.

Wilson, J. L., & Laman, T. T. (2007). "That was basically me": Critical literacy, text, and talk. *Voices from the Middle, 15,* 40–46.

Wise, B. (2007). Turning reading research into policy. *Reading Research Quarterly, 42*(3), 407–411.

Wortham, S. (2004). The interdependence of social identification and learning. *American Educational Research Journal, 41,* 715–750.

Wortham, S. (2006). *Learning identity: The joint emergence of social identification and academic learning.* New York: Cambridge University Press.

Yang, G. (2008). Graphic novels in the classroom. *Language Arts, 85*(3), 185–192.

Yolen, J. (2004). *The devil's arithmetic.* New York: Puffin.

Zwiers, J. (2008). *Building academic language: Essential practices for content classrooms, grades 5–12.* San Francisco: Jossey-Bass.

Index

231